824.8 ARN
SOT

MONMOUTHSHIRE TRAINING COLLEGE

This book is due for return on or before the last date shown below.

15. MAR. 1996	.27 OCT 2005	
26. APR. 1996		
13. MAY 1996		
30. MAY 1996		
18. MAR. 1997		
18. APR. 1997		
20 MAY 1997		
-2. JUN 1997		
-5. JUN. 1997		
25. JUN 1997		

5

MATTHEW ARNOLD AND THE ROMANTICS

MATTHEW ARNOLD
AND
THE ROMANTICS

by
Leon Gottfried

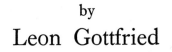

Routledge & Kegan Paul
LONDON

*First published 1963
by Routledge and Kegan Paul Ltd
Broadway House, 68–74 Carter Lane
London, E.C.4*

*Made and printed in Great Britain by
William Clowes and Sons, Limited
London and Beccles*

Copyright Leon Gottfried 1963

TO MY MOTHER

CONTENTS

ACKNOWLEDGEMENTS

OF the previous writers on Matthew Arnold, two stand out as having been so generally useful to me that I feel impelled here to express my general indebtedness to their labours over and above what is implied by my numerous footnote references to their work. I refer to Lionel Trilling and Louis Bonnerot, whose books on Matthew Arnold must stand as milestones of Arnold criticism. Although I have not in every case agreed with one or the other of them, I have found them both to be consistently stimulating and informative. Of special studies that have had the most direct relevance to my work, I should like to select for special acknowledgement the chapters on Arnold in George H. Ford's *Keats and the Victorians*, notable both for their incisiveness of thought and lucidity of expression. I should also like to mention in this place two studies of Arnold which cover some of the same ground as my book, although both appeared after my book was written. I refer to William A. Jamison's *Arnold and the Romantics* and D. G. James's *Matthew Arnold and the Decline of English Romanticism*. Part of Chapter IV first appeared in *Review of English Studies*, and is reprinted with the permission of the editors and of the Clarendon Press, Oxford.

Both the University of Illinois and Washington University have extended aid which made my work possible. A University Fellowship at Illinois gave me a year during which to undertake the research for this study. I am grateful to Dean Lewis E. Hahn of the Graduate School of Arts and Sciences and to Thomas S. Hall, formerly Dean of the College of Liberal Arts, both of Washington University, for their help in procuring various grants which have enabled me to carry this work to completion.

I wish to thank personally William E. Buckler of New York University for his generous co-operation in permitting me to study his collection of transcripts of Arnold's correspondence with his publishers, and for permission to quote from unpublished portions of that correspondence. Neville Rogers, now of Brandeis

ACKNOWLEDGEMENTS

University was most helpful in his comments on my fifth chapter. I am grateful to Joseph H. Summers of Washington University for his kind support and advice in many ways. To Royal A. Gettmann of the University of Illinois my personal and intellectual indebtedness is so ancient and profound that I can find no adequate means to express it. Finally, I should like to thank my wife for her criticism, her encouragement, and her endurance.

L.G.

Washington University
St. Louis

I

INTRODUCTION

WITH the passage of time, Matthew Arnold's eminence in English literature becomes increasingly plain. Both as a transitional figure linking his era to our own and as the central man of letters in his own period he fully deserves the thorough, searching study he has been receiving in recent years. The special quality of Arnold's eminence which has earned this attention is not easy to define, but perhaps just because it is elusive and paradoxical, Arnold continues to occupy his unique place of interest. His weaknesses must be admitted. As a poet he had neither the turbulent energy of Browning nor the virtuosity of Tennyson; indeed, some of his verse can scarcely be called competent and is readable only because it is his. As an observer of society he was often limited by provincialism, the very vice he made it his life's work to oppose. He had no profound political philosophy, he could be as guilty as the most crass Philistine of viewing history as a prologue to the age of Victoria, and he apparently knew nothing about economics. His religious writings are marred by inconsistencies of reasoning and a dearth of precision—not to mention the want of any sort of intuition of the supernatural. Even as a literary critic he frequently showed and, on more than one occasion, virtually boasted of a lack of sound scholarship; furthermore, his overriding propagandist intentions sometimes prevented a disinterested analysis and evaluation of the literary object before him.

These are a few of the major criticisms which have been brought against Arnold. In the face of these attacks, what remains to account for our increasing sense of Arnold's stature and centrality? Although a total critical placement of Arnold is beyond the scope of this study, some generalizations may be relevant. There is one outstanding quality, to my mind, which gives Arnold his unique place in the English literature of his period, a place of special relevance to our times. He possessed a profound intuition of the historical irrevocability of the disruptive, atomizing forces of modern life, and a keen instinct for the problems and perils these forces were bringing and would continue to bring into being. Furthermore, he dedicated himself to a lifelong struggle to do something about the situation by attempting to construct viable compromises between the past and the future. True, others were as aware as he of the direction in which the world was moving. Some, like Leslie Stephen, Thomas Huxley, or Frederic Harrison, had a far more systematic understanding of modern intellectual trends, but tended to underestimate the problems and dangers for the moral and artistic life which would eventually be entailed; hence they welcomed the future with, on the whole, few misgivings. Still others possessed as shattering a sense of the problems of modern life, but were prompted, like Ruskin, Morris, Pater, and their lesser intellectual heirs, to a defiant or terrified retreat, hoping perhaps to sweep back the tide of the future with the broom of aestheticism or Utopian socialism. Compromisers too were not wanting, as the cliché of the 'Victorian compromise' reminds us, but typically their solutions were likely to include a degree of voluntary self-blindness or, as it seemed to later generations, ignominious capitulation to the god of things as they are. Arnold's two great contemporary poets, Tennyson and Browning, fall to some extent within this category.

Of the literary figures of the epoch there were two of outstanding talent who struggled most diligently to achieve a perilous balance, accepting much of the new without blinking its dangers and confusions, striving to preserve what they thought valuable in the old without stumbling into the fright or anger of reaction, and who attempted to speak to their age in terms it could understand, without pandering to the age's self-satisfaction. Consequently, our own age, reaping the harvest of the social and philosophical revolutions of the nineteenth century, and still struggling with the same problems, continues to find a more than historical significance in the work of these two writers, the novelist George Eliot and the poet-critic Matthew Arnold.

But Arnold is a singularly interesting literary figure to us not only because of his position as a prophet of the modern age; he is also a bridge that connects us with the earlier period which was drawing to a close when he was born in 1822. He grew up under the personal as well as literary influence of Wordsworth, in an age when Keats, Shelley, and Byron were dominant poetic forces and Coleridge a seminal thinker on social and religious problems. The great Romantics were not only positive influences, but also negative. Like any generation of giants, this one created severe artistic and psychological problems for the next generation. But in addition to this typical situation, the Romantic movement tended to divorce the Victorian writer from the past in a special way. It stood like the Chinese Wall separating the nineteenth century from the dominant literary tradition of the eighteenth century represented by such key figures as Dryden, Pope, and Johnson, and from the antecedent tradition of wit going back to Donne. This tradition, with its feeling for the social organism and its ability to absorb widely disparate and contradictory intellectual elements, might have been useful to the Victorian poets had they been able to regard it as poetry ('true' poetry, as they would have phrased it), but it was not until the present century that it has again been made usefully and respectably available to poets. Indeed, it is scarcely exaggerating to say that the general effect of Romanticism on the Victorian landscape of the literary past was virtually to destroy the fruitful availability of two centuries of work. In the immediate past towered Wordsworth and Coleridge, Keats, Shelley, and Byron; looming like distant mountain peaks over these stood Shakespeare, Milton, and perhaps Spenser and Chaucer. Here and there a slight poetic eminence—Herbert, Gray, Burns—might be discerned by the careful seeker. But between the gigantic Rockies in the distance and the Appalachians of the immediate past lay a poetic prairie virtually as extensive and undifferentiated as the American midwestern flatlands.

Matthew Arnold was both a cartographer and a product of this version of the landscape. But of equal importance was his acute sense of its limitations. He possessed, for his time, a strongly European consciousness, and he looked to Europe, ancient and modern, to help fill in the great gaps in the English map of the mind and spirit. This European consciousness in turn, with its rationalist and authoritarian bias, contributed to the conviction he had formed early that the great Romantics, insulated and deprived of a centrist tradition, had failed to solve the problem of making an adequate home for the spirit in the modern world, in spite of the magnitude of their talents and efforts. Moreover, he saw the Romantic cult of the individual as a dangerous extension of

3

prevailing English provinciality and cultural anarchism. Thus in Arnold we find a deep split between his inherited conditioning toward Romanticism as the only available 'great tradition' at once modern and English, and his belief that it was a tradition inadequate to the needs of the modern world. Because of the latter belief, the great Romantics and their Elizabethan forebears were obstacles to be overcome and pitfalls to be evaded. However, the former conditioning, operating at least as much on the unconscious as on the conscious level, contributed decisively to the formation of the mental, spiritual, and aesthetic patterns of perception by which Romanticism itself was to be judged.

In view of Arnold's complex and ambiguous position in modern literary history, as both continuator and severe critic of the Romantic tradition, and as interpreter and critic of his own age in terms of problems possessing continuing relevance to us, it would seem that a detailed examination of his relations with the Romantics might help to define more precisely the nature of that position, and of Arnold's own literary objectives and accomplishments. The present study attempts to provide such an examination by exploring and evaluating the full range of Arnold's reactions to the major Romantic poets over his whole career: the nature and extent of their poetic, critical, and personal influence upon him, and the quality and limits of his critical reaction to them. Although my primary interest is literary, I also consider social and religious interactions in so far as they are relevant to literary considerations.

When this study was projected, it seemed desirable if possible to unify the material by grouping it around certain key ideas, such as 'Idea of Poetry', 'The Quest for a poetic Language', etc. However, closer acquaintance with the material led me to conclude that a simple division of the material by poets, while less satisfying in some respects, was more faithful to the subject itself. Arnold's own mind naturally rebelled against system, and his approach to literature was basically an approach to men. Furthermore, he was too close to the literature of the first quarter of his century to see it as a more or less solid unit of 'Romantic' poetry, with some individual divergences among the poets. Although he did on occasion refer to the literature of the period as a whole, it was more in terms of a chronological than an ideological unit, and on such occasions he tended to see the variety of the period as much as its unity. Consequently. in the ensuing chapters I have tried in each

4

case to survey all the material relevant to a specific poet and to relate, in as complete and orderly a fashion as I could, the whole story of Arnold's relations with him; however, it has been expedient to treat Shelley and Coleridge in one chapter, for reasons which are given there. As far as seemed reasonable, a similar organizational pattern has been used for the various chapters, but I have not hesitated to vary it when variation seemed required by the material. One of the disadvantages of this method is that it entails a certain amount of repetition, but I have preferred to admit this repetition in order to keep each chapter coherent within itself, and to minimize confusing cross-reference.

Because each chapter makes up a fairly self-subsistent unit, I have not devoted my concluding chapter to a résumé; instead, in it I have dealt with Arnold and Romanticism in general. In particular, that chapter raises such questions as whether and to what extent Arnold himself may properly be called a Romantic poet; what his idea of poetry owed to and how it diverged from Romanticism; and what he had to say on the rare occasions when he actually used the words *Romantic* and *Romanticism*. Such questions, except for the last, of course cannot be answered other than speculatively, for too much depends upon the critic's definitions and presuppositions. Such answers as I propose, therefore, will have served a sufficient purpose if they help clarify the terms of the discussion and illustrate the nature of Arnold's quandary as a man virtually unable to express his sense of the bankruptcy of Romanticism except in Romantic terms.

II
SUCH NEED OF JOY:
WORDSWORTH

. . . who, ah! who, will make us feel?

I. WORDSWORTH'S INFLUENCE ON MATTHEW ARNOLD

Personal and Philosophical

THROUGHOUT a long and varied literary career, spanning some forty years, Matthew Arnold never tired of admiring, criticizing, imitating, and rebelling against William Wordsworth. Consequently, a study of Arnold's criticism of Wordsworth becomes, in effect, a survey of Arnold's life—for his relationship with Wordsworth began early, an outgrowth of the friendship between Dr. Arnold and the poet. It is natural that no single utterance of Arnold upon Wordsworth should possess the finality of such essays as those on Joubert, Gray, or Maurice de Guérin. These personalities left their unique impressions; Arnold had his say about them and passed on. Wordsworth, on the other hand, belongs with the group of plastic forces which helped create Matthew Arnold, and taught him that which was to become a permanent part of him. A list of such formative influences may be expanded or abridged according to the degree or permanence of influence we wish to use as criteria; the fuller list would certainly show such names as Keats, Burke, Renan, and others whose influence applied to a certain portion of Arnold's life or affected one of his various literary careers. But no list, however abridged, could afford to omit the name of Wordsworth. In a letter to Cardinal Newman, Arnold himself supplies his own roster of leading influences:

> There are four people, in especial, from whom I am conscious of having learnt—a very different thing from merely receiving a strong

6

impression—learnt habits, methods, ruling ideas, which are constantly with me; and the four are—Goethe, Wordsworth, Sainte-Beuve, and yourself.[1]

Since by his own estimate Arnold learned so much from Wordsworth it may be well to review the background of personal and family relationships before taking up more specifically literary matters. Matthew Arnold's acquaintanceship with Wordsworth began when the former was still an infant, since Dr. Arnold and Wordsworth were friendly from at least 1824. Dr. Arnold had become so enamoured of the Lake Country that, with the added attraction of Wordsworth's company, he regularly moved his household to Westmorland twice a year during the thirties, and when the educator decided in 1833 to build a home in the Lake District for his rapidly expanding family, the proximity of Wordsworth was a determining factor in choosing a site. In this task Wordsworth himself assisted, the site selected for Fox How being near Wordsworth's own Rydal Mount. Wordsworth also helped oversee the building of the house, and we may well imagine that the shrewd north-countryman tolerated no nonsense from the builders. His sister-in-law, Sara Hutchinson, planned the gardens for the future Arnold home, and the poet, finally, contributed the capstone in the form of a dedicatory sonnet.[2]

The families remained on intimate terms for many years. Dora Wordsworth Quillinan was particularly close to the Arnolds, and the home of Jemima Quillinan, a stepdaughter of Dora's who lived until 1894, long remained a centre for the younger branches of the Wordsworth family and for the descendants of Matthew and his brother Thomas Arnold.[3] Wordsworth himself took an early and continued interest in the rather insouciant youth who was carefully husbanding beneath the surface of wit and dandy 'a hidden ground of austerity'. There is no evidence for assuming it, yet one would like to speculate on the possibility that the youth confidentially discussed some of his poetic plans with the aged poet; indeed, otherwise it is not easily apparent what attracted the austere old man to the seemingly frivolous lad. We know on the authority of Clough that Wordsworth tried to help young Matthew, a rather indifferent student, with his college work. He had 'taken Matt under his special protection as a 2nd classman' and so had every right to be 'well pleased' when the latter was elected fellow of Oriel.[4] (This

7

information casts an ironic sidelight on the dictum later to be promulgated by the critic, that the great Romantic poets suffered because 'they did not know enough'.) Furthermore, the effect of this personal relationship was reinforced for Arnold at Oxford, where Wordsworth was one of the prominent 'voices' of the forties, and was even claimed by the Tractarians as 'their poet'. What remains to be said of the personal relationship between the two men has best been summed up in 'Wordsworth' by Arnold himself, with undoubted fervour if somewhat negatively:

> It is not for nothing that one has been brought up in the veneration of a man so truly worthy of homage; that one has seen him and heard him, lived in his neighbourhood, and been familiar with his country. No Wordsworthian has a tenderer affection for this pure and sage master than I, or is less really offended by his defects.

Evidence of the abiding personal influence of Wordsworth and his poetry may be found in Arnold's letters, in his notebooks, and in the many incidental references to Wordsworth in the public writings. In 1864 Arnold recommends his essay on Joubert to Mrs. Davy, a friend of his mother, because 'the true old Wordsworthians to which band she and I both belong, are just the people for whom Joubert is properly meant'. In 1866, acknowledging a letter from his mother which evidently contained some reminiscences of Thomas Arnold, Wordsworth, and Coleridge, Arnold comments that 'everything about Wordsworth and Coleridge is interesting'. From another letter to his mother in 1871 we learn that reading Wordsworth aloud was a practice in Arnold's household. In the letters, too, we find a recurring tendency for Arnold to associate impressions of external nature with the poetry of Wordsworth. This is particularly noticeable in the letters he wrote to his unmarried sister Fan, an ardent nature lover. In a letter of 1873 after the death of their mother we find Arnold recommending Wordsworthian therapy for grief, Wordsworth's consoling and healing power being a commonplace of Victorian opinion:

> And so you are again at Fox How. That is well, if you are able to bear it. It will be a long time before you feel of your grief, as you look out on the hills and the fern and the trees and the waters.
> > It seems an idle thing, which could not live
> > Where meditation was—
> and yet that is undoubtedly the right thing to feel, and that the

thought of dearest mamma should be simply a happy memory and not a gnawing regret. But one cannot say that dear old Wordsworth succeeded in complying with his own teaching when he lost Dora. Perhaps he was too old and had not his strength and spirits enough left to him. But he was right in his preaching for all that, and not in his practice. I like to think that you so deeply feel the beauty of that beloved country, that it will be a real help and solace for you, however you make use of it: whether precisely in the way Wordsworth would have meant, or in some other of your own.

In 1879, when Arnold was busy with his selections from Wordsworth, he mentions in another letter to Miss Arnold that the effect of reading so much of Wordsworth lately 'has been to make me feel more keenly than usual the beauty of the common incidents of the natural year'. As late as 1886, writing to the same correspondent from the Continent, Arnold wishes (alas, in vain) for the milder spring weather in terms of a line of Wordsworth's poetry, and a few weeks later he contrasts his mode of travel with 'how much better Wordsworth saw the valley of the Meuse by the sort of travelling in his day!'[5] This nostalgia for an earlier, simpler day, expressed here merely in connection with modes of travel, is a dominant note in all of Arnold's thought and writing about Wordsworth.

Let us now consider briefly three special areas where Arnold may be said to have learned 'habits, methods, ruling ideas' from Wordsworth: morality, religion, and politics. We have already seen one example of a central moral idea of Wordsworth in Arnold's letter about the death of his mother. This idea may be expressed negatively as the necessity to overcome grief and melancholy, and positively as the attempt to transmute sorrow, if possible, to joy; it forms a leading motif in nineteenth-century attitudes toward Wordsworth, as men sought the consolations they had been accustomed to seek in religion while unable to believe in the objective validity of religion, and consequently in its power to give those sorely needed consolations.[6]

Other instances of Arnold's personal attempt to make use of Wordsworth's consolatory power may be found in his notebooks. A poignant entry of 1870 consists of the single line: 'For all things are less dreadful than they seem.'[7] This line, from one of the *Ecclesiastical Sonnets*, comes with the force of a cry, scarcely of

9

hope, but rather of wish, in Arnold's lifelong war against melancholy. We can only guess about the biographical significance of this prayerful entry. It might refer to the loss of his two children, Basil and Tommy, but seems belated in that connection, Tommy having died in November, 1868, and Basil the preceding January. Little information has been allowed to leave the family about the reaction of Mrs. Arnold to these heavy losses, but there is a story that she was seriously overcome, and that during the following year or two spent many hours sitting by their graves in morbid grief. The line may have some reference to Arnold's feelings about his wife's unsettled state of mind at this time. The other passages of Wordsworth's moralizing appear in the notebook for 1884, probably jotted down during one of Arnold's numerous rereadings of *The Prelude*. Although not as dramatic as the line given above, both of these quotations relate the trials of life to 'something loftier' in us, or at work for us, 'In the unreasoning progress of the world.' It is possible to conjecture, only half facetiously, that these passages[8] bear some relation to Arnold's weariness at the unending drudgery of his work as Inspector of Schools, and were a reminder of hope in the midst of 'the common aspect, daily garb, / Of human life' in its 'most unfruitful hours'. 'Wise men everywhere', said Arnold in an essay published in the year of these notebook entries, 'know that we must keep up our courage and hope; they know that hope is, as Wordsworth well says,

> "The paramount *duty* which Heaven lays,
> For its own honour, on man's suffering heart."[9]

For Arnold, as for Wordsworth and Coleridge, joy was of fundamental importance to life, and if he could not transmute sorrow to joy, he could at least find in Wordsworth plenty of support for his efforts to do the next best thing, perhaps more congenial to his temperament, that is, to cultivate stoic calm.

In the area of religion, where Arnold expended so much thought and feeling, it would be surprising not to find signs of Wordsworth's pervasive influence, in spite of the great and obvious differences between the fundamental religious beliefs of the two men. Neither Wordsworth's early flirtations with Deism, nor his later orthodoxy suited Arnold's needs. Arnold's universe, the universe of nineteenth-century mechanistic science, was too cold and empty for the former, while his religious views were too 'advanced' for the latter; natural science and biblical criticism had erected barriers too high for Arnold to traverse. Nevertheless, Arnold, like such Broad Church leaders of the preceding generation as Maurice and Dr. Arnold, was attracted by the undogmatic but profound 'sentiment of the numinous' to be found in Wordsworth. And in spite of Arnold's resigned but firm elimination of the supernatural from his 'religion', his intense desire to hold fast to a traditional and national church as an instrument of moral education, national unity, and spiritual enlargement undoubtedly derives some of its force from the influence of Wordsworth. Arnold's view of poetry as a kind of substitute for religion, and the corollary of the poet-priest, also derive in part from both the precept and example of Wordsworth, although going to lengths that would certainly have been unacceptable to the sage of Rydal. Finally, Arnold's use of Wordsworth's poetry for incidental reference in his religious writings and his borrowing of the Wordsworthian phrase 'stream of tendency' as one of his circumlocutions for 'God' reveal that Wordsworth was never far from his thoughts on religion.[10]

In Arnold's political and social thought, as in religion, there was more fundamental disagreement than agreement between him and Wordsworth; in both areas, moreover, the lines of influence are tangled by such cross-fertilizing forces as Burke, Coleridge, and Dr. Arnold. Nevertheless, certain significant parallels and points of likeness are worth noting. Arnold was a Liberal, but certainly of a very special stamp, so that his efforts to raise the level and expand the horizons of Liberal thought often struck other Liberals as rank disloyalty to their principles.[11] Foreseeing that the future belonged to the party of change, he chose to work with it, and criticized Wordsworth for burying himself in the past. Nevertheless he made it his political mission to try to temper the quantity, quality, and direction of change with a historical attitude, a respect for tradition, and a scepticism of modern man's 'eigene grosse Erfindungen', the excessive devotion to which Arnold saw as the parent of anarchy. Arnold's distaste for 'system', the pet plaything of Jacobinism, may have been due partly to his confessed—and evident—weakness as an abstract thinker. But perhaps an even more important factor in the formation of his special and complex blend of conservative Liberalism was the influence of counter-Liberal forces such as Newman and the Tractarians, Burke, and Wordsworth.

Probably the most solid link between Wordsworth's social thought and Arnold's is the powerful conviction shared by them that the true direction for reform lay in the inward improvement of the individual. *Estote ergo vos perfecti!*, the motto for *Culture and Anarchy*, is written repeatedly in Arnold's notebooks and forms the recurrent theme not only of his political writings but of his literary criticism as well. A cognate mistrust of legislative action as the *unum necessarium*, of 'natural rights', of 'machinery', and of unbridled democracy are further cross-ties. However, some of their social ideas are in contrast. Probably the most striking of these contrasts is in their attitudes towards the role of the State in bringing about the much-needed improvement of the individual. Although sceptical of the benefits of direct legislative action, Arnold believed in a strong State, to which he looked for leadership in educational reforms (here speaks the school inspector and the son of his father) to bring about the elevation of public attitude and intelligence so desperately needed for successful democracy. That democracy would come he felt to be inevitable and, under the right conditions, desirable; Wordsworth, on the other hand, feared democracy and wanted a government representative of the mind of the country, that is, of its best thought, not of its masses.[12] With this ideal Arnold did not altogether disagree, but he believed that the only hope for achieving a reconciliation between the Wordsworthian ideal and the actualities of political democracy lay in educating and humanizing, as rapidly as possible, the *demos*. He had little hope of doing much directly for the proletariat ('Populace') in the near future,[13] and concentrated most of his efforts on the class which was already possessed of political power, set the tone for the nation, and, he believed, established the standards and ideals for the aspiring proletarians—the great middle class. Arnold believed, certainly with justification, that he was labouring for the future, but that Wordsworth had been able to maintain his conservative attitudes only by resolutely turning his back on the modern world with its harassing and complex problems. The deep-rooted, local, provincial culture which Wordsworth so earnestly struggled to defend and preserve was also attractive to Matthew Arnold. But where Wordsworth ardently longed and worked for the preservation of this way of life,[14] Arnold was ruefully aware that, aside from any other objections to such a programme, it was impossible, for it contradicted 'the way the world was going'. And since this impossibility was visible even during Wordsworth's lifetime, Arnold, though he loved Wordsworth for what he was, could only feel that the sage poet had diminished his effectiveness both as a poet and as a social force by allying himself with the past. Nevertheless, the strong strain of conservatism in Arnold's Liberalism, seen against the background of his early personal relationship with and lifelong veneration for Wordsworth, clearly indicates that the older man exerted a considerable modifying influence upon the social thought of the younger.

We have briefly seen, then, evidence of the deep and long-lasting effect of Wordsworth upon Matthew Arnold, the poet and teacher who assumed for his age something of the prophetic mantle of the earlier poet, and who during his whole mature life taught that the poetry of Wordsworth was 'the most important work done in verse, in our language', of the nineteenth century.[15] This formative relationship provides an interesting, appealing, and illuminating background for the study of the indirect criticism and appreciation of Wordsworth to be found in Arnold's poetry, and of his articulated criticism both in verse and prose—subjects to which we shall now direct our attention.

Literary Influence

Arnold as a poet was, in part, a disciple of Wordsworth, although in theory he also thought of himself as a reformer and rebel. His poetic practice and his assumptions about the nature of poetry reveal, I believe, that the influences established by Wordsworth and the other Romantic poets were too powerful to be put aside without a more drastic reconsideration of poetic questions than Arnold was prepared to make. The literary influence of Wordsworth may be seen in Arnold's own concept of the nature of a poet, his ideas of what poetry should be and do, and in the frequent appearance of Wordsworthian allusion in Arnold's own lyric and meditative verse.

Ludwig Lewisohn has written that Wordsworth's work

seems to have determined Arnold's standard of poetic excellence. 'The noble and profound application of ideas to life is the most essential part of poetic greatness', not so much because it actually is, but because Wordsworth's greatness does consist of it. And this is natural. Our theories of poetry and art are not mathematical; they have flesh and blood. We do not approve of a certain poet because he fits our theory; but our theory is the practice of the poets whom we love. The definition of poetry as a criticism of life has its origin in Wordsworth's work.[16]

And of Arnold's poetry, Herbert Paul has said:

> His spiritual father was Wordsworth, from whose grave his own poetry may be said to have sprung.[17]

Both of these observations must be seriously qualified. Much of Arnold's theory, and some of his practice, is in direct reaction against Wordsworth; furthermore, poetic influences other than Wordsworth's must be allowed. Most notably of the moderns, it was from Goethe that Arnold derived many of his ideas of how modern poetry could gain the intellectual and critical enlightenment it needed in order to become a true *magister vitae* for modern life. Still, when all qualifications have been allowed for, it must be accepted that the greatest single literary influence upon Arnold was that of Wordsworth, according to Arnold the greatest English poet after Milton and, barring Goethe, the greatest nineteenth-century poet in any language.

Central to Arnold's idea of the nature of poetry is the Wordsworthian belief expressed in the Preface to the *Lyrical Ballads*:

> Poetry is the breath and finer spirit of all knowledge; it is the impassioned expression which is in the countenance of all science.

Arnold called Wordsworth a great critic on the basis of this preface; he inscribed this quotation from it in his notebooks more than once, and adopted it as his own definition in 'The Study of Poetry' (1880). Putting the idea in his own words, and diluting the image somewhat, he asserted that 'Poetry attaches its emotion to the idea', although the implied hypostatization of content and expression seems like a step backward to Neo-Classical theory.[18] Although much of Arnold's dissatisfaction with English poetry stemmed from his critical allegiance to the idea, it is clear that his basic poetical faith is in the emotion. In a famous and representative remark in his essay on Gray, Arnold was the spokesman for a whole generation of post-Romantics:

> The difference between genuine poetry and the poetry of Dryden, Pope, and all their school, is briefly this: their poetry is conceived

14

and composed in their wits, genuine poetry is conceived in the soul.[19]

Of course, it was Wordsworth who had called the primary endowment of the poet 'that first great gift, the vital soul', and we find the line duly transcribed in Arnold's notebooks.[20] Much of Arnold's criticism is based on this idea. Although soul may be called 'personality' in 'Byron' or 'character' in 'Keats' or even 'manner' in discussing Homer's 'nobility', Arnold makes it clear that one cannot have nobility of style without nobility of soul. In 'Thomas Gray' Arnold argues that the true poet, even in an unpoetical age, is known by his qualities of soul; and elsewhere, in passing remarks on Charlotte Brontë and Flaubert he applies this standard to novelists. This being so, the poet must be careful to guard his soul against the world's contamination, like Senancour in his mountain fastness or the scholar-gipsy pursuing his gleam. Again Arnold could find ample corroboration in Wordsworth. For example, he copied the following passage from *The Prelude* into his notebook, under the Miltonic heading 'Keep thyself pure':

> Far better [than the 'heartless chase of trivial pleasure']
>   had it been to exalt the mind
> By solitary study, to uphold
> Intense desire through meditative peace.[21]

And Arnold's vision of the soul as a Palladium recalls Wordsworth's great vision on Snowdon in Book XIV of *The Prelude*:

> So, in its lovely moonlight, lives the soul.
> Mountains surround it, and sweet virgin air;
> Cold plashing, past it, crystal waters roll . . .[22]

Since the soul is the source of 'genuine' poetry, the effects of poetry will also be on the soul, which is the basic element not only in the composition but also in the appreciation of poetry. As Wordsworth said, in words twice transcribed by Arnold in his notebooks, 'To be incapable of a feeling for poetry, in my sense of the word, is to be without love of human nature and reverence for God.'[23] We find this belief incorporated in Arnold's lifelong defence of the humanizing power of humane letters, especially poetry, from the early *Essays in Criticism* to the late essays on 'The Study of Poetry' and 'Literature and Science', and it permeates the religious writings. Arnold's elevated notion of poetry as the enduring part of religion, and indeed as a virtual substitute for religion, is well known. Here, too, Arnold could find some support in Wordsworth, as we can see from the characteristic comments of Wordsworth on his own poems that Arnold copied into his notebooks. The following passage was taken down in 1867:

> They will co-operate with the benign tendencies in human nature and society, and will, in their degree, be efficacious in making men wiser, better and happier.[24]

Arnold used this passage again as the close of his Wordsworth essay in 1879; in that year he also copied into his notebook another passage from the same letter of Wordsworth's:

> Trouble not yourself upon their present reception: of what moment is that, compared with what is, I trust, their destiny!—To console the afflicted; to add sunshine to daylight by making the happy happier; to teach the young and gracious of every age to see, to think and feel, and therefore to become more actively and securely virtuous;—this is their office; which I trust they will faithfully perform long after we (that is, all that is mortal of us) are mouldering in our graves.[25]

Although Arnold valued intelligence in poetry, although he judged the Romantics, Wordsworth included, as deficient in this quality, it is worth noting and underscoring his own basic Romanticism as revealed in his rejection of Pope and Dryden and his exaltation of Gray according to the criterion of 'soul'. That for Arnold the 'soul' dwelt apart in a moonlight atmosphere, remote from the 'battle in the plain', a Palladium on a 'lone fastness high', may be an indication of the loss of vitality of the Wordsworthian tradition. But in the picture of 'soul' as both the source and prime recipient of poetry, and in the relationship between it and 'the freshness of the early world',[26] we may see how thoroughly the influence of Wordsworth helped establish the criteria and values by which poetry was to be interpreted and judged by Matthew Arnold.

Arnold's own poetic practice further reveals the influence of Wordsworth. By way of qualification, it would be well to bear in mind a remark once made by T. S. Eliot, that in prose a writer may say what he wants but in poetry what he can. Nevertheless, one of the most striking features of Arnold's poetry is the extent of its divergences from the classicist demands of his criticism, in the direction of Romantic and especially of Wordsworthian poetry.

Arnold's earliest published poem, *Alaric at Rome*, the Rugby
prize poem of 1840, is determinedly Byronic, but three years later
in *Cromwell*, a prize poem at Oxford, the major influence is clearly
Wordsworth's. Arnold himself in a note calls attention to an
allusion to the twelfth of Wordsworth's *Sonnets to Liberty*; a
specific image derived from natural scenery was borrowed and
developed by the young collegian. But in addition to this specific
allusion the accents of Wordsworth are heard repeatedly in the
poem, especially when external nature is brought in. Indeed, that
so much external nature is decidedly 'brought in' might alone
help establish the foster paternity of the poem's style, but the case
is proved when we see passages like:

> Yet all high sounds that mountain children hear
> Flash'd from thy soul upon thine inward ear;
>
> [ll. 27–8]

> . . . thine eye
> In common sights read secret sympathy;
>
> [ll. 31–2]

> . . . a lonely tree,
> On some bare headland, straining mournfully,
> That all night long its weary moan doth make
> To the vex'd waters of a mountain lake!
>
> [ll. 189–92]

(The exclamation point that concludes the last passage is, however,
pure Arnold, and not merely juvenile, for surely there was never
another important poet so free with this shrill mark.)

If we skip nearly four decades from the juvenilia of 1843 (Oxford
published the poem but Arnold never did) to the last major poem
of Arnold's career, *Westminster Abbey* (1881), we shall still find
traces of the deep influence of Wordsworth. In that poem Arnold
eulogized Dean Stanley, his friend and his father's biographer, as
one who possessed

> love of all things pure,
> And joy in light, and power to spread the joy.
>
> [ll. 79–80]

The key words 'pure', 'joy', and 'power' are precisely those which
are leading motifs in Arnold's handling of Wordsworth. The
passage as a whole seems to echo that line from Wordsworth

which Arnold himself chose as offering the key to the poet's greatness, his power to 'bring us word "Of joy in widest commonalty spread".'[27] The strength of the echo should not cause us to lose sight of another key word, 'light', nor to forget that Arnold criticized the Romantic poets for their lack of 'light' or intellectual largeness and freedom. But the stress in the quoted passage is not merely on light, but on *'joy* in light', and it is this emphasis which relates the idea to Arnold's evaluation of Wordsworth. Writers like Bishop Colenso or Voltaire might offer 'light', but their light was worse than darkness because of their failure to offer it in such a way as to rejoice the soul. It was Wordsworth's special glory, in Arnold's opinion, that he did offer that which sustains the soul, what Arnold, like Coleridge and Wordsworth before him, called 'joy'.

It would be otiose to attempt to trace all the signs of Wordsworthian influence through the whole body of poetry between the early and late poems cited above. Arnold's Wordsworthianism was recognized early. Swinburne, whose review of Arnold's *New Poems* in 1867 is still a useful critique, pointed out its pervasiveness with some sympathy, although later, in a mood of disaffection, he sneered at Arnold as a 'pseudo-Wordsworth'.[28] Other contemporaries as diverse as John Duke Coleridge and Herman Melville also noticed specific echoes, as have numerous modern critics; these citations of parallels, along with some others I have observed, are reviewed in a note.[29] Two lines from *Empedocles on Etna* have been especial favourites. After being called by Swinburne 'verses in the highest tone of Wordsworth', they have been pointed out again by Douglas Bush, Louis Bonnerot, and E. K. Brown:

> But we received the shock of mighty thoughts
> On simple minds with a pure natural joy.[30]

But in truth there are many Wordsworthian passages in *Empedocles on Etna*. Perhaps just as striking as the couplet above is the following passage from Act I:

> ... Our youthful blood
> Claims rapture as its right;
> The world, a rolling flood
> Of newness and delight,
> Draws in the enamour'd gazer to its shining breast.
>
> [ll. 352–6]

which may be compared with Wordsworth's *Ode: Intimations of Immortality*, ll. 78–85. Arnold himself indicates in a letter that he was trying in *Thyrsis* to attain something of a Wordsworthian style, or, in his terms, lack of style:

> ... the diction of the poem was modelled on that of Theocritus, whom I have been much reading during the two years this poem has been forming itself. ... I meant the diction to be so artless as to be almost heedless.[31]

This may be set alongside Arnold's later comment on Wordsworth's style:

> But Wordsworth's poetry, when he is at his best, is inevitable, as inevitable as Nature herself. It might seem that Nature not only gave him the matter for his poem, but wrote the poem for him. He has no style.[32]

Still speaking of *Thyrsis*, Arnold continues in the letter quoted above:

> The images are all from actual observation, on which point there is an excellent remark in Wordsworth's notes, collected by Miss Fenwick.

The observant reader of Arnold could continue such a catalogue at considerable length, but I believe that enough has been shown to document the mere existence of a significant influence. *Resignation*, one of Arnold's important poems, seems to me to have so many relevant points of contact with *Tintern Abbey* that it may almost be considered a reply to it. However, I reserve the detailed discussion of this poem for an appendix.[33] Now let us return to the more important problem of attempting to ascertain the significance of what Arnold borrowed, and of what he was unable to use —that is, to determine the elements of implicit criticism of the older poet in the practice of the younger. I shall, in general, restrict my examination to subject matter, tone, and style, omitting 'ideas' in the sense of 'consciously held attitudes or beliefs about society, Nature, etc.', except as these are directly relevant.[34]

Arnold's most important manifesto on the proper subject matter for poetry is the Preface to the 1853 edition of his poems. The lyric is not considered, the discussion being limited to narrative and dramatic poetry. Arnold's plea for classical objectivity, for a poetry of great actions, and for self-effacement on the part of the poet is well known; equally well known, to the point of triteness, is Arnold's failure as a poet to satisfy his own classical standards.[35] The dramatic poems may, from this point of view, be dealt with rapidly. *Empedocles on Etna* is a great poem in many respects, but it was dropped from the canon by the author for fifteen years, his reasons for the suppression making up the occasion and much of the substance of the 1853 Preface. The poem, failing to resolve itself into action, failed likewise to provide the feeling of satisfaction, of catharsis, which Arnold desiderated. It is virtually impossible not to see in it, in spite of Arnold's disclaimers, 'a true allegory of the state of one's own mind', the very thing Arnold as a critic was rejecting, holding Wordsworth largely responsible for encouraging such poetry.[36] But whatever its failures by Arnold's critical standards, *Empedocles on Etna* remains an interesting poem, and the briefest comparison with Arnold's only other considerable dramatic poem suggests that *Empedocles* is interesting because of those very failures. *Merope*, written in 1857 to inaugurate Arnold's Professorship at Oxford, is an imitation of Greek tragedy composed in strict conformity to the classical standards of the 1853 Preface. Arnold hoped it possessed the 'character of Fixity', and, alas, it does—the fixity of a monument of academic poetry; occasionally rising to moments of beauty, it is as a whole unprofitable and dull.[37]

With his narrative poetry Arnold has been more successful, some of these poems being among his most widely loved compositions. Their success, however, is surely not due to the poet's adherence to classical standards. The one narrative, *Sohrab and Rustum*, which represents Arnold's most successful attempt in the 'grand style' is very far, for all its Homeric trappings, from exemplifying the rapidity and the plainness and directness of expression which Arnold marked as two of the four leading characteristics of Homer's style.[38] But to say that Arnold is, in comparison to Homer, literary and artificial is little to the point. What I should like to stress is that Wordsworth himself when he turned his full powers most successfully to narrative, as in *Michael*, is Arnold's superior precisely in terms of those criteria which Arnold set up—total subordination of part to whole, classic simplicity, and objectivity. For all Arnold's critical objections in his Preface to the idea that 'A true allegory of the state of one's own mind . . . is perhaps the highest thing that one can attempt in the way of poetry', he was

20

even less able as a poet to escape from subjectivism than was Wordsworth.

Only in that meditative-lyric verse in which Arnold attempts to deal with modern ideas that were reshaping the European mind do we find the subject matter making anything like an adequate criticism against Wordsworth's poetry. Even this point, if it be allowed, must be seriously qualified, however. Arnold did not attempt to make poetry of the very 'unpoetrylessness'[39] of the modern world; his characteristic poetic response to modernity was one of evasion. We need only call to mind such poems as *Obermann*, *The Scholar-Gipsy*, and *Stanzas from the Grande Chartreuse*, to see that they represent an attempt to fly *from* the modern world *into* poetry rather than an attempt to fuse the two. It may also be argued that the ideas which were bringing into existence the modern world are as deeply interfused into the ground-structure and method of *The Prelude* and even the *Lyrical Ballads* as in anything of Arnold's. With the possible exception then of his dealing with the modern sense of alienation, we shall not find that the subject matter of Arnold's poetry makes a radical criticism of Wordsworth's in the sense, say, that Wordsworth's does of Pope's. If Wordsworth is to bear the responsibility of establishing the poet's own states of mind as the main subject of poetry, Arnold surely is equally responsible for furthering, and further limiting, this establishment in his practice in spite of his intended rebellion against it, and thereby for furthering the divorce between 'poetry' and 'life'.

Twentieth-century poets, faced with the problem of this divorce and striving for a reconciliation, have found it necessary to make a radical revision of the idea of the 'poetic' itself. Most notably, these attempts are reflected in the handling of tone. Seeking ways to make poems out of the complexity of an atomized civilization, our poets have gone to school to Donne, Marvell, Herrick, even to the once discredited Dryden, Pope, and Johnson; irony has become a dominant mode. Arnold, too, felt that he had such a task, or at least that modern poetry had such a task, to accomplish, but if we look in his poetry for signs of a complementary revision of attitudes towards poetry itself, we shall not find them. He was probably the most skilled and witty ironist of his era in prose, using the medium to articulate the manifold ironies and paradoxes to which he was keenly alive in modern life and in himself. But his concept of the 'poetic', inherited from Milton and Wordsworth, prohibited the use in poetry of whole ranges of tone, particularly the ironic tone or method.[40] To be sure, some of these contraries were used as the subjects for poems—e.g., in *Dover Beach*, or in the three poems named in the last paragraph—but contrariness is not reflected in the texture or tone of the verse itself. In Arnold's acquiescence, not always conscious, in the limitation of poetic tone to the expression 'of simple emotions, and these of a limited class: the tender, the exalted, the poignant, and in general, the sympathetic',[41] he is most evidently uncritical of the Romantic tradition. Where we do find complexity of tone in the Romantics, it is likely to be achieved by stylistic means proscribed by Arnold, such as the dazzling wit and satiric thrusts of Byron or the rich metaphorical complexity of Keats and Shelley. Like Wordsworth, however, Arnold rarely used metaphor. He deplored Keats's and Shelley's (and Shakespeare's) addiction to complex imagery, and preferred on principle the more direct modes of expression. To make this observation of Arnold's poetry is to risk being unfair to Wordsworth's greater variety. What is indicated, however, is something of the nature of what Arnold was able to learn poetically from Wordsworth and the depth to which the influence, even though it represented but a part of Wordsworth, penetrated.

It would not be quite fair to Arnold, on the other hand, to suggest that he has in this respect merely taken and narrowed what Wordsworth had to offer. Arnold too had his distinct note, to use one of his own favourite words. That we may best define this note by negation when we compare Arnold with Wordsworth is, however, significant. Arnold's poetry is totally lacking in the one tonal quality for which he most highly prized the poetry of Wordsworth —the quality of joy. Arnold's poetry, as W. C. Brownell has said, 'is never joyous; joyousness is the one quality above all others which it never has'.[42] This difference may be in part attributed to temperament, but that alone is an insufficient explanation. Wordsworth, like Arnold, had been dangerously threatened by melancholy; Wordsworth had even had to live through, what Arnold had not, a period of despair which we might today call a nervous breakdown. But Wordsworth was able to find springs of strength in early experience from which to derive a poetry and a philosophy ('emotion recollected in tranquillity' is more than a poetic stratagem). This was precisely what Arnold, who felt that his whole life had fallen upon an iron time, could not do. He yearned intensely for the 'freshness of the early world', he could derive many things from it—recreation, pleasure, refreshment— but not strength. And this is no wonder since the early experience to which he turned was not his own; it was Wordsworth's, or Europe's, or civilization's. Thus there is a quality of sentimentalism in Arnold's 'soft primitivism' which is lacking in Wordsworth; Arnold is the week-end visitor, the self-conscious nature-lover (cf. *Lines Written in Kensington Gardens*) who does not feel direct contact with and can derive no spiritual invigoration from 'the Mothers', the profound and mysterious sources of being. And what he could not find as a man, he could not offer as a poet.

But moreover, Arnold was unable himself 'to construct something / Upon which to rejoice.'[43] Brought up in a Christian tradition in which joy and salvation were contingent upon certitude of faith, the loss of certitude meant equally the loss of joy:

> the world, which seems
> To lie before us like a land of dreams,
> So various, so beautiful, so new
> Hath really neither joy, nor love, nor light,
> Nor certitude, nor peace, nor help for pain;

the weather of the heart is left cold and bleak, a 'wintry clime.[44] Ernest Renan, who helped form Arnold's theological thought, has expressed the forlornness of the man who has known faith and lost it:

> The fish of Lake Baikal, we are told, have spent thousands of years in becoming fresh-water fish after being salt-water fish. I had to go through my transition in a few weeks. Like an enchanted circle Catholicism embraces the whole of life with so much strength that when one is deprived of it everything seems insipid. I was terribly lost. The universe produced upon me the impression of a cold and arid desert. For the moment that Christianity was not the truth, all the rest appeared to me indifferent, frivolous, barely worthy of interest. The collapse of my life upon itself left in me a feeling of emptiness like that which follows an attack of fever or an unhappy love affair.[45]

Arnold, too, sees himself as a fish out of water,

> Wandering between two worlds, one dead,
> The other powerless to be born,
> With nowhere yet to rest my head.[46]

But if the loss of faith stood like a barrier between Arnold and traditional sources of joy, it is ironic that this loss was itself the by-product of the great critical effort of modern European thought which Arnold believed to offer the intellectual deliverance of the age. More than the loss of religion, even, it is this 'march of mind , this 'current of fresh opinion' which Arnold felt stood between his generation and Wordsworth's.

As a consequence, there is in Arnold's most characteristic poetry a tone of melancholy and regret which renders a stern though implicit judgement on Wordsworth. It is all the more stern because it represents an unconscious force in Arnold directly counter to his conscious rejection of melancholy self-indulgence and escapism in poetry. Arnold was quick to see, if he could not avoid, these qualities in his work; for example, we may refer to his criticism of *Empedocles on Etna* in the 1853 Preface and his remarks to Clough on *The Scholar-Gipsy*:

> I am glad you like the Gipsy Scholar—but what does it *do* for you ? Homer *animates*—Shakespeare *animates*—in its poor way I think Sohrab and Rustum animates—the Gipsy Scholar at best awakens a pleasing melancholy. But this is not what we want.
> > The complaining millions of men
> > Darken in labour and pain—
> what they want is something to *animate* and *ennoble* them—not merely to add zest to their melancholy or grace to their dreams.— I believe a feeling of this kind is the basis of my nature—and of my poetics.[47]

For all that Arnold could get from Wordsworth, the one thing that was not available to him as a poet was that very thing for which Arnold the critic most prized Wordsworth—his 'deep power of joy'. The nearest thing that Arnold could try in his poetry to achieve is peace, calm, stoic resignation; Wordsworth's influence was insufficient to provide him with any spiritual value more positive. The healing force, the solace, the refreshment which Arnold, like so many other Victorians, seemed to find in Wordsworth was insufficient to bring to the poet more than a melancholy sense of the increasing alienation between all that he most valued and the life around him, vulgarized, materialized, and brutalized.

If, however, Arnold was unable to gain poetic guidance from Wordsworth in meeting the poetic problems of his own age it certainly need not be considered the fault of Wordsworth, who had had different problems to cope with. F. R. Leavis argues that:

> It was possible for the poets of the Romantic period to believe that the interests animating their poetry were forces moving the world, or that might move it. But Victorian poetry admits implicitly that the actual world is alien, recalcitrant and unpoetical, and that no protest is worth making except the protest of withdrawal.[48]

Arnold, in his critical capacity, recognized this situation more clearly than any of his contemporaries, and he demanded a poetry which would offer more than escape. He wanted poetry to engage the whole attention of mature readers by meeting the demands of the intellect and not merely engaging the feelings, or some feelings. And yet as a poet he was able to go little further than his contemporaries in solving the attendant poetic problems. As a poet, his characteristic response to modern life, as Leavis argues, is evasion, differing from his fellow poets 'mainly in the cool, meditative lucidity of his waking dream'.[49] No critic has been more conscious than Arnold of the importance of milieu in the formation of poetry, and in some of his verse he seems to blame his hard luck in having been born too late (e.g., in *Obermann*, ll. 61–80). But when we consider the accomplishment of a poet like Gerard Manley Hopkins, although to be sure in isolation, we must recognize that it is more than a matter of the luck of having been born in one or another milieu that accounts for Arnold's failure in his own work to heal the breach between poetry and 'life'. He could see clearly the weaknesses of the contemporary poetical situation, he could distinguish in general the nature of the changes that modern poetry would have to undergo in order to re-establish contact with the serious interests of intelligent men like himself, and he saw himself indeed as a 'reformer in poetical matters'.[50] But Wordsworth, a more vigorous and independent poetic genius, had known that a true reform of poetry involved new concepts of the nature of poetry, and he had recognized that these new concepts implied the most drastic changes in the approach to language itself, the stuff of poetry. Arnold was insufficiently independent as a poet to break away from the dominant tradition of the 'poetic', and so he was unable to do much more than record mournfully, with 'sad lucidity', the nature and impact of the widening breach. Hence 'the poetic' comes to be more and more removed from those 'forces moving the world', it comes to be literary and Alexandrian in a way that Pope and Johnson would not have tolerated. The road from Wordsworth's *Michael* to Wilde's *Sphinx* goes past, among other signposts, Arnold's *Obermann* and *Scholar-Gipsy*.

It is in the characteristic tone of his poetry, then, that Arnold offers his most poignant implicit criticism of Wordsworth, or at least indicates the limits of Wordsworth's usefulness to him. In his style generally, Arnold offers Wordsworth the high critical tribute of emulation. Although he sometimes drew upon Milton, Keats, and Shelley among the English poets, there appear in almost every important poem of Arnold's cadences and turns of phrase, diction and imagery, which reveal an implicit acceptance of Wordsworth's style as a general standard. Above all, we find the influence of Wordsworth in Arnold's general rejection of verbal sensuousness, complexity, and 'conceitedness'—even to the point of being prosaic—and in his pursuit of an austere purity of diction. And I am not thinking of mere mechanical imitation; at his best Arnold was a poet of real if slight genius, and so could transform even what is most clearly borrowed to his own purposes. A glance at a whole poem may reveal this more clearly than any number of parallel passages. *Requiescat*, probably Arnold's most exquisite short lyric, is so purely Arnoldian that there is no stanza, scarcely a line, which is not evidently his own; yet there is probably no other poem which indicates more surely the line of his poetic descent from Wordsworth, and so it makes a fitting conclusion for this discussion of influence.

> Strew on her roses, roses,
> And never a spray of yew!
> In quiet she reposes;
> Ah, would that I did too!
>
> Her mirth the world required;
> She bathed it in smiles of glee.
> But her heart was tired, tired,
> And now they let her be.
>
> Her life was turning, turning,
> In mazes of heat and sound,
> But for peace her soul was yearning,
> And now peace laps her round.

Her cabin'd, ample spirit,
It flutter'd and fail'd for breath.
Tonight it doth inherit
The vasty hall of death.

II. CRITICISM IN VERSE

Although from his earliest poems, letters, and criticism, to his latest there is evidence of Arnold's continuing interest in Wordsworth, it is notable that certain attitudes seemed to be fixed so early that there is no special need to take account of chronological development. It is convenient, however, first to examine Arnold's explicit criticism of Wordsworth in verse, all of which was written before he published any prose criticism at all. In three poems written between 1849 and 1852 Arnold expressed the sum of his evaluation of Wordsworth. These are *Stanzas in Memory of the Author of 'Obermann'*, first published in 1852 but dated by the author November, 1849 (hereinafter called *Obermann*); *Memorial Verses*, composed after Wordsworth's death in the spring of 1850 and first published in *Fraser's Magazine* in June of that year; and *The Youth of Nature*, first published in 1852. In both *Obermann* and *Memorial Verses* Arnold uses a favourite technique, that of comparing and placing two or more writers; in *Obermann* he deals with Senancour, Goethe, and Wordsworth, and in *Memorial Verses* with Goethe, Byron, and Wordsworth. In *The Youth of Nature* Wordsworth appears alone; elegiac reflection becomes the occasion for raising certain questions about the relationship between man and nature. Of the three, I take *Memorial Verses* as the central document, the other two poems adding to or qualifying but not materially altering its criticism of Wordsworth.

In an undated letter presumably of May 1850, Arnold wrote to Arthur Hugh Clough, in familiarly flippant style, 'I would fain see thee as I have at Quillinan's sollicitation [*sic*] dirged W. W. *in the grand style* and need thy raptures therewith.'[51] This 'dirge' voices attitudes towards Wordsworth that are highly representative of Arnold's period, as witness Swinburne who in 1867 commented that these verses 'at once praise and judge the great poet, then newly dead, better than any words of other men'.[52] But the *Memorial Verses* are not only representative of an era; they also make up a document of central importance to our understanding of Arnold himself. T. S. Eliot has called the passage on Wordsworth

27

'not so much a criticism of Wordsworth as a testimonial of what Wordsworth had done for *him*'.[53] This, if true, is at the same time one of the most representative qualities of the critique. Consequently, it may be useful to review some of the many points of contact between this poem and other areas of Arnold's interest.

At least two features of the poem may be traceable to undergraduate influences on Arnold. The general grouping of Wordsworth with Byron and Goethe, and the relationship between them and Arnold's sense of *maladie du siècle* may derive from Carlyle, a significant influence on Arnold's youth.[54] At the same time, the therapeutic use of poetry and of Wordsworth's poetry in particular was being prescribed by John Keble, whose tenure of the chair of poetry at Oxford (1832–41) overlapped Arnold's undergraduate period there. Keble gave his lectures on poetry the significant title *De poeticae vi medica*, and in a lengthy Latin dedication to Wordsworth he used a number of phrases echoed by Arnold. Wordsworth is the *vates sacer* (cf. Arnold's 'he was a priest to us all' in *The Youth of Nature*) who lifted up men's hearts to holy things (*legentium animos ad sanctiora erigeret*) with his high and sacred truth (*divinae veritatis*) which is all the more precious in perilous times (*labente saeculo*).[55] In *Memorial Verses*, Arnold, somewhat more sentimentally, also tells how Wordsworth, in a 'wintry clime' and an 'iron time', worked upon the heart: 'He spoke, and loosed our heart in tears.'

In addition to these critical influences, at least three poets— aside from Wordsworth himself—seem to have contributed to the Wordsworth section of *Memorial Verses*. Thomas Gray, in Arnold's view a misplaced Romantic, may have contributed an important image. In his essay on Gray, Arnold associated him with Wordsworth, and he had high praise for *The Progress of Poesy*, in which appear these lines on Shakespeare:

> Far from the sun and summer-gale
> In thy green lap was Nature's darling laid.
> [ll. 83–4]

In *Memorial Verses* we are told that Wordsworth

> . . . laid us as we lay at birth
> On the cool flowery lap of earth.
> [ll. 48–9]

Another, more definite literary allusion, this time to Dante, strikes closer to the heart of Arnold's praise of Wordsworth. The story of Ugolino in the thirty-third canto of the *Inferno* seems to have spoken to something deep in Arnold. From this episode he later chose one of his touchstones, 'that incomparable line and a half of Dante, Ugolino's tremendous words—

> "Io no piangeva; si dentro impietrai.
> Piangevan elli . . ."'[56]

The petrifaction of the soul resulting from suppressed emotion is a common theme in Arnold's poetry, and it is as a liberator or emotion that Wordsworth is praised in *Memorial Verses*. The 'prison-cell' in the following passage from the periodical version of the poem indicates that the great passage of Dante was probably in Arnold's mind:

> He found us when the age had bound
> Our spirits in a brazen round:
> He spoke, and loosed our heart in tears.
> He tore us from the prison-cell
> Of festering thoughts and personal fears,
> Where we had long been doom'd to dwell.

The last three lines were later suppressed, and the second line became 'Our souls in its benumbing round', the passage thereby losing some of the force of the allusion. Arnold may have felt that the language was too violent for the context, or that they exaggerated, since Wordsworth did not actually liberate him from the Victorian inferno.

The third poetic parallel comes from Virgil, 'the most beautiful, the most attractive figure in literary history'. In his second book of the *Georgics* Virgil contrasts a philosophical poet, presumably Lucretius, with another kind rather like himself:

Happy he who hath availed to know the causes of things, and hath laid all fears and immitigable Fate and the roar of hungry Acheron under his feet; yet he is no less blessed, who knows the gods of the country, Pan and old Silvanus and the Nymphs' sisterhood.

Arnold almost certainly had this passage in mind in his comparison of Goethe and Wordsworth.[57] Here is Arnold on Goethe:

> And he was happy, if to know
> Causes of things, and far below
> His feet to see the lurid flow
> Of terror, and insane distress,
> And headlong fate, be happiness.   [ll. 29–33][58]

29

Arnold's emphasis upon the pastoral-idyllic element in Wordsworth's poetry is reminiscent of Virgil's description of the joys of
the nature poet:

> What fruits the boughs, what the gracious fields bear of their own
> free will, these he gathers, and sees not the iron of justice or the
> mad forum and the archives of the people.[59]

This sentiment is given a more sinister implication in *Obermann*:

> But Wordsworth's eyes avert their ken
> From half of human fate

and there is a related passage, but without the note of depreciation,
in *The Youth of Nature*:

> The complaining millions of men
> Darken in labour and pain;
> But he was a priest to us all
> Of the wonder and bloom of the world.
>
> [ll. 51–4]

Arnold confessed to 'a profound, an almost affectionate veneration' for Virgil in language almost identical to that used more than
twenty years later in his personal tribute to Wordsworth, and in
his 'Wordsworth' essay he quotes a line about the 'pii vates' from
Virgil. But his final judgement on Virgil, like that on Wordsworth,
was that he was not adequate. However, where Wordsworth's
inadequacy was intellectual, Virgil's was temperamental: 'Over the
whole of the great poem of Virgil, over the whole Aeneid, there
rests an ineffable melancholy . . . which is at once a source of charm
in the poem, and a testimony to its incompleteness.'[60] In characterizing Virgil's deficiency, Arnold might have been speaking of
himself, while at the same time illuminating his admiration for
Wordsworth's 'deep power of joy'.

Out of this rich ground in Arnold's reading and experience grew
the *Memorial Verses*. A significant clue to the nature of this tribute
may be found in the word 'soothing' [l. 35]; Wordsworth's voice,
more than those of his two great contemporaries Goethe and
Byron, more even than the voice of any other poet since Orpheus,
was 'soothing'. Allowing for some poetic hyperbole, the choice of
Orpheus for the comparison is notable. It was Orpheus whose singing could enchant the very stones and trees, bring the inanimate
to life, and even suspend the torment of the damned. The Hades

of Orpheus is comparable to the 'wintry clime' of Modern England,

> this iron time
> Of doubts, disputes, distractions, fears.
>
> [ll. 43–4]

The allusion mentioned above to Dante's story of Ugolino reinforces the Orpheus–Hades parallel, although the hell has become the modern inferno of subjective isolation and sterility. T. S. Eliot in *The Waste Land* alluded to the same passage of Dante in expressing a similar sense of spiritual isolation and desiccation:

> I have heard the key
> Turn in the door once and turn once only
> We think of the key, each in his prison
> Thinking of the key, each confirms a prison.

But what did Wordsworth offer to the sufferers of 'this strange disease of modern life, / With its sick hurry, its divided aims'? Not strength to bear, not wisdom to understand—the gifts of Byron and Goethe—but rather a respite, a source of refreshment from the fount of primal feeling,

> The freshness of the early world.
>
> [l. 57]

Precisely what world this is is not clear. Some critics of Arnold assume that in stressing the pastoral he is merely, or at any rate mainly, valuing Wordsworth as a 'nature poet'. It is true that Arnold did probably pay more attention to this aspect of Wordsworth's genius than some modern critics would like, but I believe that he is by no means simply making a conventional undergraduate assessment. Although the imagery involves 'hills' and 'fields', the total force of the central passage indicates a symbolic and psychological identification of 'nature' with root emotional experience, so that the landscape of the poem becomes an almost mythic lost garden, and this mythic quality is enforced by the comparison of Wordsworth to Orpheus and by the resultant associations of Orphic resurrectionist mystery. I am not trying to turn Arnold into a twentieth-century poet fresh from reading *The Golden Bough*, of course, but it seems to me that the poem itself demands a recognition of its symbolic intentions. If these are granted, it appears that

31

Arnold may have possessed a deeper understanding of Wordsworthian wisdom (as distinguished from formal philosophy) than
he is commonly credited with:

> He laid us as we lay at birth
> On the cool flowery lap of earth,
> * Smiles broke from us and we had ease;
> The hills were round us, and the breeze
> Went o'er the sun-lit fields again;
> Our foreheads felt the wind and rain.
> Our youth return'd; for there was shed
> On spirits that had long been dead,
> Spirits dried up and closely furl'd,
> The freshness of the early world.
>
> [ll. 48–57]

The landscape elements of this passage should be seen against the
context of the earlier description of the infernal landscape of
'mournful gloom' [l. 39] associated with the 'benumbing round'
[l. 46] of modern life, rather than as recollections of summer
vacations in the Lake Country. Wordsworth's 'healing power'
[l. 63] lies in his ability to put us in touch with our own deeper
selves, that 'central stream of what we feel indeed' that courses
through 'our buried life'.[61]

But this power has its limitations, implied in the word 'soothing',
and perhaps in the Orpheus comparison as well; Orpheus did not,
after all, manage to lead his Eurydice back to the upper world.
Wordsworth offered healing respite from the problems of self, and
the problems of modernity, but he did not adequately interpret the
modern world and so does not help us to master it:

> The cloud of mortal destiny,
> Others will front it fearlessly—
> But who, like him, will put it by?
>
> [ll. 68–70]

This cloud cannot forever be put by; for Arnold, only the great
tragic poets succeed in 'breasting in full the storm and cloud of
life' and so rising to liberation, to 'content and joy'.[62] Arnold has
been interpreted to mean that Wordsworth ignored or underestimated the problem of evil; I do not believe, as I shall argue
further below, that this is a correct interpretation. Rather, he is
saying that Wordsworth, by turning his back on modern life and

ideas, by failing to expose his consciousness fully to the disintegration of the old order, had limited the possibilities of his interpretative relevance. What he did was much; he helped nourish and keep alive the very springs of life during a wintry season. But this, though necessary, is not sufficient for that total interpretation of life in all its fullness which Arnold posited as the highest goal of literature. Nevertheless, Wordsworth's gift, in spite of limitations, is precious and rare. In one of the *Switzerland* poems Arnold said

> That will, that energy, though rare
> Are yet far, far less rare than love.

Not only will and energy, but even supreme intelligence is less rare than the power of true feeling, Wordsworth's power, according to *Memorial Verses*:

> Time may restore us in his course,
> Goethe's sage mind and Byron's force;
> But where will Europe's latter hour
> Again find Wordsworth's healing power?
> Others will teach us how to dare,
> And against fear our breast to steel;
> Others will strengthen us to bear—
> But who, ah! who, will make us feel?
> [ll. 60–7]

If it is implied in *Memorial Verses* that Wordsworth's value is limited, these limits are indicated more directly in *Stanzas in Memory of the Author of 'Obermann'*. Here Wordsworth is placed with Goethe and Senancour as one of the three reigning spirits of 'our troubled day' [l. 46], the only three who have 'attain'd . . . to see their way' [ll. 47–8]. But his 'sweet calm' [l. 79] was bought at the expense of turning away from the harassing problems of an age of change:

> But Wordsworth's eyes avert their ken
> From half of human fate.
> [ll. 53–4]

The context should make it clear that Arnold does not mean either that Wordsworth's retirement to the Lake Country was in itself an evasion, since Senancour also withdrew from Paris and retired to the Swiss Alps, or that Wordsworth ignored the darker aspects of life *per se*. The grouping of writers shows, rather, that Arnold is again concerned with the matter of interpretative adaptation to the special problems of modern life, especially the problems of loss and change in the intellectual realm.

To Arnold, it seems, Senancour was more representative of the modern spirit than either Wordsworth or Goethe. The teachings of the former are true but limited in scope. The latter, called in *Memorial Verses* the 'physician of the iron age', did attain a 'wide and luminous view' [*Obermann*, ll. 79–80], but his path may scarcely be followed by moderns who have had no opportunity like his to reach their prime in the stability of a 'tranquil world' [l. 67]:

> Like children bathing on the shore,
> Buried a wave beneath,
> The second wave succeeds, before
> We have had time to breathe.
>
> [ll. 73–6][63]

Arnold amplified his judgment of the special significance of Senancour in his essay on 'Obermann':

> His constant inwardness, his unremitting occupation with that question which haunted St. Bernard—*Bernarde, ad quid venisti?*— distinguish him from Goethe and Wordsworth, whose study of this question is relieved by the thousand distractions of a poetic interest in nature and man.[64]

This remark might seem to indicate that Senancour averted his eyes from more of human fate than Wordsworth. The point, however, is that Senancour's more perfectly detached introspection gave him a purer and sharper vision of the special disintegrative conditions of modern life.

That this unremitting occupation led to disillusion with the world's goods and to 'icy despair' [l. 88] helps account for Arnold's temperamental attraction to and critical overestimation of Senancour. Undoubtedly Senancour's rejection of the world in favour of the pursuit of inward truth made a powerful appeal to Arnold, in whose poetry the theme of withdrawal and solitude is one of the most persistent. Perhaps this melancholy was even more appealing to him than Wordsworth's power of joy. Nevertheless, if Arnold pays due tribute to the lesson of Senancour, the lesson of solitude and the refusal to be carried away by the teachings of the world

and its confusion, he also insists that the poet is driven by two
desires:

> Ah! two desires toss about
> The poet's feverish blood.
> One drives him to the world without,
> And one to solitude.
>
> [ll. 93–6][65]

And so he, or the narrator representing him in the poem, at last
turns consciously away from 'the master of his wandering youth'
and returns to the world, leaving but half his life with the 'melancholy shade' [ll. 132, 138].[66] Perhaps he recalls the lesson of
Wordsworth as a corrective to the attraction of Senancour, the
lesson that hope is

> The paramount *duty* which Heaven lays,
> For its own honour, on man's suffering heart.

At any rate, the apostrophe to Senancour,

> O unstrung will! O broken heart!
>
> [l. 183]

is immediately and conclusively followed by

> A last, a last farewell!
>
> [l. 184]

Even if Arnold was temperamentally able to make but limited
use of Wordsworth's power of joy—and if Wordsworth himself
only achieved the power at the cost of limiting his purview—the
lesson of Wordsworth's joy is ultimately of more value than the
example of Senancour's icy despair. Senancour belonged to
Arnold's youth. In *Obermann*, written in 1849, Arnold already bids
him farewell; in *Stanzas from the Grande Chartreuse* (1855)
Senancour is one, with Byron and Shelley, of a trio of failures.
And almost twenty years after *Obermann*, in *Obermann Once More*,
it is Senancour himself, introduced dramatically, who is made to
remind Arnold that 'men have such need of joy' [l. 237], and who
instructs him:

> Despair not thou as I despair'd,
> Nor be cold gloom thy prison!
> Forward the gracious hours have fared,
> And see! the sun is risen!
>
> [ll. 281–4]

No wholly new ideas on Wordsworth as a poet are introduced in
The Youth of Nature written a little more than two years after
Obermann and about a year and a half after *Memorial Verses*.
Arnold, taking a lonely walk along Rydal and Grasmere on a bright,
windy January day in 1852, was moved to deal again with the world
of Nature and with Wordsworth.[67] The hieratic elements latent in
the imagery of *Memorial Verses* here become overt; Wordsworth
is characterized as

> . . . a priest to us all
> Of the wonder and bloom of the world,
> Which we saw with his eyes, and were glad.
> [ll. 53–5]

Again there is the theme of 'the dissolving throes / Of a social order'
[ll. 31–2]; the loss of a 'sacred poet' is the more poignant 'In an
age which can rear them no more!' [ll. 49–50]. But a different aspect
of Wordsworth is emphasized in the picture of the aged seer who
has outlived his time, an idea reminiscent of *Empedocles on Etna*
which was being written about this time. A comparison is made
between Wordsworth and Tiresias:

> He grew old in an age he condemn'd.
> He looked on the rushing decay
> Of the times which had shelter'd his youth;
> Felt the dissolving throes
> Of a social order he loved;
> Outlived his brethren, his peers,
> And, like the Theban seer,
> Died in his enemies' day.
> [ll. 28–35]

This is followed by an apparently digressive strophe on the death
of Tiresias, concluding:

> Nor did reviving Thebes
> See such a prophet again.
> [ll. 46–7]

The comparison with Tiresias may be intended to stress
obliquely both Wordsworth's place in English poetry as the
successor to Milton, and a general view of poetry as a species of
prophecy. However, a few lines further on there is an elliptical and
rather ambiguous 'But' which may offer further explanation for
the elaboration of the Tiresias comparison:

36

> The complaining millions of men
> Darken in labour and pain;
> But he was a priest to us all
> Of the wonder and bloom of the world,
> Which we saw with his eyes, and were glad.   [ll. 51–5]

The *But* of line 53 may be taken in a positive sense: 'We were troubled and in darkness; at least he was of some help . . .' or, more negatively, suggesting the same limitation as that mentioned in *Obermann*: 'At a time when all is so darkened and troubled, he can only preach no longer attainable values. . . .' Probably Arnold consciously intended the former, but the latter interpretation suggests an interesting ambiguity in the Tiresias comparison: is Wordsworth being compared with Tiresias as much for his blindness ('Wordsworth's eyes avert their ken') as for his vision? Such subtle ironies were probably far from Arnold's conscious intentions, whatever they may unconsciously reveal. Arnold believed in plainness of style; hence submerged ambiguities in his poetry are likely to be the result of unclear thought, loosely connected imagery, or emotional ambivalence, rather than of a carefully planned poetic strategy.

Still, the ironic implication of blindness in vision has its attractiveness in interpreting this poem, for it provides a structural link between the first section, fifty-eight lines of mourning for Wordsworth, and the second section, seventy-six lines of philosophizing rather loosely connected with the first section. The specific limitation of vision implied of Wordsworth–Tiresias may be expanded to cover the inherent limitations of finite Man puzzling himself in an unsuccessful quest for significance in infinite and inscrutable Nature. In the second part of the poem, Arnold raises the question of the nature of external reality, most of this section being assigned as a dramatic speech to personified Nature. Arnold's musings about the nature of Nature are often obscure and frequently contradictory, but in general we may say that although he loved landscapes, flowers, dogs, fishing, etc., he reflected the advanced ideas of his time in regarding Nature as inscrutable and indifferent to man, if not outright hostile; this attitude in turn helps account for his limited ability to accept Wordsworthian philosophy. The title of the poem itself returns us to the 'early world' of *Memorial Verses*, while the anti-Wordsworthian indifference of Nature to Man expressed in her speech in the poem implies again the limited value of Wordsworth's philosophy in a more 'mature' age. In quality this section of *The Youth of Nature* is inferior to the first section, which is full of concrete and delicate evocations of the Wordsworth country. The inadequacy of the second section has been well described by Joseph Warren Beach:

> This is feeble poetry and perfunctory morality. The poem is highly inadequate either as a criticism of Wordsworthian nature-philosophy or as a defense of it—this futile questioning as to whether nature is or isn't there. It exhibits too dim a sense on Arnold's part of the complex and massive implications of the term nature to Wordsworth's generation.[68]

Before turning now to Arnold's criticism of Wordsworth in his prose works, let us summarize the early criticism that we have found expressed in verse. Most of Arnold's abiding attitudes have already been expressed; the only totally new matter will be the criticism of style. Most insistent is the theme of Wordsworth as a priest of nature whose special gift was his ability to revive and stimulate the emotions and recall to us the joy in the primal affections. This theme is related to that of the *maladie du siècle*; Wordsworth's gift is of special value because of its timeliness, helping to bring the refreshing waters of life into a parched desert. On the other hand, there is the theme of Wordsworth's limitations and the consequent restriction of his usefulness. Wordsworth's helpfulness is restricted partly because his readers are the victims of the very malady which gives Wordsworth his specially poignant value; they can no longer feel as he felt. But partly it is the fault of Wordsworth, who achieved his equilibrium at the expense of turning away from those problems which moderns most feel the need of solving. Finally, the true value of Wordsworth lies in his experience, not in his interpretation of it, what F. R. Leavis has called his wisdom rather than his philosophy.[69] The effort to extract a philosophy from Nature is mocked by Nature herself:

> Race after race, man after man,
> Have thought that my secret was theirs,
> Have dream'd that I liv'd but for them,
> That they were my glory and joy.
> —They are dust, they are changed, they are gone!
> I remain.
>
> [*The Youth of Nature*, ll. 129–34]

38

III. CRITICISM IN PROSE

Style

Two elements loom up and tend to dominate Arnold's formal prose criticism of Wordsworth. One is his rejection of Wordsworth's philosophy, the other is his criticism of Wordsworth's style. The first element, the rejection of the philosophy, is not wholly new, having already been adumbrated in some of the poetic criticism, as we have seen. Arnold has been accused of undervaluing the philosophy partly because of his popularizing intentions; this point is of especial relevance to the selections from Wordsworth which he edited in 1879, and will be discussed further in connection with that volume. In addition, as he hinted in *The Youth of Nature*, Arnold found Wordsworth's experience of far higher value than the philosophy derived from it; here Arnold also shows not only his general distrust of system, but his sound sense of how poetry works. Finally, Arnold's attitude towards the philosophy is related to his specifically poetic criticism of Wordsworth, and connects with his discussion of style. Arnold's intention in dealing with Wordsworth was always to emphasize his greatness as a poet. To bring into clear relief the best poetry, and the truth in the best poetry, he felt it necessary to prune away the jungles of prosy moralizing, no matter how virtuous it might be as preaching. True poetry, he said repeatedly, is

> a criticism of life under the conditions fixed for such a criticism by the laws of poetic truth and poetic beauty.[70]

In the essay on 'Wordsworth', Arnold states this essential, if somewhat vague, qualification twice over, and explicitly denies that by 'treating in poetry moral ideas' he means 'composing moral and didactic poems'. He even rewrites history in this essay in order to emphasize the aesthetic element. In *Last Words on Translating Homer* he had said:

> Poets receive their distinctive character, not from their subject, but from their application to that subject of the ideas (to quote the *Excursion*)
> 'On God, on Nature, and on human life',
> which they have acquired for themselves.[71]

4   39

In 1879 he recalled the statement with a significant addition (my italics):

> Long ago, in speaking of Homer, I said that the noble and profound application of ideas to life is the most essential part of poetic greatness. I said that a great poet receives his distinctive character from his application, *under the conditions immutably fixed by the laws of poetic beauty and poetic truth*, from his application, I say, to his subject, whatever it may be, of the ideas
>
> 'On man, on nature, and on human life',
>
> which he has acquired for himself.[72]

Arnold did not see any inconsistency in rejecting the Words-worthian 'philosophy', considered as a set of ideas abstracted from the poetry, while at the same time praising the truth and beauty of Wordsworth's 'criticism of life' in his poetry. Arnold was not acting the part of philosophical critic, sorting out good ideas from bad. The point which so many of Arnold's critics have tended to overlook is that he was engaging himself as a literary critic, sorting out good *poetry* from bad, and he was, moreover, implicitly defending the right to assume such a position. Hence Arnold's criticism of Wordsworth's style, a second major element in his prose criticism, is particularly significant. No explicit and little successful implicit stylistic criticism of Wordsworth is to be found in Arnold's verse; for this we must turn to his prose.

In the essay 'Maurice de Guérin' (1863), Arnold puts forward the idea that 'The grand power of poetry is its interpretative power.' He then distinguishes between two types of interpretation, that of the natural world, producing at its best *natural magic*, and that of the moral world, producing at its best moral profundity. Although Wordsworth's glory is ultimately to be made to rest mainly upon the latter, he was also outstanding in his capacity for the former. His

> voice . . . heard
> In springtime from the cuckoo-bird
> Breaking the silence of the seas
> Among the farthest Hebrides

is selected for quotation along with passages from Shakespeare, Chateaubriand, Senancour, and Keats to demonstrate how poetry, not science, gives us the 'true sense of animals, or water, or plants' by making us 'participate in their life'. Although later in the same essay what Arnold affirms tentatively of Shakespeare—that in those poets who unite both kinds of interpretation the moral usually ends by making itself master—is 'yet more strongly affirmed of Lucretius and Wordsworth', the emphasis on Wordsworth's power of natural interpretation is never neglected.

Indeed, some critics have gone so far as to claim that Arnold tried to reduce Wordsworth to a kind of Celtic bard.[73] Some warrant for this point of view may be derived from Arnold's poetic dealings with Wordsworth, but the place where he seems nearest to adopting such a limiting view is in *On the Study of Celtic Literature* (1866). There he recapitulates at one point in a discussion of 'natural magic' the catalogue of quotations from 'Maurice de Guérin', with some minor alterations; Wordsworth's cuckoo-bird, however, is still prominent. And in the conclusion of *Celtic Literature* Wordsworth is significantly paired with Keats as a poet of natural magic.[74] However, in these lectures, it should be remembered, Arnold scarcely considers the question of moral interpretation, at least directly. Most of the book is a plea for the English to give freer play to the Celtic element in them, which is to say their feelings for beauty and passion. They need to be incited to a richer emotional life. However, they also need to broaden and enrich their intellectual life, and this point forms the other pole of this study. Hence, in one of his characteristic turns, Arnold in the end awards the palm in modern poetry to the Germans—that is, Goethe—after having devoted most of the book to praising the Celtic qualities lacking in the German. The award is made for the high success of German poetry with 'the immense serious task it had to perform'. Arnold's description of this task, out of context, is ambiguous: 'the grand business of modern poetry,—a moral interpretation, from an independent point of view, of man and the world'.[75] Seen against the background of Arnold's thought, the words which should emerge are 'from an independent point of view'; that is, modern German poetry has succeeded in applying modern ideas to life, succeeded more than any other body of modern poetry in taking full account of modern intellectual developments in making its moral interpretation of life. Consequently it is not inconsistent for Arnold to stress in this context the nature poet aspect of Wordsworth, since in his capacity as a 'priest of nature' he offers something the Germans cannot, while at the same time

> the one thing wanting to make Wordsworth an even greater poet than he is,—his thought richer, and his influence of wider application,—was that he should have read more books, among them, no doubt, those of that Goethe whom he disparaged without reading him.[76]

It is characteristic of Arnold as a critic 'ondoyant et divers' that he considers only those aspects of whatever literature is under discussion which are relevant to his immediate purpose, and that purpose is generally involved with addressing a specific argument or a specific audience, the literary criticism being subordinate to the occasion.

In the essay on Wordsworth (1879), the value of Wordsworth's moral interpretation is given a leading place, as it is again in the later 'Byron' essay. There is, moreover, no mention of 'natural magic', although 'nature' still plays a fairly prominent role even in the discussion of style. The twofold source of Wordsworth's greatness, according to Arnold, is in his 'extraordinary power' to feel 'the joy offered to us in nature' and 'the joy offered to us in the simple primary affections and duties;' his greatness is exhibited by 'the extraordinary power with which, in cases after case, he shows us this joy, and renders it so as to make us share it'. His power to feel these things is a part of his good fortune as a man, presumably, but his power to 'show' and 'render' is what makes him a poet: it is his style. Faced, however, by the great disparity between the poetic quality of Wordsworth's best poetry and his worst lapses, Arnold flounders. He quotes exquisitely, but when it comes to explaining the special quality of Wordsworth's style, and its special defects, he makes little headway.

On his critical perception of the poor quality of much of Wordsworth's verse, and on his belief that the poet's later alterations of his poetry are in general not improvements,[77] Arnold bases his conclusion that Wordsworth was not at best a conscious artist, and that when he tried too hard he often produced his worst work:

> Work altogether inferior, work quite uninspired, flat and dull, is produced by him with evident unconsciousness of its defects, and he presents it to us with the same faith and seriousness as his best work.

Wordsworth's greatness in expression, when he is great, is more a matter of luck ('inspiration') and character ('sincereness') than of mastery of his medium. At his best, 'He has no style':

> It might seem that Nature not only gave him the matter for his poem, but wrote the poem for him.

He learned much from Milton and occasionally rises to heights of Miltonic eloquence, and much from Burns, too, who could show him

> a style of perfect plainness, relying for its effect solely on the weight and force of that which with entire fidelity it utters.

At his best, however, Wordsworth is

> unique and unmatchable. Nature herself seems, I say, to take the pen out of his hand, and to write for him with her own bare, sheer, penetrating power.

'This arises from two causes', Arnold continues, as though he were about to give an explanation:

> from the profound sincereness with which Wordsworth feels his subject, and also from the profoundly sincere and natural character of his subject itself.[78]

Even the reader who agrees fully with the general tenor of this criticism is bound to feel dissatisfied with such pseudo-analysis; it would be difficult to match this example of question-begging and circularity in any other critic of comparable power and scope. For surely poetry as great as Wordsworth's greatest cannot be produced—and Arnold as a poet must have known this—without great artistry. The poet's worthiness as a person is not sufficient to account for it; and what can Arnold mean by the 'sincere and natural character' of the subject of a poem? And how can what style utters possess 'weight and force' apart from the language in which it is uttered?

The explanation for such aberrations seems to be that as Arnold ceased to be a practising poet, the tact with which he could select poetry and pass general judgements on it did not desert him, at least when he was dealing with poetry that fell within his range of appreciation. But his powers as an analytic critic suffered from a kind of inattentiveness to how poems are actually made. Consequently, the touchstone method came into increasing prominence as a way of avoiding particular analysis. A striking example of the confusion into which this failure to see clearly the relation of style and subject can betray the critic follows immediately after the passage just quoted above. With his usual good taste Arnold selects *Resolution and Independence* as a poem illustrating Wordsworth's special power. But when he says that Wordsworth's expression in this poem 'is bald as the bare mountain tops are bald, with a baldness which is full of grandeur', it is clear that his eye is not on the object, to use against him one of his own favourite Wordsworthianisms. Walter Pater, in an earlier essay, was certainly closer to the truth, as any reader can confirm by glancing at the poem, when he compared *Resolution and Independence* to Keats's *The Eve of St. Agnes* 'for its fulness of imagery'.[79] The greater refinement of Arnold's insight into the particularities of style in his earlier criticism may be illustrated by another passage on Wordsworth's style, from what is undoubtedly Arnold's finest work of sustained literary criticism, the lectures *On Translating Homer*. Moved to speak for once about a contemporary by the 'ridiculous elevation' of Tennyson above Wordsworth,[80] Arnold defines with absolute precision the difference between the authentic simplicity of Wordsworth and the artful imitation of it by Tennyson. It is true that he does not offer detailed analysis in support of his intuition, but the aptness of his quoting and the delicacy of his general comments tend to make such analysis almost superfluous:

> French criticism, richer in its vocabulary than ours, has invented a useful word to distinguish this semblance (often very beautiful and valuable) from the real quality. The real quality it calls *simplicité*, the semblance *simplesse*. The one is natural simplicity, the other is artificial simplicity. What is called simplicity in the productions of a genius essentially not simple, is, in truth, *simplesse*. The two are distinguishable from one another the moment they appear in company. For instance, let us take the opening of the narrative in Wordsworth's *Michael*:—
>
>> 'Upon the forest-side in Grasmere Vale
>> There dwelt a shepherd, Michael was his name;
>> An old man, stout of heart, and strong of limb.
>> His bodily frame had been from youth to age
>> Of an unusual strength; his mind was keen,
>> Intense, and frugal, apt for all affairs;
>> And in his shepherd's calling he was prompt
>> And watchful more than ordinary men.'

Now let us take the opening of the narrative in Mr. Tennyson's *Dora*:—

> 'With Farmer Allan at the farm abode
> William and Dora. William was his son,
> And she his niece. He often looked at them,
> And often thought, "I'll make them man and wife."'

The simplicity of the first of these passages is *simplicité*; that of the second, *simplesse*. Let us take the end of the same two poems: first, of *Michael*:—

> 'The cottage which was named the Evening Star
> Is gone,—the ploughshare has been through the ground
> On which it stood; great changes have been wrought
> In all the neighbourhood: yet the oak is left
> That grew beside their door: and the remains
> Of the unfinished sheepfold may be seen
> Beside the boisterous brook of Green-head Ghyll.'

And now, of *Dora*:—

> 'So those four abode
> Within one house together; and as years
> Went forward, Mary took another mate:
> But Dora lived unmarried till her death.'

A heedless critic may call both of these passsages simple if he will. Simple, in a certain sense, they both are; but between the simplicity of the two there is all the difference that there is between the simplicity of Homer and the simplicity of Moschus.[81]

There is no confusion here between the appearance of an old leech gatherer and the language of a poem about him; the critic's eye is plainly on the object.

Arnold's doctrine of 'unconsciousness' and 'inspiration' at any rate does have the virtue of taking account of Wordsworth's unevenness, and it also allows Arnold to offer some explanation of the weaker efforts, particularly in blank verse. Wordsworth's 'true and most characteristic form of expression', says Arnold, 'is a line like this from *Michael*—

> 'And never lifted up a single stone"'

with its noble plainness, or in the 'natural magic' of the cuckoo passage of *The Solitary Reaper*; at times he rises to heights even of

Miltonic grandeur. However, where Milton was master of his style, Wordsworth is not; when he is trying too hard to have a style, he is most likely to fail by falling into 'ponderosity and pomposity'. This judgement in 'Wordsworth' is essentially a recapitulation of an earlier discussion in *On Translating Homer*:

> ... what distinguishes the greatest masters of poetry from all others is, that they are perfectly sound and poetical in these level regions of their subject,—in these regions which are the great difficulty of all poets but the very greatest ... when Wordsworth, having to narrate a very plain matter, tries not to sink in narrating it, tries, in short, to be what is falsely called poetical, he does sink, although he sinks by being pompous, not by being low.

> > 'Onward we drove beneath the Castle; caught,
> > While crossing Magdalen Bridge, a glimpse of Cam,
> > And at the Hoop alighted, famous inn.'

> That last line shows excellently how a poet may sink with his subject by resolving not to sink with it. A page or two farther on, the subject rises to grandeur, and then Wordsworth is nobly worthy of it:

> > 'The antechapel, where the statue stood
> > Of Newton with his prism and silent face,
> > The marble index of a mind for ever
> > Voyaging through strange seas of thought, alone.'

> But the supreme poet is he who is thoroughly sound and poetical, alike when his subject is grand, and when it is plain: with him the subject may sink, but never the poet.[82]

In a later essay ('A French critic on Milton', 1877) Arnold again contrasts Milton's accomplishment in blank verse with the 'ever-recurrent failure, both in rhythm and diction' of Thomson, Cowper, and Wordsworth, and again quotes the same offending line, exclaiming over it: 'To render a platitude endurable by making it pompous!'[83] This passage from Arnold's later criticism incidentally illustrates further his increasing crudeness in the handling of critical vocabulary as more time and different interests separated him from his own days as a poet; the objectionable line is weak neither in rhythm nor diction, considered in themselves, but rather in *tone*, as Arnold's exclamation indicates. In *Homer* (1861) and earlier he had seen this distinction quite clearly. For example, in a letter of 1853 he refers to a recent article on Wordsworth:

> Perhaps it does not sufficiently praise his *diction*: his *manner* was often bad, but his diction scarcely ever—and beyond Moore's etc.—constantly.[84]

A résumé of the main points and overall tendency of Arnold's criticism of Wordsworth's style shows that it is of a piece with his general estimate of Wordsworth, or rather runs parallel with it. Arnold's judgement that Wordsworth was not a master of style, particularly in blank verse, has its counterpart in his general rejection of the most ambitious works from the canon of the most successful: 'The *Excursion* and the *Prelude*, his poems of greatest bulk, are by no means Wordsworth's best work.' In fact, Arnold goes so far as to concur with Jeffrey's judgement of the *Excursion* as regards poetic style: 'This will never do.' Wordsworth at his best is an inspired bard who can reach unmatched heights, but not through conscious control of his craft ('In Wordsworth's case, the accident, for so it may almost be called, of inspiration, is of peculiar importance'), just as his moral insight into 'the truest and most unfailing source of joy' is deep but restricted, limited by his narrowness of intellectual culture. His deficient power to sustain the style needed for long poems is related to the lack of philosophic breadth needed for a mastery of modern problems—the breadth, say, of a Goethe. This limitedness of his 'criticism of life' is, finally, reflected in the limitedness of his self-criticism as a poet shown by the frequent juxtaposition of good pieces with inferior ones, by his 'ingenious but far-fetched' arrangement of his poems, and by his general inability to revise his earlier work without marring it.[85]

Wordsworth's Thought

Although Matthew Arnold's 1879 essay on Wordsworth contained little criticism that was strikingly original, it probably did more than any other piece of Wordsworth criticism to specify and bring to a focus most of the issues which have been argued and expounded ever since by scholars and critics. Probably none of these issues has proved more controversial than the problem of Wordsworth's philosophy; since Arnold, almost every writer on Wordsworth has been compelled to deal with the question more or less in the terms in which Arnold left it. These terms are in the main resolvable into two points, which may be considered separately for purposes of discussion: first, the question of the validity, breadth, and usefulness of the philosophy; and second, the question of its relevance to Wordsworth's greatness. A recent compendium of Wordsworthian criticism by a number of eminent critics shows clearly that the controversy is still very much alive a century after Wordsworth's death; I refer to *Wordsworth: Centenary Studies Presented at Cornell and Princeton Universities*, which contains contributions by such eminent writers as Douglas Bush, Lionel Trilling, John Crowe Ransom, and others. The trend of most criticism since A. C. Bradley's essays early in this century has been to pay serious attention to the philosophy; this may be seen from the title of the essay in *Centenary Studies* in which Douglas Bush substantially reiterates Arnold's arguments, or attitudes: 'A Minority Report.'

Professor Bush, citing Arnold's poetry for support, carries on one side of the argument; namely that Wordsworth 'withdrew from the problems of the modern mind', and 'slighted the darker and grimmer elements in life'. Another side of Arnold's argument has been carried on by F. R. Leavis, who, like Arnold, believes that 'even if Wordsworth had a philosophy, it is as a poet that he matters'.[86] The latter side of the argument may be dealt with simply, since I suppose that it is won for our time. It would be difficult today to find an advocate for any view which attempted to elevate as great art any purportedly imaginative literature solely, or primarily, on the grounds that it contains sound doctrine or valuable philosophy. Indeed, when this view is expressed thus baldly, it is difficult to imagine a significant critic of any age who would defend such a critical standard—least of all Wordsworth himself, who, in his criticism, emphasized the *dulce* of poetry quite as much as the *utile*. That Arnold felt called upon to attack this didactic view at all may be attributed partly to the low state of Victorian criticism, and perhaps even more to the unique position occupied by Wordsworth as a spiritual force in the nineteenth century.[87] Today Wordsworth may still be a spiritual force, and he is certainly still a literary force, but the age of 'Wordsworthianism' is gone.

It should, of course, be remembered that Arnold was no enemy of thought in poetry but the reverse, provided the emphasis is on the poetry. Indeed, he argued that the failure of the poetry of the

48

great Romantics was not due to inadequacy of energy or of creative talent, but to its inadequacy of ideas;

> This makes Byron so empty of matter, Shelley so incoherent, Wordsworth, even, profound as he is, yet so wanting in completeness and variety. Wordsworth cared little for books and disparaged Goethe. I admire Wordsworth, as he is, so much that I cannot wish him different; and it is vain, no doubt, to imagine such a man different from what he is, to suppose that he *could* have been different. But surely the one thing wanting to make Wordsworth an even greater poet than he is,—his thought richer, and his influence of wider application,—was that he should have read more books. . . .[88]

Furthermore, in the essay on Wordsworth it is not Wordsworth's thought as such that is rejected; on the contrary, so far as it is made concrete in great or good verse it is welcomed.[89] And more than welcomed, even, for Wordsworth's superiority to many poets who surpassed him in individual pieces is made to lie precisely in the greatness of his power in dealing poetically with moral ideas. To be sure we are told of limitations: he was insufficiently immersed in modern culture to deal adequately with the intellectual needs and problems of the period, and, after the great decade beginning in 1798, there was a falling off of poetic power reflected in a tendency toward prosy didacticism. But in spite of these, Arnold's high praise of Wordsworth remains, that he was a poet who produced a sufficient mass of work which united 'profound truth of subject with profound truth of execution' to rank as a modern classic.

Hence, when we see that Arnold's function is that of a literary critic, there is no inconsistency as some have charged in his rejection of Wordsworth's 'philosophy'.[90] Because, says Arnold, the Wordsworthians tend to overlook the fact that Wordsworth is great because he is a great poet, because they 'are apt to praise him for the wrong things', we must be on guard against them:

> His poetry is the reality, his philosophy,—*so far at least, as it may put on the form and habit of 'a scientific system of thought' and the more that it puts them on,*—is the illusion . . . we cannot do him justice until we dismiss the *formal* philosophy. [My italics.]

Arnold, that is, is defending the right of poetry to establish its own standards of value, and this defence need not be invalidated as mere rationalization by our recollection of his own hostility to systematic philosophy. What Arnold has said here of Wordsworth, if the words I have italicized are given their due weight, would be equally applicable to Milton, Dante, or Lucretius, whose value is surely not based on their cosmology, pneumatology, or other elements of their official 'thought'. Arnold did not criticize *The Excursion* or the philosophical poetry generally because it contained ideas, or because the ideas were not good ones, but because they were all too often spun into 'a tissue of elevated but abstract verbiage, alien to the very nature of poetry'.[91]

To be sure, Arnold did also criticize Wordsworth's ideas, but this is another matter. He did not say that Wordsworth's beliefs were wrong; he was not for dismissing them, but repeatedly stressed their value. Only, he believed that Wordsworth's thought was limited. This criticism is generally held to involve two points: first, that Wordsworth avoids the grim and tragic aspects of life; and second, that Wordsworth was deficient in intellectual culture and in his awareness of the modern situation.

As for the first point, I do not find the evidence convincing that Arnold actually believed this, although to be sure there is some ambiguity in his criticism of Wordsworth. Miss Edith Batho has accused Arnold of setting the example, 'which has been far exceeded, of representing [Wordsworth] as ignorant of or as deliberately ignoring the harsher sides of Nature and life', and critics like Douglas Bush, who believe Wordsworth to be guilty of such intentional blindness, are likely to turn to Arnold for support.[92] But such evidence as there is that Arnold felt this way must be derived from his poetry, even if his fully developed later criticism must be partially discredited in the process (as in Professor Bush's essay). It is true that in his poetic criticism Arnold tended toward the bard-of-Nature view of Wordsworth; the relevant passages have already been considered. Further support for this interpretation of Arnold's views might be adduced from his own poetic treatment of Nature, seeming to discredit Wordsworth's Nature philosophy:

> Man must begin, know this, where Nature ends;
> Nature and man can never be fast friends.[93]

Certainly Arnold, although a lover of scenery and outdoor activity, never had the kind of spiritual relationship with Nature that formed so important a part of Wordsworth's youth.⁹⁴ Furthermore, the Nature which was being revealed by nineteenth-century science was increasingly felt to be vast, inscrutable, and indifferent, if not actually hostile to man. But the poet who wrote the lines just quoted can hardly have failed to recognize the significance of Matthew's speech in Wordsworth's *The Fountain*, mentioned in the preface of 1879 as one of the 'poems of a kind most perfectly to show Wordsworth's unique power':

> The blackbird amid leafy trees,
> The lark above the hill,
> Let loose their carols when they please,
> Are quiet when they will.
>
> With Nature never do they wage
> A foolish strife; they see
> A happy youth, and their old age
> Is beautiful and free:
>
> But we are pressed by heavy laws;
> And often, glad no more,
> We wear a face of joy, because
> We have been glad of yore.

Or we may choose a passage from *Tintern Abbey*, another favourite poem of Arnold's, and one in which Wordsworth is speaking in his own person:

> For I have learned
> To look on nature, not as in the hour
> Of thoughtless youth; but hearing oftentimes
> The still, sad music of humanity.
> [ll. 88–91]

Or could Arnold have overlooked the attitude towards Nature, and towards human suffering, in *Elegiac Stanzas Suggested by a Picture of Peele Castle*? Indeed, it is striking how many of Wordsworth's poems on the 'harsher sides of Nature and life' are included in Arnold's volume of selections, including the above-mentioned poems, *The Brothers*, *Fidelity* (to mention some of those listed by Miss Batho), and numerous others such as *The Affliction of Margaret*, *Michael*, *Margaret*, *The Small Celandine*, etc.

Wordsworth's poetry may be charged with the gloom and harshness of life, but Wordsworth consistently returned to the power of joy that lay beyond: 'Not without hope we suffer and

mourn.' Arnold, too, emphasizes this power of joy in his evaluation of Wordsworth, and consequently finds Wordsworth's
'criticism of life' to be more profound and true than the pessimism
of Leopardi with which it is compared in 'Byron'. But this is not
the same as saying that Wordsworth's power of joy is based upon a
refusal to recognize the presence of evil in the universe. According
to Arnold, even tragedy rises to 'content and joy; this is its value.[95]
Wordsworth could not have ranked so high in Arnold's esteem if
he had not possessed 'high seriousness', and high seriousness he
could not have possessed if his moral ideas had seemed unearned
or had represented a facile optimism; surely no candid reader of
Arnold could think otherwise on this point. A. C. Bradley in his
contributions to Wordsworth criticism, emphasizing the darker
and deeper aspects of Wordsworth's thought, did not attempt to
controvert Arnold so much as to complete him, and at that
Bradley took his point of departure mainly from Arnold's verse
criticism.[96]

On the second point, however, the alleged narrowness of
Wordsworth's intellectual culture and his withdrawal from the
modern situation, Arnold expressed himself quite unambiguously.
On this point, which Arnold indubitably believed, he has not been
as seriously challenged. While numerous critics both before and
since Bradley have brought out for us the importance of Wordsworth's mystical tendencies and his perception of human suffering
—even at the hands of Nature—no equally successful effort has
been made, I believe, to establish the view that the poet who
called Voltaire dull dealt adequately with the moving ideas of his
time. Which is not to say that Wordsworth contributed nothing, or
that Arnold thought that he had contributed nothing, to an understanding of the modern situation. In a letter written even earlier
than *Obermann*, Arnold compared Wordsworth to Goethe for his
'Thorough sincerity—writing about nothing that he had not
experienced.' However, he continued, 'the difference between the
range of their two experiences is immense, and not in the Englishman's favour'.[97] This is similar to a remark of thirty-five years later
in the 'Address to the Wordsworth Society':

> Dealing with no wide, varied, and brilliant world, dealing with the
> common world close to him, and using few materials, Wordsworth
> ... is yet so profoundly impressive because he has really some-
> thing to say.[98]

52

The special nature of what it is that Wordsworth has to say, and its peculiar relevance, as Arnold saw it, is defined by a comparison of Wordsworth to Burke. In a letter of 1880 to a French correspondent, Arnold speaks admiringly of Burke as 'one of the best and deepest spiritual influences of our century'. He continues:

> Burke, like Wordsworth, is a great force in that epoch of concentration, as I call it, which arose in England in opposition to the epoch of expansion declaring itself in the French Revolution. The old order of things had not the virtue which Burke supposed. The Revolution had not the banefulness which he supposed. But neither was the Revolution the commencement, as its friends supposed, of a reign of justice and virtue. . . . An epoch of concentration and of resistance to the crude and violent people who were for imposing their 'renouvellement' on the rest of the world by force was natural and necessary. Burke is to be conceived as the great voice of this epoch. He carried his country with him, and was in some sort a providential person. But he did harm as well as good, for he made concentration too dominant an idea with us, and an idea of which the reign was unduly prolonged. The time for expansion must come, and Burke is of little help to us in presence of such a time.[99]

Elsewhere Arnold had said of Burke that, because he 'saturates politics with thought', his writings are distinguished, 'for those who can make the needful corrections', by their 'profound, permanent, fruitful, philosophical truth'.[100] Burke, that is, had a solid hold upon a certain aspect of truth—if not all of the truth, nevertheless sound and valuable truth so far as it goes. For how much can any one man know?

> To try and approach truth on one side after another, not to strive or cry, nor to persist in pressing forward, on any one side, with violence and self-will,—it is only thus, it seems to me, that mortals may hope to gain any vision of the mysterious Goddess, whom we shall never see except in outline, but only thus even in outline.[101]

Of Wordsworth's relevance to modern life, as of Burke's, Arnold's judgement is balanced and dialectical, not final and unequivocal. Of the chief English writers of the early nineteenth century:

> The gravest of them, Wordsworth, retired . . . into a monastery. I mean he plunged himself into the inward life, he voluntarily cut himself off from the modern spirit. Coleridge took to opium. Scott

became the historiographer-royal of feudalism. Keats passionately gave himself up to a sensuous genius, to his faculty of interpreting nature; and he died of consumption at twenty-five . . . their works have this defect,—they do not belong to that which is the main current of the literature of modern epochs, they do not apply modern ideas to life; they constitute, therefore, minor currents. . . .[102]

Minor currents, that is, with respect to the specific point of view underlying the *Essays in Criticism*, the attempt to deal with the problem of modernity. But then, is the work of Byron and Shelley more valuable because they did try to deal with the modern spirit? No; these poets were the true failures. The times, the cultural milieu, the 'Zeitgeist', could not in England at that time support such an effort, and so 'The best literary creation of that time in England proceeded from men who did not make the same bold attempt as Byron and Shelley.'[103] It proceeded, that is, from Scott and Keats and above all from Wordsworth. Is this inconsistency? Rather, I believe it is an excellent example of Arnold's putting into practice his critical ideals of objectivity and flexibility, of his refusal to let his critical judgement be swayed (and this is not necessarily the same as saying he was right) by even his own preconceptions of what literature ought to do.

For Arnold insisted repeatedly that Wordsworth, in spite of his limitations of experience and intellectual culture, did produce the best and most significant work in English not only of his own period, but of the whole era since Milton. If Wordsworth's vision was limited, it is nevertheless supremely valuable. In that 'inward life' to which he retired he found deep sources of joy and consolation perennially valuable, of 'moral strength' perpetually useful. Consequently Arnold concluded of him that his superiority to Burns, Keats, Heine, and other lesser lights lies in this:

. . . he deals with more of *life* than they do; he deals with *life*, as a whole, more powerfully.[104]

Wordsworth's Greatness

Hence, for all his limitations, Wordsworth is a great, an exceedingly great, poet. And because he is great as a poet, Arnold correctly says that we ought to focus our attention where his true greatness is to be found—on the poetry. Arnold chose the moment of his presidential address to the Wordsworth Society to reassert this basic, and in that company somewhat heretical, attitude. The Society itself, dedicated to the enlargement of Wordsworth's fame and the spread of his moral teachings, may be regarded as the inevitable culmination of the nineteenth-century tendency to insist upon Wordsworth's greatness as a moral influence, and very nearly to sanctify the poet himself, a tendency which Coleridge had observed as early as 1817.[105] Consequently, when the Society selected Arnold as its third president in 1883, he was probably chosen for his great authority as a man of letters and for the contribution he had made to Wordsworth's fame with his volume of selections, despite his defections from orthodox Wordsworthianism.

Arnold, naturally, was conscious of the differences which separated him from the orthodox, and alluded to them in his opening remarks. With his customary 'vivacity' he went on to compare the Society itself to a monastery with its rules of poverty, chastity, and obedience. Members of his audience who were familiar with his writings might have been reminded of his remark in 'Heinrich Heine' that Wordsworth himself had retired into a monastery, or disturbed by the evident allusion of his remark to his reference in 'Wordsworth' to the 'small band of devoted followers', the Wordsworthians, against whom the 'disinterested lover of poetry' must be on his guard. Indeed, the description of this meeting of the monks of the Wordsworthian order which Arnold sent in a letter to his wife written on the day of the speech comes depressingly close to the image he had called up in 'Wordsworth' of a Social Science Congress listening raptly to a reader declaiming some particularly dull and preachy lines of Wordsworth, while 'in the soul of any poor child of nature who may have wandered in thither, an unutterable sense of lamentation, and mourning, and woe!'[106]

After a complimentary reference to the Wordsworth criticism of Stopford Brooke and Aubrey de Vere,[107] Arnold proceeded to summarize his own ideas. Admitting his view of Wordsworth's imperfections, he adds:

> But I doubt whether anyone admires Wordsworth more than I do. I admire him, first of all, for the very simple and solid reason that he is in such an exceedingly great poet.

Then we find the (by now) familiar placing of Wordsworth after Shakespeare and Milton, the tribute to Shakespeare's incomparability and to Milton's superior artistry, and the summation of Wordsworth's special merits: first, his spiritual passion unmatched even in Milton; second, that although his materials are limited, he has something to say; and third, and most distinctive, 'his power of happiness and hope, his "deep power of joy".'[108]

Although E. K. Brown has rather convincingly argued that Arnold often, perhaps generally, fell short of his critical ideal of disinterestedness,[109] I believe that this 'Address to the Wordsworth Society' is an example of serious striving toward this goal. A slight impurity of motive may be suggested of his willingness to yield certain points against Wordsworth in the more thorough and famous 'Wordsworth' essay; Arnold was there trying to popularize the poet. But there could be no such motive in this address to the inner circle of already devoted readers. It is equally certain that Arnold was moved by no mere motive of iconoclasm; there is no reason to doubt the sincerity and fervour of his own admiration. His lifelong preoccupation with Wordsworth is shown, for example, by his frequent use of Wordsworthian lines and phrases in his miscellaneous writings. No other poet is quoted so frequently, and we must conclude that for all Arnold's admiration of other poets, it was Wordsworth above all whom he loved. But his devotion to high and objective critical standards, and his intense desire to see Wordsworth recognized as a poet and not merely as the prophet of a cult, compelled him to set aside his own personal prejudices ('I can read with pleasure and edification ... everything of Wordsworth, I think, except *Vaudracour and Julia*') and those of his audience, and praise Wordsworth only in those terms which he believed were true, but which must to the more fervent have seemed grudging and limiting.

And limiting, in a sense, Arnold's judgements on Wordsworth certainly are, but not as limiting as has often been suggested. Over and over he said that Wordsworth's great and distinctive gift was his 'deep power of joy', and only by exploring the central concept of 'joy' through some of its ramifications in Arnold's thought can we come to understand more fully its profound and far-reaching meaning to him.[110] Above all, joy is not a passive state of mind or a mere feeling. It is associated, as it was for Coleridge and Wordsworth, with power, energy, force, with the full activity of a harmonious spirit, with religion, and with the greatest art. Its absence is equivalent to a spiritual death:

> Fulness of life and power of feeling, ye
> Are for the happy, for the souls at ease,
> Who dwell on a firm basis of content!
> But he . . .
> Who has no minute's breathing space allow'd
> To nurse his dwindling faculty of joy—
> Joy and the outward world must die to him,
> As they are dead to me.[111]

Arnold personally knew the flavour and perceived the dangers of dejection. He wrote in 1856 to his favourite sister:

> To make a habitual war on depression and low spirits, which in one's early youth one is apt to indulge and be somewhat interested in, is one of the things one learns as one gets older. They are noxious alike to body and mind, and already partake of the nature of death.[112]

This is a recurrent theme in his correspondence. Moreover, Arnold's preface to the 1853 edition of his poems is a famous example (there are others in his correspondence with Clough) of his ability to censure his own poetry when it failed—as it so often did!—to reach beyond melancholy, when it failed to *animate*.

To animate, that is, to inspirit, to make alive in the fullest sense —this is the priceless gift offered both by poetry and religion at their best; so Arnold believed. If the rational core of religion is morality, it is nevertheless true that man cannot live by reasoned morality alone. The power of religion is proportionate to its ability to engage the whole man, to make its moral truth not merely known but felt and loved. This is what makes the high and pure morality of Marcus Aurelius and the exalted intellectual religion of Spinoza fall so far short of meeting the needs of all but the most exceptional of men. But 'the power of Christianity', wrote Arnold in the preface to *God and the Bible* (1875), 'has been in the immense emotion which it has excited; in its engaging, for the government of man's conduct, the mighty forces of love, reverence, gratitude, hope, pity, and awe,—all that host of allies which Wordsworth included under the one name of *imagination*, when he says that in the uprooting of old rules we must still ask:

"Survives imagination, to the change
Superior ? Help to virtue does she give ?
If not, O mortals, better cease to live!" '113

Critics of Arnold's religious writings, such as A. W. Benn, F. H. Bradley, and T. S. Eliot, have found it easy to indict him for amateurism, inconsistency, triviality, and ignorance. Eliot, moreover, taking a hint from Paul Elmer More, has damned Arnold for opening the way to aesthetic religion (going to church for the sake of the beautiful ceremony) and the religion of aesthetics (art for art's sake); he protests that a position like that in the passage quoted above from the preface to *God and the Bible* amounts to 'a counsel to get all the emotional kick out of Christianity one can, without the bother of believing it'.[114] But whatever his unorthodoxy Arnold was preserved from a mere flabby religiosity by precisely that deep strain of piety and moral fervour which led him into the alien and repellent field of religious controversy and compelled him to make the Herculean effort to save for an infidel generation, which included himself, what he felt to be the inestimable value and human truth of Christianity. Following the example of Coleridge, he sought to ground the sanctions of religion not in a book, nor in a system of thought, nor in a human institution, nor in a body of dubious external fact, but in the emotional and moral needs of man. Only there, in man's heart, could those sanctions be proof against the new learning of geology, biology, Biblical criticism, and all the forces of the modern world which were dissolving the old alliance between imagination, in the high Wordsworthian sense, and human conduct. Accepting and even furthering the dissolution of the old, orthodox grounds of this alliance, the grounds of tradition and authority, Arnold sought to be among those who were attempting to keep the alliance itself alive by basing it upon new grounds that could not be undermined by scientific discovery. The pragmatic approach to religion has its dangers, as Arnold seems at times to have recognized, but it was the only path he could find between a desiccating naturalism and an obscurantist supernaturalism. The truth, that is, scientific truth, must be faced and accepted, but religion itself must not be allowed to perish. 'Dissolvents of the old European system of dominant ideas and facts we must all be, all of us who have any power of working', he had written in the first *Essays in Criticism* (1865); 'what we have to study is that we may not be acrid dissolvents of it.'[115]

Religion for Arnold was not, then, mere morality; the great human truth which he was trying to conserve was not just the lesson of righteousness, but of *joy* in righteousness:

> And yet men have such need of joy!
> But joy whose grounds are true.[116]

Jesus, even if he was not supernatural, was still 'divine' in some sense because of the great truth and beauty of his moral vision and because of his power to make this truth and beauty felt as joy:

> And never certainly was the joy, which in self-renouncement under-lies the pain, so brought out as when Jesus boldly called the suppression of our first impulses and current thoughts: *life, real life, eternal life.* So that Jesus not only *saw* this great necessary truth of there being, as Aristotle says, in human nature a part to rule and a part to be ruled; he saw it so thoroughly, that he saw through the suffering at its surface to the joy at its centre, filled it with promise and hope, and made it infinitely attractive.[117]

Similarly, he continues, 'Israel . . . is "the people of righteousness", because, though others have perceived the importance of righteous-ness, Israel, above every one, perceived the happiness of it.' The Bible, then, is not to be regarded as a work of science or of his-tory; its true function, Arnold wrote in *God and the Bible*, is to 'animate and fortify' faith in righteousness through its truth and power and beauty.[118] If humanity could become sufficiently 'humanised' through the development of its powers of 'flexibility, perceptiveness, and judgment', it could appreciate this kind of truth. Men would then love and be taught by the Bible without demanding supernatural sanctions.

So deep is the feeling in Arnold for joy as the *animating* or life-giving force, that he unconsciously misquotes Wordsworth in praising George Sand's renunciation of 'idolatrous' popular reli-gious beliefs and anthropomorphism: 'She does not attempt to give this divinity an account much more precise than that which we have in Wordsworth,—"*a presence that disturbs me with the joy of animating thoughts.*"'[119] Wordsworth (*Tintern Abbey*) has '*elevated* thoughts', although *animating* was one of his favourite words. As for *joy*, the importance to Wordsworth of both word and concept need not be dwelt upon. In *Tintern Abbey* alone we find

Arnold's favourite 'deep power of joy', 'healing thoughts / Of tender joy', and three other occurrences, as well as one each of *joys* and *joyless*.

It is true, however, that the concept of 'joy' had a far richer and more profound significance for Wordsworth than it did for Arnold. The lack of joy in Arnold's own poetry perhaps explains why Wordsworth's was so precious to him. There is sounded repeatedly in Wordsworth's poetry a note completely beyond Arnold's range; this is apparent at once in the passage from *Tintern Abbey* from which Arnold took the key phrase 'power of joy':

> ... we are laid asleep
> In body, and become a living soul:
> While with an eye made quiet by the power
> Of harmony, and the deep power of joy,
> We see into the life of things.

Arnold, completely lacking in the mystical sensibility that formed so important a part of Wordsworth's poetic equipment, possessed neither the temperament nor the experience to understand the full Wordsworthian import of the 'joy' in the passage above. Wordsworth's 'eye made quiet by the power / Of harmony' is an admirable metaphor for just that spiritual gift, the lack of which all of Arnold's poetry both expresses and mourns. But if, as one critic has it, Arnold was unable to see beyond the power of joy to the power of Vision which Wordsworth sometimes attained,[120] he was still able to see much that was of central importance in Wordsworth and in Arnold's own life and thought, as well as in his social and missionary activities. As a matter of fact, Arnold seemed to feel that Wordsworth's visionary powers were less, not more, significant than his power of joy, for the former were unique and idiosyncratic, while the latter was based on universal emotions and was universally accessible. Consequently he was rendering Wordsworth the most serious kind of praise when he chose the word *joy* as the keynote of his essay on Wordsworth.

IV. THE WORDSWORTH SELECTIONS

As early as the beginning of 1877 Matthew Arnold was approached by George Macmillan, the publisher, to edit a volume of Wordsworth selections for the Golden Treasury Series. Arnold liked the idea, but in the press of other work apparently forgot about it until he was reminded two years later. He worked on selecting and editing the poems during March and most of April of 1879, and then began to write the preface. It was completed and sent to the printer by May 22, only a week later than the date Arnold had hoped for back in April; it appeared in the July issue of *Macmillan's Magazine*. As the weeks went by, Arnold grew irritated at the delays in the publication of the book due to Macmillan's use of Edinburgh printers (R. and R. Clark), for he had wanted it to be out early in July at the latest, in time for summer travellers to buy for vacation reading. Arnold was fresh from working on his *Six Chief Lives from Johnson's Lives of the Poets*, and his tone in speaking of the Scottish printers is reminiscent of the great doctor's as he expostulates with Macmillan on June 30: 'Why do you use these provincial and imperfectly awakened people?' At last, by August 27, the book was printed, bound, and ready for publication.[121]

The first edition of *Poems of Wordsworth* contained 165 poems, arranged and organized in six 'natural' groups: Poems of Ballad Form (nine, unchanged in subsequent editions); Narrative Poems (thirteen, unchanged later); Lyrical Poems (thirty-six, with four more subsequently added to make forty); Poems Akin to the Antique, and Odes (nine, unchanged); Sonnets (sixty, number unchanged but six dropped, six added, and five removed to different positions); and Reflective and Elegiac Poems (thirty-eight, one later added to make thirty-nine). Although a few poems were dropped and a few added in subsequent printings,[122] the general organization remained the same. The groups themselves move generally in the direction of starting with lesser forms and ending with those in which Arnold believed that Wordsworth had achieved unique greatness. In accordance with the preference he had expressed in his preface, Arnold chose most of the poems (about four-fifths) from collections published during the great years 1798–1807 (in the preface Arnold, perhaps to get a round decade, refers to the date 1808, one which is meaningless in the publishing history of Wordsworth). Indubitably, Arnold's collections contain most of the poems which have come to be Wordsworth's most popular or most highly praised work in the shorter forms.[123]

Even a fairly cursory examination of one section, the sonnets, reveals that Arnold's arrangement was carefully planned for overall

effect. Moreover, this is the section that seems to have caused the
most difficulty and to have undergone the greatest number of
changes. There are sixty sonnets, a total number which remained
unchanged in later editions. In the first edition they are chosen in
the following proportion from Wordsworth's own groupings:
sixteen from *Poems Dedicated to National Independence and Liberty*,
revealing Arnold's consciousness of Wordsworth as Milton's
successor as a patriotic sonneteer, a point not mentioned in
Arnold's preface; nineteen from *Miscellaneous Sonnets* (this number
eventually rose to twenty-two); seven from *Poems Composed or
Suggested during a Tour, in the Summer of 1833* (these shrunk to
five); three from the *Ecclesiastical Sonnets* (although Arnold confessed that he was not especially partial to these, their representation later grew to five, one of the additions being the fine sonnet
'Mutability'); and the remaining fifteen (later twelve) from six
other groups. These poems are not arranged in their Wordsworthian
categories. Instead, Arnold has put together those on similar or
related subjects in such wise that there is a definite movement or
rhythm in the group as a whole. Of course, in some instances
sonnets which were placed together by Wordsworth remain
together, but where Arnold found one from another group which
fit his own vision of order, he placed it where he felt it belonged.
In Arnold's sequence in the first edition, the first clear grouping
consists of eighteen sonnets on political, national, and social
subjects, beginning with the patriotic 'Fair Star of Evening'. The
final poem of this group, 'Here pause: the poet claims', provides
a transition to the next group of seven more personal poems in
which Wordsworth deals with his art and himself. (The essential
nature of this group was unchanged, but it was subsequently
improved by the replacement of 'Pelion and Ossa flourish side by
side' by the sonnet beginning 'Surprised by joy', and of 'Adieu,
Rydalian Laurels!' by 'To the Author's Portrait' which had formerly
not been as logically placed in the sequence.) The twenty-sixth
sonnet, 'A flock of sheep that leisurely pass by', also concerns the
poet's personality, but its images of nature lead to the next ten
poems which deal with landscapes, seascapes, etc., though not
necessarily unmixed with moral observation. (Although there was
some rearrangement in this group, it, too, remains essentially
unchanged.) The last of these, 'I thought of Thee, my partner and
my guide', a poem that appears to be clearly related to Arnold's

own *The Youth of Nature*, turns us from scenery back to the soul, and so leads to the last and largest group of twenty-four. It is perhaps misleading to call these a group, for they are fairly miscellaneous in subject, dealing with religion, history, art, and personal or family matters. However, they are all personal in approach and a religious note runs like a thread through the group as a whole. In the first edition Arnold seemed to want to have the closing sonnets connect to the beginning ones. The first sonnet was a patriotic poem, and the last two, 'Admonition' and 'Wansfell! this Household has a favoured lot' (referring to Fox How, the Arnold home near Rydal Mount), bring us to that specific corner of England with which Wordsworth was most intimately connected, the Lake Country. Subsequently, however, these two poems were moved back with other 'landscape' poems, and their terminal position was taken by a pair of profoundly visionary sonnets called 'Death' ('Methought I saw the footsteps of a throne') and 'The Everlasting Temple' ('In my mind's eye a Temple, like a cloud'). This final, miscellaneous, group caused the most trouble. Of the six new sonnets five were added here; of the six dropped from the collection, two came from this section; and of the five sonnets from the original list which were moved to new locations, three came from here.

Like the sonnets, the prefatory essay may also be divided, for purposes of summary, into five sections, although a formal outline does a certain amount of violence to the sinuous movement of Arnold's thought and prose style. Opening the essay there is a disquisition on 'glory' containing a review of the history of Wordsworth's fame of no particular critical significance, but of considerable relevance to the general purpose of the volume. After this section on fame, Arnold proceeds boldly and explicitly to claim for Wordsworth a rank, as we have seen, above all English poets since Shakespeare except for Milton,[124] and, moreover, above all Continental poets since Molière except for Goethe. Admitting that this is a high claim to make, he asks what obstacles have hitherto prevented the general recognition of its justice. The two principal obstacles have been, first, that Wordsworth's longest poems are not his best and the best shorter poems are mixed with work quite flat and dull, and second, that the poet's own arrangement of his work based upon 'supposed unity of mental origin' is far-fetched and artificial, the traditional categories being more natural and satisfying. Arnold concludes this portion of the argument by asserting that when Wordsworth's best work is disengaged from the inferior, there remains not merely a few masterpieces, as with Keats or Coleridge, but so great and ample a 'body of powerful and significant work' that his superiority will prove itself.

Next Arnold turns to the question, in what does Wordsworth's superior worth consist? After referring to his own earlier dictum in *On Translating Homer* that 'the noble and profound application of ideas to life is the most essential part of poetic greatness', he claims for Wordsworth precisely this kind of greatness. The main quality of greatness in English poetry is its 'energy and depth' in dealing with moral ideas; Arnold strikingly calls upon Voltaire as authority for this generalization. Now Arnold intends to make clear that he is not supporting a Philistine doctrine of didacticism which would be vulnerable to attack by aesthetic critics, but at the same time he had no sympathy with the 'art, for art's sake' attitude and wants to show its superficiality. Therefore, he says, the word *moral* is not to be interpreted too narrowly, for human life is in so great a degree moral that any poetry which rejects moral ideas may be said to reject life itself. After further reference to authority—Epictetus now—and a contrast of Wordsworth with the French poet Gautier, the English poet is again praised for being intent on 'the best and master thing', that is, the question how to live, and in this he is in the main stream of great English poetry.

But now, in the fourth section of the essay, a qualification is to be made. Some, the Wordsworthians, would go too far by insisting 'that Wordsworth's poetry is precious because his philosophy is sound'; they lay too much stress on Wordsworth's thought as a system (here Arnold is glancing at Leslie Stephen's essay on 'Wordsworth's Ethics'). Their approach is harmful, partly because the philosophy itself may have its limitations or flaws as a system, but also, and this is more important, because the Wordsworthians, primarily concerned with philosophy, are too likely to praise the worst poetry—the most abstract, dull, and didactic. Therefore, says Arnold, we must dismiss the philosophy, at least in any systematic sense, to do justice to the poetry. The greatness of Wordsworth's criticism of life is not in his system, but in his profound intuition of the deep, primary, and common human sources of all that makes life harmonious and valuable—what

Arnold, following Wordsworth, calls *joy*—and in his power as a poet to make us share it.

The rest of the preface consists of the discussion of Wordsworth's style dealt with above, and of a conclusion in which Arnold recapitulates briefly the reasons for Wordsworth's eminence and states the aim of the volume of selections: 'To disengage the poems which show his power, and to present them to the English-speaking public and to the world.' He admits that this anthology does not contain all of Wordsworth's interesting work, but it does contain 'nearly everything which may best serve him' and 'nothing which may disserve him'. Finally, in a graceful coda, Arnold places himself personally with the Wordsworthians who can read even the dullest of the master's works with 'pleasure and edification', and pays his personal tribute to his 'pure and sage master'. He ends, however, with a plea to let Wordsworth make his way with the wider audience of European literature, so that his poems may do their work (in Wordsworth's words) of co-operating 'with the benign tendencies in human nature and society . . . in making men wiser, better, and happier'.

It is apparent, then, that the general purpose of the book and direction of the preface is to augment Wordsworth's fame and help spread his influence. Earlier, in 1874, Pater, in a notable essay on Wordsworth which foreshadows Arnold's in certain respects, had pointed out the mixture of good and bad in the poet and had called for such a volume of selections which would exhibit his unique power.[125] When the opportunity presented itself to Arnold to make up such an anthology, he set to work with ever-increasing enthusiasm. He has been much criticized for some of the results of his intention to popularize Wordsworth. A. C. Bradley argued, with justice, that 'Arnold wished to make Wordsworth more popular; and so he was tempted to represent Wordsworth's poetry as much more simple and unambitious than it really was, and as much more easily apprehended than it ever can be.'[126] Professor Bonnerot has made a similar charge. Lane Cooper, in a violent and angry attack on Arnold in 1929, even made it a major criticism of Arnold as a critic and editor that he made money from the Wordsworth anthology, implying, it seems, that Arnold had simplified and popularized Wordsworth for venal reasons.[127]

Certainly we may agree with, at least, the sounder and more temperate of these criticisms such as Bradley's. Wordsworth's

65

simplicité, even as a technical achievement, is probably not so easily apprehended as, say, Tennyson's *simplesse.* But Arnold's final purpose was not merely to popularize; rather, he saw in this immediate goal a means to a greater end. And that end was related to his general and unceasing effort to teach, to humanize, to spread sweetness and light, and to help create 'a current of true and fresh ideas'. Moreover, Arnold in seeing himself as an apostle to the Gentiles felt that his mission, whether he was at the moment dealing with religion, social problems, or literature, was always at bottom a moral, indeed, a religious one. This central purpose provides the unifying theme which runs through all of Arnold's work and without which none of it can be fully understood.

Arnold was not an originator but a disseminator of ideas; this is the way he saw himself and his mission. He was willing whenever necessary to make tactical sacrifices if by so doing he could advance his strategic purpose. And so the technique he used in attempting to spread the influence of Wordsworth is not singular. In his religious writings we see him prepared and even happy to jettison dogma if only he could win acceptance for the Bible and the religious spirit on other terms. In his lecture on Emerson he used the same technique: Let us give up, he says, 'to envious time as much . . . as time can fairly expect ever to obtain' in order to save what is truly and perpetually valuable.[128] It is the same in his treatment of Byron and Keats and other literary figures. Moreover, Arnold was always conscious of addressing a particular audience at a particular time. Such an approach has its dangers for the literary critic, well summarized by E. K. Brown who observed that 'A critic who is consciously rectifying an error into which he believes that a generation of readers have fallen becomes in an attenuated sense, to be sure, a victim of provinciality', and that his work may readily suffer obsolescence.[129] Although Arnold had higher hopes for his poetry, he willingly accepted that much or even most of his prose after serving its purpose would be given up to time. What is remarkable is the amount of it which remains interesting and viable.

All this is well known. However, before we can apply these generalizations usefully to a specific piece of work such as the Wordsworth preface, we must take account of developments in both Arnold's thought and in the historical situation, and here we must notice a special feature of his late literary criticism which has not generally been remarked. But first we must go back to the beginning of the 1870's, the 'ecclesiastical decade'. The readers for whom Arnold had designed his earlier literary criticism, his books on education, and his essays on social questions—in other words, all the main prose works of the 1860's—were of the Middle Class of England, the Philistines, or at any rate the more teachable among them. Arnold's intention in these writings had been to work on this class, as he put it in *Culture and Anarchy*, 'inwardly and cure their spirit'. The principal therapeutic agent was to be an 'intellectual deliverance' which he called in his inaugural lecture at Oxford 'the peculiar demand of those ages which are called modern'.[130] But in turning to religion at the end of that decade Arnold was also turning in considerable part to a new audience, and the emphasis in his work became less intellectual and more plainly moral. Much of that new audience belonged to the recently enfranchised Populace; Arnold believed that there was great work to be done with this emergingly powerful class. The preface to *Literature and Dogma* makes this turn quite clear.[131] That book was not designed, as some have appeared to think, to weaken the faith of believers; the orthodox Philistine, if he could be brought to read it, would of course see in it only vicious and perverse infidelity. Nor was its purpose primarily the intellectual one of introducing its readers to the new developments in Biblical criticism. Assuming the existence of an audience already influenced by the critical attitude, Arnold meant to do with them what he had earlier accused Bishop Colenso of failing to do: he meant to edify. The principal theme of these religious books may be summed up in the question and answer with which Arnold concluded a sonnet first published in 1867 called *The Better Part*:

> Was Christ a man like us? *Ah! let us try*
> *If we then, too, can be such men as he!*

He was not addressing believers at all. He was writing as an apologist, even a missionary, more than as an educator. His audience, as he conceived it, was made up of those who, in being deeply influenced by the current climate of opinion, had not so much lost their faith but rather failed to see any reason for faith, and who were yet troubled about the significance of life in a universe bereft of its old symbols and sanctions. Starting from the assumption that the Bible was not historically or scientifically true, they were willing to ask 'What then?' These people who, in rejecting received dogmas, were rejecting the Bible as well, might come from all classes, but specifically Arnold appealed to the intelligent and positivistic members of the working class.[132]

Arnold's urge to reach the lower classes increased with the years. His missionary zeal may be inferred from his insistence, against his publisher's objections, on bringing out a half-crown edition of *Literature and Dogma* in 1884 when the standard edition was still selling well; later, again at his instance, a similar edition of *God and the Bible* was brought out.[133] It was the working class, Arnold had long believed, which was the most accessible to ideas (see the essays on 'Democracy' and 'Equality' of 1861 and 1878 respectively, in *Mixed Essays*), because its members had no vested interest—social, economic, or moral—in the existing order. But because they did lack these attachments to tradition, their accessibility to new ideas, a good thing in itself, was a source of danger as their political power increased.[134] Arnold's aim in reaching this audience with his religious books, then, was not to destroy faith in the Bible, but to animate it on what he considered to be intellectually tenable grounds: that the Bible, whatever it was not, remained the truest source of moral inspiration and the greatest agent of spiritual refinement that the world had ever known.

Much regret has been expressed over Arnold's wasted years in the wilderness of theology where he was an amateur and an alien (although not so much an amateur as some of his opponents have lightly assumed), and there was rejoicing when he returned to his true home in the Holy Land of literature. To be sure, the admirer of Arnold's criticism must wish that he had devoted the thought and energy of those years to producing more essays in criticism. It has also been urged that not only are his religious writings amateurish, but that they failed to reach and influence the audience for whom they were designed, or that even if they did have some pertinence and influence in the 1870's, they are no longer of interest. Some of this censure may be merited, but much is not. There is, for instance, ample evidence that Arnold's religious writings did indeed exert a fairly widespread influence.[135] However, it is not my intention here to enter into a defence of these writings, but rather to argue that if we put them into a separate or aberrant category, we risk overlooking the unity of intention by which they are related to Arnold's earlier and even more significantly to his later literary criticism. The nature of Arnold's earlier development from a critic of literature to a critic of society to a critic of religion is reasonably well understood. What I wish to stress is the subsequent continuity between the religious criticism and the literary work which followed it.

In the preface to the last of his religious books, *Last Essays on Church and Religion* (1877), Arnold pointed out this unity and continuity of intention. He explained that, as for explicit attention to religion, 'what I wished to say has been said. And in returning to devote to literature, more strictly so-called, what remains to me of life and strength and leisure, I am returning, after all, to a field where work of the most important kind has now to be done, though indirectly, for religion.' This work is to provide the ulterior purpose of his late literary criticism. Arnold goes on to explain the nature of that work and the field where it most needs to be done: 'I am persuaded that the transformation of religion, which is essential for its perpetuance, can be accomplished only by carrying the qualities of flexibility, perceptiveness, and judgment, which are the best fruits of letters, to whole classes of the community which now know next to nothing of them, and by procuring the application of those qualities to matters where they are never applied now.' That is, he announces that his subsequent literary work will be popularizing, and explains why. After pointing out the low state of religion in the minds of the 'masses of men', Arnold proceeds to argue that religion cannot be made appealing to those 'gross and materialising' minds by keeping religion materialistic and anthropomorphic, for these minds are already rejecting that kind of religion on other grounds, while their 'grossness of perception and materialising habits' render them unfit for any other kind of religion. Hence what is called for is indirect action. As he had earlier tried to 'work inwardly' to cure the spirit of the Philistines, he now urges a remedy for the current situation by what he called 'a gradual transformation of the popular mind, by slowly curing it of its grossness of perception and of its materialistic habits, not by keeping religion materialistic that it may correspond to them.'[136] Arnold was writing his preface not only to *Last Essays on Church and Religion,* but to 'The Study of Poetry' and to all the literary work of the last decade of his life.

Arnold's turning to the Populace as the class where the greatest things now needed to be done is further indicated in another document of the period of his return to literature. In January,

1879, Arnold delivered an address to Ipswich Working Men's College. This address was published on February 1 in the *Fortnightly Review* under the revealing title, 'Ecce, Convertimur ad Gentes' (reprinted in *Irish Essays and Others*). Writing to a sister about his audience, Arnold observed in his characteristically schoolmasterish way that 'They are said to be an intelligent set, and I do not despair of making them follow me.'[137] His own bourgeois mentality, the possession of which he never denied, is revealed in this speech by his implicit assumption that the middle class is and must remain the most important for all its faults, and that from this class the aspiring proletarians must take their values. But he expressed a strong note of weariness and discouragement with his labours in the field of middle-class education, and he called upon the workers to exert their influence towards the improvement of schools for the enlightenment of the middle class, that these workers might have something truly valuable to aspire to, or, as he put it in the same letter to his sister, 'a more civilised middle class to rise into, if they *do* rise'. The great work of civilizing mankind, Arnold urged upon the working men, 'is not nearly done yet; and our Judaic and unelastic middle class in this country is of no present service, it seems, for carrying it forward. Do you, then, carry it forward yourselves, and insist on taking the middle class with you.'[138]

For Arnold, the great civilizing agency in general was literature, but he believed that it had an especially urgent task to perform in his time, for only literature could reconcile and atone the religious and the scientific attitudes. He expressed this Wordsworthian faith in the high utility of literature repeatedly, both in public and in private. For example, he wrote in a letter of 1870 that Lord Salisbury (Robert Cecil), recently appointed chancellor of Oxford, was a dangerous man 'chiefly from his want of any true sense and experience of literature and its beneficent function'. Salisbury was a great believer in the future of physical science, and at the same time was a dogmatic traditionalist in religion—a most explosive combination when, as Arnold put it, 'the immense work between the two, which is for literature to accomplish, he knows nothing of'.[139] Ten years later in 'The Study of Poetry', Arnold made his most famous and most ambitious claim for literature: 'We should conceive of it as capable of higher uses, and called to higher destinities than those which in general men have assigned to it hitherto. More and more mankind will discover that we have to turn to poetry to interpret life for us, to sustain us. Without poetry, our science will appear incomplete; and most of what now passes with us for religion and philosophy will be replaced by poetry.' And in the Wordsworth preface of 1879 he prophesied: 'Perhaps we shall one day learn to make this proposition general, and to say: Poetry is the reality, philosophy is the illusion.'[140]

Moved by his compelling sense of the need to spread the influence of the best that had been thought and said in the world, and perhaps relieved to have finished his theological labours, Arnold turned with a remarkable burst of energy to the popular dissemination of literature during the years 1877–81. In 1877 and 1878 there were the *Six Chief Lives from Johnson's Lives of the Poets* with an essay on Johnson, and a projected selection of sermons from Hales, Whichcote, and Cudworth. (Although Arnold apparently did a considerable amount of work on the latter book, to have been called *The Broad Church in the Seventeenth Century*, it never saw the light.[141]) In 1879 there was the Wordsworth and in 1881 the Byron anthologies which Arnold edited for Macmillan's Golden Treasury Series, with their famous prefaces. Also in 1881 he edited the *Letters Speeches and Tracts on Irish Affairs*, a selection from Burke with a critical preface. The other most considerable critical essays of this period, 'The Study of Poetry', 'John Keats', and 'Thomas Gray', along with his choice of selections from Keats and Gray, were all contributed in 1880 to Humphry Ward's popular anthology, *The English Poets*. And all of this is only a part of his output during those fertile four years, the part of most direct relevance here. But Arnold also contributed during this period no fewer than fifteen other essays and speeches to *The Fortnightly Review*, *The Nineteenth Century*, *The Quarterly Review*, and *The Cornhill Magazine*, including one on Milton, one on Goethe, and a well-known essay on George Sand.

Probably Arnold's most successful effort at popularization, and perhaps the one which meant the most to him, was his Wordsworth anthology. In the first place, Arnold was a disciple of Wordsworth and had derived many of his ideas about the nature and function of poetry from him. Moreover, he believed Wordsworth to be, of all modern poets, uniquely qualified by the purity, truth, elevation, and at its best, beauty of both his style and his moral vision for carrying on among the populace the beneficent spiritual labour which he, like his master, considered to be poetry's high calling. It is significant that the young poet who had written to Clough that those who knew no Greek should read only Milton and parts of Wordsworth should, as a middle-aged critic, write to Jemima Quillinan, Wordsworth's step-granddaughter, that he hoped to make the 'great public' buy Wordsworth's poems as they bought Milton's.[142] To be sure, the use of Wordsworth's poetry for spiritual healing or as a substitute for religion was no new thing in the nineteenth century. But the establishment of Wordsworth's fame among the many as a true English classic remained to be done. Probably Ruskin expressed the common opinion when he observed that reading Wordsworth was, for the vulgar, a labour rather than a pleasure.[143] Arnold, too, was willing to admit that the poetry of, for example, Byron, 'will always, probably, find more readers than Wordsworth's, and will give pleasure more easily'.[144] But perhaps by seeing Arnold's popularization of Wordsworth in its context of his lifelong effort to spiritualize the materialized upper class, to humanize the brutalized lower class, and to refine the vulgarized middle class, we may become somewhat less ready to condemn and more inclined to understand, if not to excuse, some of the simplifying tendencies of his preface for which he has been so roundly criticized.

Another charge that has been levelled against Arnold, and one against which it is difficult to find any defence, is that his editing of the poems was unsound and even unscrupulous. He frequently neglected Wordsworth's own late revisions, and sometimes even went so far as silently to manufacture a text of his own by piecing together readings from various editions. Arnold's text of *Laodamia* (which he Hellenized as *Laodameia*) will serve as an example. It is a farrago of readings from three early texts (1815, 1820, and 1827); later revisions (1836 and 1845) are ignored, and the poem Arnold printed was never seen by Wordsworth. Such editorial practices are especially damaging in view of Arnold's claim not to have given 'any piece otherwise than as Wordsworth himself gave it', although he was referring to the fact that he gave only whole poems, not excerpts.[145] If Arnold cannot be defended against the charges of editorial malpractice brought against him by Lane Cooper,[146] it is at least possible to point out that his method of procedure was not the result of indifference or of carelessness, but was entirely purposeful, although it may be questioned whether this provides an extenuation or an aggravation of the offence. At any rate, his selection of readings was based upon his conviction that most of Wordsworth's later revisions were not improvements, and that he as editor was 'restoring' more valuable original readings.[147] Arnold evidently believed that in a volume frankly designed for a popular audience, he had to rely for the establishment of text on the taste he considered best—his own, and that of the younger Wordsworth. There did not yet exist a scholarly text complete with variant readings, and even today when such a text exists, the editor of Wordsworth faces the same problems that Arnold faced. A remark he made on Shelley is indicative of his general attitude toward the problems of editing modern poets: 'Shelley is not a classic, whose various readings are to be noted with earnest attention.'[148] And if Wordsworth was a far greater poet than Shelley in Arnold's opinion, he was not a 'classic' either, certainly not for purposes of making up a popular volume of selections.

And popular it was, in spite of the doubts of Ruskin and some of the Wordsworthians such as Sir Henry Taylor.[149] Within five months of publication, the small standard edition had sold nearly 4000 copies, not to mention the sales of the large paper edition.[150] The volume went through five or six printings (I have been unable to determine whether that of 1888 preceded Arnold's death in April of that year) during the remaining nine years of Arnold's life, and has continued its vigorous life on both sides of the Atlantic through thirty-nine total printings until the present day. The hardy little book is still in print, although the type is growing worn and the printing is less bright and clear than that in 1879. It has been widely used in schools, and in 1897 Macmillan even published an eighty-eight page handbook supplementary to it (Richard Wilson, *Helps to the Study of Arnold's Wordsworth*). It would be difficult to estimate to how many readers Arnold's selections have introduced Wordsworth, and impossible to count the number of people up to the present day whose idea of Wordsworth, for better or worse, is essentially Arnold's, transmitted directly or filtered through generations of teachers. In addition to this popular success, Arnold's essay probably more than any other single piece of Wordsworth criticism defined most of the issues which have been debated ever since by scholars and critics— especially the vexed question of the relevance of Wordsworth's philosophy to his poetry. Certainly through this volume Arnold did more than any other single influence to enlarge Wordsworth's fame and secure him a place as a popularly recognized English classic. His services on behalf of the fame of Wordsworth were recognized by the Wordsworthians when he was chosen as president of the Wordsworth Society in 1883, even though he was not a member and some of his ideas must surely have offended many who were.[151] However, we may doubt whether Wordsworth himself would have felt perfectly at ease among the Wordsworthians when we recall that he spoke like a true eighteenth-century gentleman of kicking Jeffrey's breech for calling him the leader of a cult, and that this same Wordsworth at one time dreamed of printing his poems on halfpenny broadsides to be sold to the common people, and hoped that the spread of popular education would increase his public.[152] This historic Wordsworth, we must believe, would have been pleased by the success of his disciple's efforts to popularize him. And it is even more certain that Arnold, could he have foreseen his full success, would also have been deeply and disinterestedly gratified

III

THE ANGUISH OF GREATNESS: BYRON

Eternal passion!
Eternal pain!

I. BYRON'S INFLUENCE ON MATTHEW ARNOLD

NONE of the other major Romantic poets influenced Matthew Arnold's poetry and thought as profoundly as Wordsworth. Nevertheless, it was impossible for a poetically sensitive lad of Arnold's generation to escape the reverberations of Byron's unparalleled popularity. Looking back in 1881, Arnold could still 'remember the latter years of Byron's vogue'; he himself had 'felt the expiring wave of that mighty influence'.[1] Perhaps that wave is still expiring; at any rate almost three-quarters of a century later it broke over another schoolboy poet, T. S. Eliot, who found in re-reading Byron as an adult, that

> images come before the mind, and the recollection of some verses in the manner of *Don Juan*, tinged with that disillusion and cynicism only possible at the age of sixteen, which appeared in a school periodical.[2]

It may be representative of the different generations, however, that *Don Juan* offered the appropriate model for sixteen-year-old emotion in the early years of this century, while the oldest surviving poem of the nineteenth-century poet is saturated with the spirit, metre, and language of *Childe Harold*. If Arnold's later Oxford prize poem of 1843, *Cromwell*, reveals a predominantly Wordsworthian influence, his adolescent Rugby prize poem of 1840, *Alaric at Rome*, speaks even more obviously the language of Byron.[3] The fourth canto of *Childe Harold* provided the verse form, an epigraph, many verbal echoes, and the mood of brooding

75

melancholy over the evanescence of human greatness. The subject matter comes from the thirty-first chapter of Gibbon, but where Gibbon portrays the haughty, brutal conqueror, Arnold dwells upon the 'fiery spirit' [l.187] pausing at the moment penultimate to the sack of Rome to meditate on thoughts of home, death, and glory.

Though derivative, this early work is almost as notable for what it omits of the Byronic influence as for what it includes. The posturing, the melancholy, are Byron's, but it is unimaginable that Byron writing of the destruction of Rome would have stopped short at the poised moment before the attack or could have confined himself to introspection. Arnold, even at seventeen, is not interested in narrative action, battle, the clash of sword and spear, the moment of valour or cowardice, but rather in the thought—and doubt—that precedes and colours, if it does not paralyse, the action.[4]

Perhaps Arnold's characteristic interest in static passion, for which he was later to censure his own *Empedocles on Etna*, can even be seen in an incident that occurred when he was fourteen. At that age he won a competition in elocution at Winchester by the 'simplicity and distinctness of his delivery' of the grand harangue of Marino Faliero.[5] More likely, perhaps, the boy was revealing early signs of another trait, choosing the passage for its shock value:

> . . . an adulteress boastful of her guilt
> With some large gondolier or foreign soldier.

In his choice we may detect a trace of the Byronic dandyism of his early manhood. At any rate, after the Rugby poem the influence of Byron was more apparent in young Matt Arnold's mannerisms than in his poetry—in his proudly flowing mane of hair, 'guiltless', in the words of Clough, 'of English scissors',[6] in his bantering, half-cynical conversation, and in his taste for European literature and actresses. Lionel Trilling has provided an incisive analysis of the young poet's use of this rather gaudy façade as a self-protective device, but this superficial Byronism had only an indirect, psychological connection with the maturing poet within. Arnold's brother tells us that it was at Oxford during Matthew's undergraduate days that 'Goethe displaced Byron in his poetical allegiance', and the shift was permanent.[7]

Nevertheless, Byron, or a sort of Byron-*gestalt*, does appear as a shadow or submerged image fairly frequently in Arnold's mature poetry, as the type of impetuous, violent action and undivided will. Thus the early sonnet *To the Duke of Wellington* praises the Iron Duke not for what he did, but for his singleness of purpose, his wit 'which saw one clue to life, and follow'd it'. Arnold's deeply felt need for such integrity of purpose is the dominant motif of his correspondence with Clough, and of many of his poems, the major example being *The Scholar-Gipsy*. In *A Farewell* Arnold expresses the (partial) desire for the energy which for him is the outstanding quality of Byron:

> I too have long'd for trenchant force,
> And will like a dividing spear;
> Have praised the keen, unscrupulous course,
> Which knows no doubt, which feels no fear.

> [ll. 33–6]

However, Arnold saw too the dangers in the Byronic expansion of the ego to fill a universe emptied, like that of Raskolnikov and Ivan Karamazov, of the old gods. Such egotism may lead to the sensual anarchy and arrogance depicted in *Mycerinus*,[8] or, as in *Stagirius*, to spiritual pride with its corruption in the ultimate triviality of self-infatuation:

> When the soul, growing clearer,
>   Sees God no nearer;
> When the soul, mounting higher,
>   To God comes no nigher;
> But the arch-fiend Pride
> Mounts at her side,
> Foiling her high emprise,
> Sealing her eagle eyes,
> And when she fain would soar,
> Makes idols to adore,
> Changing the pure emotion
> Of her high devotion,
> To a skin-deep sense
> Of her own eloquence;
> Strong to deceive, strong to enslave—
>   Save, oh! save.[9]

> [ll. 14–29]

Passion itself, in *Tristram and Iseult*, is

> a diseased unrest,
> And an unnatural overheat at best,

> [ll. 135–6]

and the song of the nightingale in *Philomela* evokes the cry:

> Eternal passion!
> Eternal pain!
> [ll. 31–2]

There are dangers from without as well; Empedocles bitterly rejects an age inhospitable to great and passionate spirits:

> The brave, impetuous heart yields everywhere
> To the subtle, contriving head;
> Great qualities are trodden down,
> And littleness united
> Is become invincible.
> [Act II, ll. 90–4]

It is a Titan of whom Empedocles is speaking here and again a little further on, when he laments the

> anguish of greatness
> Rail'd and hunted from the world.
> [Act II, ll. 104–5]

Arnold repeatedly criticized his own age in similar terms, and he liked to characterize Byron as a rebellious Titan.

A further limitation on the value of a soul strong in passion, energy, and courage, is that, if untempered by Goethean wisdom and self-control or by Wordsworthian natural piety, it may simply shatter itself against the problems of the impenetrable and inscrutable universe, neither gaining relief from the problems nor making progress in solving them. There is more than a touch of Byronism in Empedocles, who can live neither with men nor with himself;[10] but, unlike Byron with his insoluble moral dilemma, Empedocles is tortured by the intellectual fever of unsatisfied thought, a torture

> Whose weariness no energy can reach,
> And for whose hurt courage is not the cure.
> [Act II, ll. 13–14]

The Byronic virtues are of no help here, as they were of no help finally to Byron himself, or at least to the Byron of Arnold's conception. Empedocles possesses the passion of a Byron, directed entirely, however, to the world of thought. Like Byron, he lacks the sanative qualities of

> Wordsworth's sweet calm, or Goethe's wide
> And luminous view,[11]

and so he finds himself not liberated but enslaved:

> Slave of sense,
> I have in no wise been;—but slave of thought?
>
> [Act II, ll. 389–90]

The natural feelings that bind man to nature and to his kind are extinguished in his monomaniac passion and he cries out, in the lines whose tone is to my mind the most reminiscent of Byron in all Arnold's adult work:

> Oh, that I could glow like this mountain!
> Oh, that my heart bounded with the swell of the sea!
> Oh, that my soul were full of light as the stars!
> Oh, that it brooded over the world like the air!
> But no, this heart will glow no more; thou art
> A living man no more, Empedocles!
> Nothing but a devouring flame of thought—
> But a naked, eternally restless mind!
>
> [Act II, ll. 323–30]

The significance of Byron, then, in the poetry of Matthew Arnold is not to be found in direct poetic influence. Outside of the youthful *Alaric at Rome*, actual echoes of Byron's poetry are rare.[12] It is rather the Byronic personality and the complex of qualities—and defects—that it represents for Arnold which is a recurring element in his poetry, sometimes as an overt symbol, more often as a form looming dimly in the background, the shadow of a Titanic failure.

This shadowy form may also be seen, more remotely, as an example of courage to dare use poetry to challenge the routine thinking of the time, to dare ask the great modern question which Arnold puts in Goethe's mouth: 'But is it so? is it so to *me*?'[13] Byron did much to free poetry from moralistic restrictions, but this freedom was employed in various ways by later poets. The vaguely defined group known as the pre-Raphaelites used this freedom to abjure morality altogether as a component of art, or rather they attempted to forge a self-sufficient aesthetic morality. Elevating subtle refinement of craftsmanship and polish to the highest level of value, they rejected the claim to greatness of the slovenly and slipshod Byron, not conscious perhaps that his rebelliousness had helped clear the way for their freedom.[14] Arnold, of course, was no more a believer in art for art's sake than

79

Byron could have been; concern for morality was of the essence of his personality and his poetics. But Arnold possessed the courage to write a poetry of doubt of things above the earth, anguish and even disgust over conditions upon it, and to offer this poetry to mid-Victorian England without hedging qualifications like Tennyson's

> O yet we trust that somehow good
> Will be the final goal of ill.

In this courage, far greater surely than that required in later decades simply to try to avoid moral questions altogether, we may see some inheritance of the quality which in Arnold's estimation had given to Byron, whatever he lacked, some portion of greatness.

II. EARLY CRITICISM—LETTERS AND POETRY

As with Wordsworth, Arnold's abiding attitudes toward Byron were expressed first in poetry; although these were amplified later in the prose criticism, and some new points, such as the matter of style, were taken up, there was little alteration or revision of these attitudes. However, where there is a remarkable overall consistency in the criticism of Wordsworth expressed in letters, verse, and prose from his very earliest years to the latest, with Byron there were fluxes and refluxes of opinion during Arnold's early life before he settled in 1850 on the general evaluation which was not to change much thereafter.

Like many another adolescent, Arnold came as a boy under the spell of Byron, although he was still an infant when Byron died and the fifteen-year-old Alfred Tennyson went disconsolately to a secluded wood near his home to write upon a stone 'Byron is dead.' Byron's fame, however, did not readily die; as late as 1846 when Thackeray assailed Byron he still felt constrained to add 'Woe be to the man who denies the public gods.'[15] Some results of this boyhood influence on Arnold have already been mentioned— the elocutionary exercise at Winchester and the prize poem at Rugby three years later—but we have also seen that Arnold had already obeyed the Carlylean injunction to close his Byron and open his Goethe before 1844, the year in which he was graduated from Oxford. It is more than likely that the rejection was as violent as may be expected when a young man turns away from an early idol. The disgust of extreme reaction may be discerned in a letter to Clough of September 29, 1848, although in the very force of the disgust we see something of Byron's power to make himself felt, the power for which Arnold was later to praise him so highly. Young Matt, on his travels ('Un Milton, jeune et voyageant' according to George Sand[16]), had just visited the lake of Geneva, but found that the 'whole locality is spoiled by the omnipresence there of that furiously flaring bethiefed rushlight, the vulgar Byron'.[17] Still, he must have felt that there were some rays of genuine illumination in the 'bethiefed rushlight', for just a few months earlier he had written to his mother of his first impressions (to be much revised later) of Heine, comparing him unfavourably to Byron in terms of sincerity:

He has a good deal of power, though more trick; however, he has thoroughly disgusted me. The Byronism of a German, of a man trying to be gloomy, cynical, impassioned, *moqueur*, etc., all à la fois, with their honest bonhommistic language and total want of experience of the kind that Lord Byron, an English peer with access everywhere, possessed, is the most ridiculous thing in the world. Goethe wisely said the Germans could not have a national comedy because they had no social life; he meant the social life of highly civilized corrupt communities like Athens, Paris, or London: and for the same reason they cannot have a Byronic-poetry.[18]

The ambivalence of attitude—Byron is vulgar and false, Byron is also strong and sincere—adumbrated in these two letters was to remain a salient feature of all Arnold's Byron criticism.

The influence of Carlyle upon the Oxford undergraduate and his own need for a poetry purer in form and more inward in thought certainly played their part in turning Arnold away from Byron. It is also likely that Wordsworth's influence was active here. In a passage of *Evening Voluntaries* Wordsworth is generally understood to be referring to Lord Byron, or to a 'Genius' of his type, as one who dares

to take
Life's rule from passion craved for passion's sake;
Untaught that meekness is the cherished bent
Of all the truly great and all the innocent.
[IV, 12–15]

This is criticism with which Arnold would have agreed, although perhaps 'meekness' is not precisely the quality he would have prescribed as a corrective. Other comments of Wordsworth on Byron come very close to Arnold's thought. Crabb Robinson recorded in his diary for 1812:

> We talked of Lord Byron. Wordsworth allowed him power but denied his style to be English. Of his moral qualities we think the same.[19]

Again in 1836 Wordsworth was saying:

> Byron has great power and genius, but there is something so repugnant to my moral sense that I abhor them.

Arnold was not inclined to pass a moral verdict on Byron until all his detestation of sexual irregularity was fully aroused by Dowden's *Life of Shelley*, but there is a striking similarity to Arnold's opinions in the ideas expressed by Wordsworth of 'power' and 'genius' which have failed, and of Byron's impurity and poverty of style. Elsewhere, Wordsworth dilated on Byron's deficiencies of style, and also rejected (as Arnold was to do) his taste in poetry:

> Byron seems to me deficient in feeling . . . His critical prognostications have, for the most part, proved erroneous . . . My main endeavour, as to style, has been that my poems should be written in pure intelligible English. Lord Byron has spoken severely of my compositions. However faulty they may be, I do not think that I ever could have prevailed upon myself to print such lines as he has done; for instance,
>
> > 'I stood at Venice on the Bridge of Sighs,
> > A palace and a prison on each hand.'
>
> Some person ought to write a critical review, analysing Lord Byron's language, in order to guard others against imitating him in these respects.

In 1881 Matthew Arnold, moved partly by Ruskin's recent attack on Wordsworth's style and defence of Byron's, did something to fulfil Wordsworth's desire.

This cycle of boyhood infatuation and youthful revulsion seems to have reached equilibrium by the end of the 1840's; in 1850 Arnold was sufficiently removed from emotional involvement to enrol Byron's name, with acknowledgement of his deficiencies, with Goethe's and Wordsworth's, and henceforward the three were to maintain their rank in his critical opinions as the greatest poets of the century in accomplishment, although Wordsworth was placed a considerable distance beneath Goethe, and Byron an even greater distance beneath Wordsworth. The *Memorial Verses* of 1850, that small storehouse of criticism, sums up the most important of Arnold's opinions of Byron. There is Byron's Titanism —'the strife ... / Of passion with eternal law'—which was to be further developed in the lectures *On the Study of Celtic Literature.* There is Byron's daring and his unquenchable courage, which became the main theme of the 'Byron' essay—he taught 'us how to dare, / And against fear our breast to steel'. Finally, and perhaps most important at this stage of Arnold's life, there is Byron's power to arouse and stimulate emotional life—'our soul / Had *felt* him like the thunder's roll.'

Arnold is too frequently given to using such generalizing pronouns as 'we', 'our', 'one', etc., where all that is warranted is 'I' or 'me'; in this instance, however, there is ample evidence that the 'our' is truly expressive of much typical nineteenth-century response. Edward Dowden asserts that 'Byron did much to free, arouse, dilate the emotional life of the nineteenth century.' William Hale White ('Mark Rutherford') in his novel *The Revolution in Tanner's Lane* (1887) paid tribute to Byron as a stirrer up of opinion and guide towards liberalism and towards a richer emotional life among the more advanced members of the working class during the poet's own lifetime; especially it is Byron's scorn of meanness, his love of freedom, and above all his courage, 'root of all virtue', for which he is praised.[20] White expressed other ideas similar to Arnold's in a review in 1881 of Arnold's *Poetry of Byron*:

> He was a mass of living energy, and it is this which makes him so perpetually attractive and sanative too. For energy, power, is the one thing after which we pine, especially in a sickly age. We do not want carefully-constructed poems of mosaic, self-possessed and self-conscious. Force is what we need and what will heal us.[21]

There is substantial accord between this judgement and Arnold's tribute in *Memorial Verses*—compare 'mass of living energy' with Arnold's 'fount of fiery life'—but in the last sentence it goes beyond what Arnold could accept, for he allowed Byron 'formative' power (following Goethe), but denied him 'healing' power. And that for one great reason. Force was good, but force was not enough; Byron was lacking in thought, in light, in constructive moral ideas which could lead to good, as opposed to merely rebellious ones with which to struggle against the bad. Byron had other deficiencies, but this is the main one. Although Arnold, as a poet, deplored Byron's lack of artistry, he was fairly charitable on this point, and overlooked it altogether in *Memorial Verses*, which was, after all, a tribute and so was mainly devoted to singling out the spiritually valuable qualities of the three poets. But Byron's greatest deficiency and ultimate failure could not be overlooked: 'He taught us little' [l. 8].

Before leaving *Memorial Verses* we must notice for a moment the words 'eternal law' [l. 11]. The adjective is significant; it defines the Byron with whom we are dealing. Arnold did not consider satire a very valuable literary type and doubted that it could be 'true' poetry at all; his opinions of Pope and Dryden are well known. And although Byron is prized in the 1881 Preface as an ally against Philistinism and a rebel against decayed, outmoded, and all too *human* law, the 'system of established facts and dominant ideas', it is clear that on the whole the essential Byron for Arnold is the poet of thunderous or moody passion and restless rebellious energy—the Titanic Byron of *Childe Harold*, *Cain*, and *Manfred*. This was true in 1850 and remained true in 1881. The anthology of that year allows only forty pages of two hundred and sixty-five of actual verse for satire. *Childe Harold* looms much larger than *Don Juan*; *Manfred* is given almost complete, but there are only eight stanzas of *The Vision of Judgment*.

This Promethean Byron is mentioned in two other poems of the next five years. In *Courage*, published in 1852 but not reprinted in Arnold's lifetime, Byron is compared with Cato; both are praised for their 'strength of soul'. Cato is admired not so much for his decision to commit suicide, as for the dauntlessness with which he carried it out; Byron's poetry is dismissed, his example of 'fiery courage' celebrated:

> And, Byron! let us dare admire,
> If not thy fierce and turbid song,
> Yet that, in anguish, doubt, desire,
> Thy fiery courage still was strong.
>
> The sun that on thy tossing pain
> Did with such cold derision shine,
> He crush'd thee not with his disdain—
> He had his glow, and thou hadst thine.

This glow was presumably not just 'furiously flaring bethiefed rushlight'. The personification of the sun and its 'cold derision' suggests the myth of Apollo and the Titan Hyperion, although it is also in keeping with Arnold's view of the coldly indifferent universe. The same Titanic Byron appears again in *Haworth Churchyard* (1855), where he is compared to Emily Brontë,

> whose soul
> Knew no fellow for might,
> Passion, vehemence, grief,
> Daring, since Byron died,
> The world-famous son of fire.
>
> [ll. 93–7]

Probably the most famous thing Arnold ever said of Byron came in another poem of 1855, *Stanzas from the Grande Chartreuse*:

> What helps it now, that Byron bore,
> With haughty scorn which mock'd the smart,
> Through Europe to the Ætolian shore
> The pageant of his bleeding heart?
> That thousands counted every groan,
> And Europe made his woe her own?
>
> [ll. 133–8]

Seen against its background of Arnold's thought, this stanza is remarkably rich in meaning. The fact that 'Europe made his woe her own' is important; European writers like Mazzini have testified that Byron was the first English poet who was also European, and that his influence was enormous in arousing European interest in Shakespeare and other English writers.[22] In his 'Byron' essay Arnold quotes the French critic Scherer, who, though hostile, recognized Byron as 'one of our French superstitions'. In spite of a certain sceptical reserve displayed in the verse quoted above, and in the 1881 essay, concerning this exaggerated European reputation, there is no doubt that Arnold prized Byron in part as an important ally in his lifelong struggle to bring England and the Continent closer together and to release England from its dogged and inflexible insularity.[23]

The famous phrase, 'The pageant of his bleeding heart', is sometimes taken for mere sarcasm. In context, its irony is certainly of a more complex sort. True, there is conveyed an impression of pose, strut, and falseness. But at the same time there is the suggestion of a certain dignity and true suffering. The value of this irony is that it is used not to avoid, but precisely to make a judgement, necessarily a complex and ironic judgement. As Arnold said later, developing the condensed image in literal prose, 'There is the Byron who posed, there is the Byron with his affectations and silliness, . . .' but 'whoever stops at the theatrical preludings does not know him.'[24]

If the whole stanza is put back into its place in the poem, it is noteworthy that there is here a new grouping of voices. In *Memorial Verses* Goethe, Wordsworth, and Byron were presented as the three most important poets of the era; in the *Stanzas from the Grande Chartreuse* Byron is grouped with Shelley and (of all unlikely people) Senancour. 'Together', in the words of a recent critic, 'they form a trio of defeated voices crying in the wilderness'.[25] The grouping in this poem has not to do with literary criticism in the narrower sense; Arnold is not now ranking poets but rather spirits or personalities. Senancour's was the voice which spoke, in its icy despair, most clearly to Arnold of the diseased condition of modern life. Byron and Shelley, especially Byron, did not withdraw as Senancour did from the scene of conflict, but they are aligned with him because of their failure, even though they alone of the English poets of the earlier nineteenth century made the 'Titanic effort to flow in the main stream of modern literature.' For this effort they will be long remembered, but 'their names will be greater than their writings'.[26] They, and Senancour, are magnificent failures: 'What helps it now?' Here, too, as in *Memorial Verses*, are expressed first in poetry ideas which Arnold later developed in his prose criticism. Here the emphasis is on Byron's defeat; he is the overthrown Titan, lacking ideas, sacrificing himself nobly but futilely in the struggle against the 'system of established facts and dominant ideas which revolted him'.[27]

III. LITERARY CRITICISM OF THE '60's

As we have seen, Arnold's sympathy with Byron was decidedly imperfect; nevertheless he considered Byron an important figure, if not a great poet. Consequently we find references to Byron cropping up from time to time in the writings of the great critical decade of the 1860's, although Byron's name appears by no means so frequently as Wordsworth's. The criticism of this decade does not deal directly with English literature except in passing, and where reference is made to modern English letters it is generally to point out deficiencies; the lifelong educational crusade was well under way. Thus, in spite of Arnold's healthy respect (scarcely the 'reverential awe' of *Memorial Verses*) for his great force, Byron's name is always mentioned in these years with some touch of depreciation, as in the following passage from a letter of 1864 renominating the three main poets of the era:

> I do not think Tennyson a great and powerful spirit in any line— as Goethe was in the line of modern thought, Wordsworth in that of contemplation, Byron even in that of passion; and unless a poet, especially a poet at this time of day, is that, my interest in him is only slight, and my conviction that he will not finally stand high is firm.[28]

Byron's comparatively low rank as a poet is further emphasized by the fact that in all Arnold's work (where he is not specifically writing about Byron) I can find only one direct allusion to his verse—significant in view of the very frequent incidental quotation from such moderns as Wordsworth and Goethe. The instance occurs in the preface to *Essays in Criticism*, where the line 'There are our young barbarians, all at play!'[29] provides one of the touches of affectionate irony in the famous eulogy to Oxford.

Of the three volumes of criticism of the sixties, significant comment on Byron occurs in two, the *Essays in Criticism* of 1865 (the various essays were published periodically in 1863 and 1864), and *On the Study of Celtic Literature*, Oxford lectures published serially in 1866 and in book form in 1867. There is no further mention of Byron in Arnold's letters except for some passages in 1881 about the Byron selections.[30] The rest of Arnold's criticism of Byron is contained, except for three brief passages in other late essays, in the Byron Essay-Preface of 1881.

A unifying theme in *Essays in Criticism*, perhaps the principal theme, is the narrowness and insufficiency of English culture and its need for the admission of new and animating influences. Thus, in so far as Byron appears in these essays, the emphasis is upon his failures. The example of Byron is particularly useful to Arnold because in attempting to trace the causes of failure in a genius whose native powers were so great, he has a splendid opportunity to criticize the cultural milieu which must bear a large share of the responsibility. Byron becomes a case study, useful as a weapon in Arnold's attack on the rigidity, insularity, narrowness, and intellectual intransigence—in short, the Philistinism—of the British character. In 'Heinrich Heine', first published in *The Cornhill Magazine*, August 1863, occurs a review of the writers of the Romantic period. They are divided into those who did and those who did not attempt to 'apply modern ideas to life'. Arnold admitted that members of the second group—Wordsworth, Coleridge, Scott, Keats—have left more successful work than those of the first—Byron and Shelley. But these admirable works do not belong to 'the main current of the literature of modern epochs'. Byron and Shelley, on the other hand, will be long remembered for having made the attempt to move in that current—the 'Titanic effort'—but they failed. Their failure, it is more than implied, was really the failure of their society and culture:

> Byron and Shelley did not succeed in their attempt freely to apply the modern spirit in English literature, they could not succeed in it; the resistance to baffle them, the want of intelligent sympathy to guide and uphold them, were too great.[31]

That is, to put it crudely, a large portion of their failure is due to their not having been born in France or Germany, the great homes of enlightened modernity.

However, a discrimination has yet to be made; Byron is not to get off quite so easily. True, some, even much, of his failure as a poet of a modern epoch may be attributed to circumstance and environment. But there remains the consideration that Byron was not temperamentally at home in the world of thought and ideas. A French or German Byron might have been better able to husband and utilize his genius, but the English one lacked, after all, the required intellectual equipment:

> When a spendthrift, one is tempted to cry, is Nature! With what prodigality, in the march of generations, she employs human power, content to gather almost always little result from it, sometimes none! Look at Byron, that Byron whom the present generation of Englishmen are forgetting; Byron, the greatest natural force, the greatest elementary power, I cannot but think which has appeared in our literature since Shakespeare. And what became of this wonderful production of nature? He shattered himself, he inevitably shattered himself to pieces against the huge, black, cloud-topped,

interminable precipice of British Philistinism. But Byron, it may be said, was eminent only by his genius, only by his inborn force and fire; he had not the intellectual equipment of a supreme modern poet; except for his genius he was an ordinary nineteenth-century English gentleman, with little culture and no ideas.[32]

Heine, on the other hand, possessed of both native genius and 'all the ideas of modern Europe', was also a failure because of a moral deficiency. So much is required to produce a literature which shall come up to the high standards of perfection which Arnold had set up—adequacy of culture both materially and ideologically, coupled with greatness of native genius in individual poets who shall also be morally and intellectually up to the best of their civilization, or beyond it—and so high are these standards, that out of all the world's history Arnold can exhibit as examples of supreme achievement in creating a 'modern' literature but a handful of Greeks of the age of Pericles.[33] With reference to the complex of rarities which must all come together at the right time and in the right way to produce an adequate literature of a modern epoch, we can well understand Arnold's notion of the Darwinian prodigality of nature expressed in the passage quoted above. More striking to the reader, perhaps, is the description of Lord Byron as 'an ordinary nineteenth-century English gentleman'—except for his genius. This estimate, which incidentally may help explain why Arnold is fairly lenient in moral judgement of Byron, seems extreme, even paradoxical. With new discoveries in Byron's biography, and perhaps a fuller understanding of psychology, we may no longer be able to think of Byron with the same awe as our ancestors. Nevertheless, we are no more likely than they to think of him as 'ordinary'—Byron with his lamed foot, his cruel, driven mother, his Calvinist childhood, starved ego, and compulsive sexuality, all fusing into neurotic revulsion from himself and his world. We find it difficult, too, to dissociate the intelligence from the whole personality. However, if we do so, we may discern what Arnold was getting at, and we shall probably agree that Byron's intellect was independent and, within limits, strong and incisive, but by no means extraordinary in range, depth, and fineness.

This intellectual deficiency is a strongly felt motif in what remains to be considered of Arnold's Byron criticism. In 'The Function of Criticism at the Present Time', English poetry of the early nineteenth century in general, and Byron's in particular, is again arraigned on the charge of intellectual inadequacy. But again Arnold insists more strenuously upon the general deficiencies of the English intellectual climate than upon individual defects. After discussing the situation as it applies to men generally, he specifies the case of the poet, who,

> . . . for instance, ought to know life and the world before dealing with them in poetry; and life and the world being in modern times very complex things, the creation of a modern poet, to be worth much, implies a great critical effort behind it; else it must be a comparatively poor, barren, and short-lived affair. This is why Byron's poetry had so little endurance in it, and Goethe's so much; both Byron and Goethe had a great productive power, but Goethe's was nourished by a great critical effort providing the true materials for it, and Byron's was not; Goethe knew life and the world, the poet's necessary subjects, much more comprehensively and thoroughly than Byron. He knew a great deal more of them, and knew them much more as they really are.[34]

A question must occur immediately to anyone who, like Arnold, believed that the ideas behind the French Revolution, in spite of certain retrograde and destructive features, were largely responsible for the liberation of the modern European intellect; why did the 'immense stir' of the Revolution fail to produce the lasting monuments of mind and spirit of the great age of Greece or the European Renaissance? Arnold believed, correctly I think, that the principal cause for this failure lay not in an excess but rather in a deficiency of reason in the Revolutionary movement. The great ideas produced during the *ancien régime* were almost lost, buried, and sacrificed in the crude and violent efforts to realize them prematurely. The great poets of the period who were stirred by the Revolution were swept along by emotional fervour rather than by a thorough intellectual grasp of the ideas which constituted the true Revolution:

> . . . the true key to how much in our Byron, even in our Wordsworth, is this!—that they had their source in a great movement of feeling, not in a great movement of mind.[35]

Certainly this judgement is true of Byron, the eternal rebel, with his simplification of his politics 'into an utter detestation of all existing governments'. It must, I think, be similarly acknowledged of Wordsworth, in spite of his profounder intelligence, that his relations with the French Revolution were essentially emotional:

> Bliss was it in that dawn to be alive,
> But to be young was very heaven!

The failure of the Revolution to live up to Wordsworth's emotional expectations was a factor in bringing about a loss of faith in himself and in his own feelings symptomatic of a severe emotional disorder; his resultant conservatism in practical politics led to an increasing theoretical distrust of all new ideas.[36] But the true greatness of the Revolution, Arnold insists, lay not in its actions but in its ideas:

> In spite of the extravagant direction given to this enthusiasm, in spite of the crimes and follies in which it lost itself, the French Revolution derives from the force, truth, and universality of the ideas which it took for its law, and from the passion with which it could inspire a multitude for these ideas, a unique and still living power; it is—it will probably long remain—the greatest, the most animating event in history.[37]

Byron, with 'little culture and no ideas', failed to understand this 'movement of mind', and the failure was characteristically English. This is the burden of the Byron criticism in *Essays in Criticism*: 'He taught us little.' This criticism will be further developed in the 1881 Preface where Arnold stresses the lack of constructive thought, the almost purely negative nature of Byron's revolutionary ardour: 'I am of the opposition.'

Nevertheless the blindly violent, emotional rebellion of Byron's powerful spirit against the god of things as they are is not for Arnold, without some positive value. This theme, which had already been expressed in verse, and was to be developed further in the late essay-preface, forms the keynote of the Byron criticism in *On the Study of Celtic Literature*. The value of these lectures as studies in a special field is nugatory. Arnold had not even a reading knowledge of any of the Celtic tongues and no very broad acquaintance with the literature, while his attempt to place his analysis of the special qualities of Celtic literature on a 'scientific' basis is a hopeless failure, founded as it was on a thoroughly unscientific race theory.[38] Still, the lectures are not without interest, both for their incidental literary criticism, and also for what they reveal of Matthew Arnold's political and social purposes and of his tactics in implementing these purposes. They are probably further from his critical goal of 'disinterestedness' than anything else in his literary criticism, and even more than the rest of it should be read as moral parables and sermons addressed to the nation at large.

Arnold's general attitude toward the Celts, as toward medievalism, was a mixture of affection and depreciation, with the latter, on the whole, predominating. Consequently his treatment of Celtic literature is shot through with irony; perhaps the best brief example which reveals this condescending attitude, as of an elder brother toward a charming but slightly idiotic junior, is in a letter to his friend Lady de Rothschild: 'I have a great *penchant* for the Celtic races, with their melancholy and unprogressiveness.'[39] But there is a special quality Arnold thought he discerned in the 'melancholy' that made it valuable; this was its force and vehemence. Feeling himself a victim, as all his poetry and more intimate correspondence show, of divided aims and mixed emotions, he half-envied more powerful spirits and could forgive them a great deal. 'What women these Jewesses are!' Arnold exclaims of the Rothschild ladies, 'with a *force* which seems to triple that of the women of our Western and Northern races'.[40] And it was not only a personal matter, for he felt that his problems were symptomatic of the age, or at any rate of the thinking, feeling people of the age 'With its sick hurry, its divided aims, / Its heads o'ertax'd, its palsied hearts'. Mark Rutherford, as we have seen, and other Victorians expressed much the same feeling in the very teeth of British imperialism and prosperity, and William Butler Yeats in our own times, himself partly a product of the Celtic revival to which Arnold helped give impetus, has summed it up in memorable words:

> The best lack all conviction, while the worst
> Are full of passionate intensity.

And it was force, energy, that Arnold admired wherever he found it—yes, even in the British Philistine where, however, it was too exclusively at the service of materialism, utilitarianism, and smug self-righteousness. What the Celts could contribute was a loosening of the emotional life, by helping to direct some of the practical Anglo-Saxon energy into less self-seeking channels, by infecting it with at least a touch of Celtic passion and impracticality.

And here Arnold was able to use Byron. In the *Essays in Criticism* Byron stood as a symbol of the helplessness of the impassioned individual against a harsh, crabbed, and unyielding civilization and the failure of that civilization to provide an adequate intellectual environment for the artist. But in *Celtic Literature* Arnold emphasized the inner source rather than the external results of the rebellion, and Byron now was used as a symbol of that Celtic passion which has contributed to the glory of English literature and which, because it is impractical and lies deeper than reason, can contribute something of value to the materially successful but narrow and ugly Anglo-Saxon character.[41] This Celtic element Arnold makes the equivalent of Titanism:

> Its chord of penetrating passion and melancholy, again its *Titanism* as we see it in Byron,—what other European poetry possesses that like the English, and where do we get it from? The Celts, with their vehement reaction against the despotism of fact, with their sensuous nature, their manifold striving, their adverse destiny, their immense calamities, the Celts are the prime authors of this vein of piercing regret and passion,—of this Titanism in poetry.[42]

It is of the essence of Celtic Titanism that it is at bottom inexplicable. According to Arnold, the source of discontent in Goethe's heroes is always known and explicable, unlike the Titanism of the Celt with his 'passionate, turbulent, indomitable reaction against the despotism of fact' which reminds us of Byron, and of

> all Byron's heroes, not so much in collision with outward things, as breaking on some rock of revolt and misery in the depths of their own nature; Manfred, self-consumed, fighting blindly and passionately with I know not what, having nothing of the consistent development and intelligible motive of Faust,—Manfred, Lara, Cain, what are they but Titanic? Where in European poetry are we to find this passion of revolt so warm-breathing, puissant, and sincere; except perhaps in the creation of a yet greater poet than Byron, but an English poet, too, like Byron,—in the Satan of Milton?
>
> > . . . 'What though the field be lost?
> > All is not lost; the unconquerable will,
> > And study of revenge, immortal hate,
> > And courage never to submit or yield,
> > And what is else not to be overcome.'
>
> There, surely speaks a genius to whose composition the Celtic fibre was not wholly a stranger?[43]

But the Celtic element must be used with moderation in the modern world. In accomplishing the special task of modern poetry, the task of interpreting 'human life afresh, and [supplying] a new spiritual basis to it', it is German poetry which has most nearly succeeded. This task 'is not only a work for style, eloquence, charm, poetry; it is a work for science; and the scientific, serious German spirit, not carried away by this and that intoxication of ear, and eye, and self-will, has peculiar aptitudes for it'. Not only are the Celtic virtues insufficient for coping adequately with the modern world in poetry and in practical life, but the Celtic vices, uncontrolled by other forces, may be actively destructive. They have betrayed the Celts, they betrayed Byron; and unless the English can harmonize the elements of the German, the Latin, and the Celt now clashing within them, and blend the best qualities of each instead of the worst, they too may perish by their very Celtism, with its 'self-will' and 'want of patience with ideas' and 'inability to see the way the world is going'.[44]

These 'Celtic' faults are the faults of Byron, the other side of his Titanic passion and energy. In his 'self-will' and 'want of patience with ideas' he is an 'ordinary nineteenth-century English gentleman'; his 'inability to see the way the world is going' is to be one of the major themes of the Byron essay, as it was in the brief, impressionistic critique of *Memorial Verses*. Byron failed to satisfy Arnold's supreme demand of a modern poet, the demand for light. But if Byron 'taught us little', that little, as far as it goes, is valuable, it is formative, as all experience of great and powerful things is formative. As for calling these faults, and virtues, 'Celtic' or 'Titanic', we are not likely today to accept the terms readily. To us the Byronic heroes, in so far as they seem genuine at all, are neurotic, or as the arch-exemplar of German reason Goethe put it in the psychological language of his time, '*hypochondrisch*'. And Byron's personality, though it continues to fascinate, does so not for any superhuman qualities but for its complex, tortured, and intense humanity.[45]

IV. LATE CRITICISM

Genesis and Reception of the Byron Anthology

In the late 1870's Matthew Arnold returned to the composition of literary criticism, and in his late criticism he concentrated mainly upon English writers. In 1877 alone he published four literary essays, later collected with others in *Mixed Essays*. In January there was 'A French Critic on Milton', in which Arnold expressed his own Milton criticism under the form of reviewing that of Edmond Scherer. (Arnold used the same method and the same French critic one year later in an essay on Goethe, also reprinted in *Mixed Essays*.) In March, in an essay on 'Falkland', Arnold was able to expatiate somewhat on his long-standing interest in the rational theologians of the seventeenth century. In June came the essay on 'George Sand', part memoir, part tribute, and part criticism; and in December Arnold made a number of incidental remarks on English writers in a review of Stopford Brooke's *A Primer of English Literature*. In the last-named essay Arnold foreshadowed his own later essay and selections in his remarks on Byron by minimizing the poet of *Don Juan* and emphasizing the force of the Byron personality.

This burst of production in 1877 was followed in the next few years by the selections from Johnson's *Lives*, from Burke, and from Wordsworth, the three essays contributed to Ward's *English Poets*, and the Byron anthology. Moreover, it was apparently during these years that Arnold expressed an interest in doing the volume on Shelley for the English Men of Letters Series.[46] The idea for the volume of selections from Byron apparently came to Arnold almost immediately after the publication of the *Poems of Wordsworth*, according to his opening remarks in the 'Byron' Preface. It is likely, too, that the satisfactory sales of the former volume had something to do with stimulating the production of the latter. At any rate, we learn from his correspondence with his publishers that, whenever it was conceived, the idea for the new volume was Arnold's own. That there was to be such a volume was a settled matter as early as May 1880, when Arnold was still completing his selections from Gray and Keats and his prefatory essays for *The English Poets*. Arnold's original intention, to have the Byron volume ready before Christmas, was successfully accomplished; the poems, arranged and titled, were sent off to the printers by December 2, 1880. It is not clear whether the prefatory essay had also been completed by this time, but it seems unlikely that it was. In December it was not yet certain that the Preface would first appear in *Macmillan's Magazine*, and the only Byron entries in Arnold's *Notebooks* for this period are in the one dated 1881. The essay did appear in *Macmillan's*, but not until March, 1881, and the volume was published in June.[47]

The time had grown ripe for the house of Macmillan to include Byron in their popular Golden Treasury Series. After falling to its nadir about 1850, Byron's reputation had been rising gradually but steadily. According to Professor Chew, 'the melancholy and disillusioned generation of the fifties, as represented especially by Arnold, turned on the whole with sympathy to this titanic figure of protest against the settlement of 1815 and the compromise which followed in all spheres of life'.[48] We have seen the shadow of this colossus in *Memorial Verses* and other poems of Arnold's young manhood. Ruskin emerged from a phase of anti-Byronism about 1857 and became, with Arnold, a powerful influence toward the revival of interest in Byron. Other voices were heard on Byron's behalf during the sixties, partly in reaction against Tennyson's fame and his rash of imitators. Swinburne's preface to his *Selections from the Works of Lord Byron* in 1865 was one of the most eloquent of appreciations. Arnold referred to it in his essay of 1881, and it remains a stimulating and well-balanced critique, far more attractive than the shrill vituperation against Byron in which Swinburne was to indulge later.

The sixties ended with the explosion of the 'Byron scandal'. After Harriet Beecher Stowe published 'The True Story of Lady Byron's Married Life' in *Macmillan's Magazine*, September 1869, defences, attacks, and counter-attacks followed in rapid succession. But when the controversy simmered down and the smoke cleared in 1871, Mrs. Stowe was discredited while Byron's poetry continued to gain in popularity and reputation. The rest of the seventies saw the firm establishment of respect for Byron's genius. Of course, there were dissenting voices, and even his admirers were able in general to take a clear view of his faults. Nevertheless the trend was all in his favour, starting with the publication of Alfred Austin's *The Poetry of the Period* in 1870. Although Swinburne and Browning were becoming disaffected, an increasing tide of favourable criticism told on Byron's behalf. In December 1870, John Morley published his excellent essay on 'Byron and the French Revolution' (reprinted in *Critical Miscellanies*, Vol. I). Karl Elze's ponderous life of Byron, published in Berlin in 1870, was translated in 1872 and prompted several sympathetic essay-reviews, including Roden Noel's 'Lord Byron and his Times' (*St. Paul's Magazine*, November and December 1873). William Minto's article in the ninth edition (1876) of the *Encyclopaedia*

Britannica, although mainly biographical, is critically sympathetic. Byron bulks large in Edward Dowden's article in 1877, 'The French Revolution in English Literature' (reprinted in *Studies in Literature*, 1889), and in his later book *The French Revolution and English Literature* (1897). Finally, in 1880, on the eve of Arnold's famous essay, four important publications contributed to Byron's rehabilitation: Ruskin's series of articles entitled 'Fiction, Fair and Foul'; Richard C. Jebb's essay 'Byron in Greece' (in *Modern Greece*, 1880), which defended Byron's sincerity in the concluding episode of his life; John Addington Symonds's Byron preface for Ward's *English Poets*; and John Nichol's *Byron* in the English Men of Letters Series. Arnold's Preface refers to both Nichol and Ruskin, and he certainly must have read Symonds as well.

Arnold's Byron volume offers many contrasts with its superficially similar companion *Wordsworth*. The latter was in some respects a pioneering venture,[49] while the *Byron* was merely another in a steady stream of selections from that prolific and popular poet, a stream going back at least to 1823 when the first *Beauties of Byron* listed in *CBEL* was published. Although the Wordsworth volume was suggested by the publisher, it was for Arnold clearly a labour of love to bring before a large public the best work of a poet he had special reason to revere. For Byron, on the other hand, Arnold had only partial sympathy; although the idea for the volume was his own, his approach to the poet is more than a little apologetic and deprecating. As late as 1880, when the volume was already projected, he praised Burns, whom he enjoyed but did not rank very high, for producing verses 'which have in them a depth of poetic quality such as resides in no verse of Byron's own',[50] and when he had completed the labours of editing Byron Arnold was himself surprised that the resultant body of poetry was 'much more beautiful and powerful than I had expected'.[51] In Wordsworth Arnold found a sufficient body of great or very good whole poems to make up a volume without excerpts from longer works.[52] The Byron collection, on the other hand, contains only a handful of complete poems, the bulk of the volume being made up of excerpts, some fairly lengthy, some mere snippets, from longer works, titled and arranged as though they were independent short poems. In the editing of Wordsworth Arnold allowed himself, as we have seen, a free hand to choose among various readings. With Byron the editing is even freer, as numerous silent excisions and elisions are made even in the midst of what appear to be solid excerpts.

Finally, the response to the two books was different. The *Wordsworth* aroused a little controversy, some lovers of the poet feeling that Arnold had been unjust to his philosophy and to his weightier productions, while other critics, like Ruskin, were angered that Arnold had unduly elevated Wordsworth's poetic rank. On the whole, however, the volume was well received, the general opinion being that, with whatever imperfections, it nevertheless performed a timely and useful service for the poet. *Byron*, on the other hand, received little praise and, with ironic appropriateness to its subject, stirred up a storm of controversy on all sides. Byron's detractors, and they were many, were aroused by Arnold's placing him above Keats, Shelley, and Coleridge; indeed 'aroused' is too feeble a word for the lengthy, fierce attack Swinburne was inspired to make on Byron's reputation, and other critics were not wanting to carry on what Professor Grierson has called a 'pogrom'.[53] Byron's admirers, meanwhile, carried on the battle opened by Ruskin in 1880.[54] Arnold was criticized for his claim that presenting Byron in excerpts improved the effect of his work, attacked for elevating Wordsworth above Byron, and censured for garbling some of Goethe's remarks on Byron, while the selections were severely and justly condemned for failing to represent the poet adequately. It would seem that no one was pleased.[55] Nevertheless, the volume was commercially successful, though not so successful as *Wordsworth*. Byron was still a popular poet with many people who were not ordinarily readers of poetry. Then, too, there was the prestige of the volume's position in Macmillan's Golden Treasury Series, and finally the book shared in the great authority of the name of its editor, who had by then become the prime literary critic of the age and an almost official spokesman for Culture.

The 'Byron' Essay–Preface

If the 'power of joy' is the keynote of 'Wordsworth', that of the 'Byron' essay of two years later may be said to be power, pure and simple. Such a facile simplification, of course, fails to do justice to the dialectic process by which Arnold attempts to define the special qualities of Byron and to place critically this complex poet-personality of great but not pre-eminent rank, of powerful virtues and glaring defects—still the idol of some, increasingly the abomination of others. Nevertheless, it is close enough to suggesting the guiding principle of the essay in which, after many damaging concessions about Byron as poet, thinker, and man, Arnold returns to and adopts Swinburne's earlier praise of 'the splendid and imperishable excellence which covers all his offence and outweighs all his defects: the excellence of sincerity and strength'.[56]

Arnold opens his essay with one of his several brief overall surveys of the major Romantic poets. Echoing his remark in 'Wordsworth', he admits that Keats and Coleridge have some pieces superior to anything in Wordsworth or Byron, but insists that their quantity of first-rate work is too slight to make up a satisfactory volume. Scott's work, which never rises to the level of his greater contemporaries, also never sinks far and so he is not particularly improved by selection. There may be some question about Shelley, but his work, Arnold believes, rises to a high level only in 'snatches and fragments'. Wordsworth and Byron alone not only are much improved by selection, but offer a sufficient quantity of good work to make the preparation of such a volume highly desirable. To this argument Arnold returns after a brief excursus on Shelley, concluded by the notorious judgement which caused readers like Swinburne to feel that here Arnold had virtually disqualified himself as a critic, the judgement that Shelley's essays and letters would finally stand higher than his poetry.

In defending his thesis that a volume of selections not only adequately represents but actually improves Byron, Arnold recognizes that he is treading on controversial ground. Specifically he cites Swinburne's preface to his own volume of selections (1865). Swinburne believed that Byron's virtues and defects were so inextricably tangled that he 'can only be judged or appreciated in the mass', and he asserted flatly that 'No poet is so badly represented by a book of selections', which could do no more than serve an introductory purpose.[57] The same point was to be vehemently urged by later critics of Arnold, some of whom argued that not only was Byron not 'improved' by selection, but that Arnold's own choice failed even to be representative.[58] Nevertheless, says Arnold —and certainly not without justice—'follow [Byron's] whole outpouring ... and he is capable of being tiresome'. The reason is simply that Byron was incapable of producing works which are organic wholes, which embody the virtue of *architectonicè* as do *Oedipus* and *The Tempest*. His strength is revealed in single incidents, single situations, and single bursts of sentiment. Briefly Arnold comments on some of the tales to illustrate his point, and shrewdly quotes Byron's own self-criticism to support it. Moreover, Byron must gain especially by having his best work alone presented at this time, when his vogue has expired and critics like Arnold's much-admired Edmond Scherer are contemptuously dismissing any claim to greatness for him.[59] But Scherer's disparagement can well be understood as a reaction to the exaggerated praise of earlier critics like Scott, who had claimed that 'Lord Byron has certainly matched Milton on his own ground'.[60] This remark affords Arnold an entry for some criticism of Byron's defects of style which make selection so desirable. As in the Wordsworth essay, the critique of style is the only element which is new, the rest of the essay consisting of the development of ideas which had already been expressed in other places. In 'Byron', as in all of Arnold's later criticism, there is no detailed stylistic analysis or practical criticism of the sort so well displayed in the lectures *On Translating Homer*. Instead, we find the simplification of the 'touchstone' method.

First Arnold quotes a pair of particularly feeble passages from *Cain*,[61] the work to which Scott had been referring in his high praise quoted above. Then, not directly using but indicating the touchstone technique, as though to say 'I have a weapon so powerful that I need only hint at its existence', Arnold remarks: 'One has only to repeat to oneself a line from *Paradise Lost* in order to feel the difference.' Pursuing the offensive, in anticipation of the argument that one should judge a poet by his best, not his worst work,[62] Arnold avers that these are not unusual or untypical lapses, but rather that

> Byron is so negligent in his poetical style, he is often, to say the truth, so slovenly, slipshod, and infelicitous, he is so little haunted by the true artist's fine passion for the correct use and consummate management of words, that he may be described as having for this artistic gift the insensibility of a barbarian;—which is perhaps only another and less flattering way of saying, with Scott, that 'he manages his pen with the careless and negligent ease of a man of quality.'[63]

There follow five particularly excruciating examples of limping rhythm, painful diction, and barbarous grammar and syntax,[64] and by contrast a line of Shakespeare and a couplet of Milton, who are 'of another and altogether higher order'. Arnold would surely have recognized that his comparisons were unfair, but the point he was trying to establish was that Byron, whatever his virtues, was not a truly great poet, as some of his admirers still thought. Elsewhere, too, Arnold had made consistent and flawless mastery of style one of the standards by which the greatest poets are judged.[65] Poets of the second rank like Wordsworth and Byron, on the other hand, however high they may rise at their best, are always liable to serious lapses by virtue of their incomplete mastery of their medium. This critique of Byron's style is partly in response to Ruskin's animadversions upon Wordsworth and almost unqualified praise of Byron as a far greater poet and stylist; Arnold had been reading these strictures in 'Fiction, Fair and Foul' in 1880 while he was at work on the Byron selections.[66] Instead of engaging in direct controversy, Arnold gracefully spikes Ruskin's guns first with his damaging quotations and touchstones. Then he quotes a line of Wordsworth which Ruskin had selected for special scorn: 'Parching summer hath no warrant', and couples it with an offering of his own: 'Sol hath dropped into his harbour.'[67] Thus he appears to be softening the tone of controversy implied by his quotation of the gallery of horrors from Byron. Conceding Wordsworth, he strategically concludes that *neither* poet can be ranked with such masters as Shakespeare and Milton who can display 'a poetical gift of the very highest order'.

Following the order that had by now become characteristic of his judicial criticism, that of first allowing all the concessions he intends before striking a balance, Arnold follows up the critique of Byron's style with some consideration of the defects of Byron the man. He puts aside 'direct moral criticism', but still we cannot dismiss Byron's 'most crying faults as a man,—his vulgarity, his affectation', without mention because they are related to his faults of vulgarity and crudity as an artist and to his defective critical judgement, as in his 'precious dictum that Pope is a Greek temple' and in other 'criticisms of the like force'—such as his extravagant praise of Rogers and contempt for Wordsworth, no doubt. At this point, precisely two-fifths of the way through the essay, Arnold turns from the 'negative part of the true criticism' of Byron to the positive and 'by far the more important' part of the 'whole truth'.

Adopting the attitude of refusing to be swayed by the mass of foreign testimony generally cited on Byron's behalf, Arnold confesses that there is nevertheless one such testimony, Goethe's, which is important to him. However, he continues, English critics do not always quote Goethe correctly, or with the full weight of context. Specifically, Arnold has in mind Nichol's *Byron* in the English Men of Letters series (1880); he may also have been glancing at J. A. Symonds's highly derivative 'Byron' introduction in Ward's *English Poets*.[68] There follows a certain amount of quibbling about the translation of some German words and phrases, in which Arnold does not clearly come off better than Nichol. It is also worth noting that Arnold himself was not very scrupulous about considering contexts in his quotations from Goethe.[69] This is not really of great importance, however; the main thing to realize is that Arnold is using the name of Goethe as a tactical device and not really as a 'source'. Rather than take issue directly with Goethe's encomia of Byron, he finds elsewhere in the same author remarks which will indicate precisely those qualifications which Arnold himself wishes to insinuate, while he modestly acts the part of impartial judge. Thus he pieces together out of Goethe just the equilibrium of praise and censure which he himself wishes to present—that Byron is a splendid, puissant, and unique personality, and 'the greatest talent of the century',[70] but that he was lacking both in self-knowledge, and in thinking powers generally: 'The moment he begins to reflect he is a child.'[71]

'Mark Rutherford' commented on the last point in his review, probably thinking of Arnold on Wordsworth:

> Mr. Arnold, although the very centre of his dissatisfaction with Byron is that he 'cannot reflect', would probably in another mood admit that 'reflections' are not what we demand of the poet.[72]

To be sure Arnold would have agreed that reflections alone are not what we demand of the poet, in that these do not alone constitute poetry, however sound they may be in themselves. He expressly disavows the view that had been attributed to him, that poetry has for its chief and distinguishing characteristic that it is a criticism of life; this is rather a generic quality and the main end of *all* literature, both poetry and prose. He had insisted in 'Wordsworth', and emphatically reiterates in 'Byron', that

> In poetry . . . the criticism of life has to be made conformable to the laws of poetic truth and poetic beauty. Truth and seriousness of substance and matter, felicity and perfection of diction and manner, as these are exhibited in the best poets, are what constitute a criticism of life made in conformity with the laws of poetic truth and poetic beauty. . . .

This, although vague, indicates at least generally what was for Arnold the relationship between thought and poetry. Constitutional impulsiveness, the impatience to get things said anyhow without thinking them through—these traits must show up in a poet's style, while a weakness of reflective powers must be especially hurtful to a poet who, like Byron, attempts to deal with philosophic problems, or engage in social and political criticism. For Arnold, whose demand for intellectual substance in poetry caused him to elevate Goethe above all English poets since Milton, this weakness was especially serious. In the end he related it to Byron's defective personality:

> The way out of the false state of things which enraged him he did not see,—the slow and laborious way upward; he had not the patience, knowledge, self-discipline, virtue, requisite for seeing it.

We may not wish to see the process of reflection taking place in the verse itself, but we may well feel and criticize its lack when it does not appear latent in the verse, as the felt matrix of which the verse is the crystallized and concrete result.

The kind of balance which Arnold has tried to make, using Goethe's words, he calls typical of the process of criticism whenever 'we leave the small band of the very best poets. . . . We have now to take what we can get, to forego something here, to admit compensation for it there. . . .' Among the poets of the second rank, the final judgement (i.e., *his* final judgement) will be in favour of those who offer a more sanative and useful—Arnold would say 'true'[73]—criticism of life. This principle is demonstrated by a comparison of Leopardi, Byron, and Wordsworth. Leopardi is superior to Byron in lucidity of thought, to Wordsworth in culture and awareness of the modern spirit, and to both in assurance of style, but none of the three is to be ranked with such 'true classics' as Homer, Dante, and Shakespeare. Furthermore, in spite of the fact that the Italian is strong where the Englishmen are weak, Leopardi's work as a whole is to be considered inferior to theirs. He is inferior to Wordsworth because his pessimism fails to offer to the spirit anything of comparable value to Wordsworth's deep sense of joy and his power to make us feel it. Wordsworth's criticism of life is 'healthful and true, whereas Leopardi's pessimism is not'. He is inferior to Byron in force of personality.

This comparative judgement of Leopardi and Wordsworth is perfectly consistent with Arnold's announced principles. However, when he turns to the other half of his comparison, that of Leopardi and Byron, this consistency vanishes. Arnold cannot, after what he has said about Byron's deficiency of thought, impute to him a valuable criticism of life to balance his stylistic deficiencies. Yet he believes that Byron's poetry on the whole is greater than Leopardi's. Here is one of the major inconsistencies in the essay, for it turns out that Byron's superiority lies not in what he did, but in 'something which he has and was, after all deduction has been made for his short-comings'.[74] It is the power of his personality which makes him, in Goethe's words, 'different from all the rest of the English poets, and in the main greater'; it is by his personality that he merits Swinburne's praise for 'the splendid and imperishable excellence which covers all his offences and outweighs all his defects: *the excellence of sincerity and strength*'. (Arnold's italics.) Arnold then proceeds to illustrate this sincerity and strength biographically and psychologically, not critically. Byron could not have been a Liberal peer, disbelieving but flattering the cant of British Philistinism; also the vices and hypocrisy of his own class roused him to 'irreconcilable revolt and battle'. Too strong to accept meekly the present order, too sincere to pretend, Byron found political life, which he admired more than writing, impossible. Poetry was his *pis aller*; lacking other outlets he brought to it his best as well as his worst self, and it was in his poetry that both these selves found expression. Thus Arnold comes, roundabout, back to the poetry, but it is not poetry as something made; Byron was not enough of an artist to be judged in that way. It is poetry as self-expression, pure and simple.

Consequently, the criticism of Byron's poetry is essentially a matter of delineating the dual nature of his personality. Byron's 'dual personality' is a commonplace today, and it was not rare in nineteenth-century criticism. However, when Arnold wrote there was still a tendency on the part of Byron worshippers like Taine and Ruskin to take the better side for the whole, while Byron detractors like Scherer and the later Swinburne saw only the worse. At the very centre of Arnold's judgement, however, is the simultaneous recognition of both sides. 'There is the Byron who posed', he admits. But in the best work

> at last came forth into light that true and puissant personality, with its direct strokes, its ever welling force, its satire, its energy, and its agony. This is the real Byron; whoever stops at the theatrical preludings does not know him.

It is this 'real' Byron who deserves the praise of Goethe, Taine, and Swinburne,

> in so far as it is true of him that with superb, exhaustless energy, he maintained, as Professor Nichol well says, 'the struggle that keeps alive, if it does not save the soul'.

On this matter of Arnold's admiration for Byron's force, Saintsbury comments sneeringly that Arnold had 'by that sort of reaction which often exhibits itself in men of the study, an obvious admiration for Force—the admiration which makes him in his letters praise France up to 1870 and Germany after that date—and he thought he saw Force in Byron'.[75] This slur scarcely needs detailed refutation. Arnold abhorred physical violence and brute force, although to be sure he admired vigour and direction of leadership. The true background for understanding this admiration is to be found in his poetry—*Memorial Verses*, the Marguerite poems, *Rugby Chapel*, etc.—and in his letters in such remarks as that to Clough: 'I am past thirty, and three parts iced over.'[76] Lionel Trilling sees more truly that Arnold's Byronism is related to his personal struggle with despondency and apathy.[77] This struggle is most amply documented in his poetry, it played a predominant role in the gradual decay of his relationship with the vacillating, introspective Clough, and it is an underlying common factor in Arnold's esteem for Byron and for Wordsworth, for whatever these poets lacked of art or intellect, both represented vitality and power. But it would be wrong to see Arnold's admiration for power in purely psychological terms. We must remember Arnold's sense of the high communal vocation of poetry, not just to interpret the world for us but to arouse, stimulate, animate us for a life of which three-quarters is conduct. Poetry which does this for us is, therefore, of great social, even, in an Arnoldian sense, religious value. Poetry which does not, which fails in energy—the poetry of Lucretius or of Leopardi—must thereby fail to perform its most important function.

There remain certain difficulties with Arnold's critical terminology. His use of the word *real* seems equivocal; is the theatrical, affected Byron whom Arnold so severely criticized *un*real ? Perhaps we should prefer the word *valuable*. Still, it is difficult after all allowance for Arnold's inconsistencies to disagree totally with his overall judgement, that our final interest in Byron's work is in seeing what this impressive personality had to say, at his best, about himself and the segment of the world which he knew best. And it is on the personality as it passes into the poetry where Arnold, after his discussion of biography and psychology, places the final emphasis. But the word *personality*, like the word *real*, is too ambiguous to be of much service. Perhaps we should prefer the word *persona* as it has been popularized in contemporary criticism. This term, in so far as it connotes mask, is not without its difficulties; it may carry us back to the strut and pose of the first two cantos of *Childe Harold*. But if by it we understand a personality as it is more or less successfully dramatized, made concrete, and hence artistically validated in poetry, the word may be useful in making just that distinction which is so necessary in dealing with Byron, the distinction between on the one hand the combination of folklore, biography, and self-advertisement which makes up our image of the man Byron, and on the other the artistic representation of an actor or narrator in a poem. We can then perhaps dispense with the difficult and slippery term *sincerity*, which draws us into the dubious shadowland between ethics, psychology, biography, aesthetics, and practical criticism.[78] Instead we may distinguish between *personae* which are artistically unsatisfactory because of blurriness, inconsequence, or shallowness, and hence appear to be puppets, or masks in the pejorative sense, and those which are, as far as required by their contexts, clearly realized, coherent, and solid, like the narrator of *Don Juan*.[79] Naturally, we need not 'like' even the latter, any more than we must like Coriolanus or the narrator of *The Excursion*, but when we agree that we are dealing with an achieved work of art, the question of 'liking' a character in it tends to become critically irrelevant.

In attempting to deal with the admittedly superior part of Byron's work, Arnold's belief that great writers always write greatly leads him into the same difficulties he encountered, or rather evaded, in trying to account for Wordsworth's best poetry. In both cases, his only recourse was to the doctrine or metaphor of inspiration. Byron is at his best when 'a higher power took possession of him and filled him' (higher, presumably, than even his 'real' personality).

> When he warms to his work, when he is inspired, Nature herself seems to take the pen from him as she took it from Wordsworth, and to write for him as she wrote for Wordsworth, though in a different fashion, with her own penetrating simplicity.

As criticism, this leads nowhere; as explanation it simply begs the question; but as a metaphorical repetition of the criticism that neither poet is an 'assured master of a true poetic style' it may do well enough. Byron's best verse Arnold divides into a lower class, rhetoric 'of extraordinary power and merit', and a higher, which he can only call 'truly poetic'. This, too, is not very satisfactory, and is more disappointing than the failure to account for the presence of superior work in second-rank artists, since we have a greater right to demand of a critic relevant discriminations of poetic quality than explanations of psychological mysteries. The 'truly poetic' is a stumbling block for modern readers who realize that in this category Arnold did not include *Absalom and Achitophel*, *The Rape of the Lock*, or Donne's *Anniversaries*, but Arnold's general tenor may be sensed by turning again to his touchstones. 'Rhetoric' is equally troublesome since the word's honorific value has been rehabilitated. T. S. Eliot, also writing on Byron, takes issue with the loose use of this term for censure, for, he observes, if we use the word 'rhetoric' to cover Byron's weaknesses, we have no word left for the work of such poets as Milton and Dryden, whose 'failures, when they fail, are of a higher kind than Byron's success, when he succeeds'.[80] Instead of clarifying his terms by analysis, Arnold employs his touchstone method, giving us a pair of quotations from Byron, one for each category. The lines are aptly chosen; the reader should sense the difference. If he wants more clarification, he must supply it himself.

Most of the rest of the essay is recapitulation. Arnold wishes to gain more readers for his subject, and enable 'those readers to read him with more admiration'; this is the best service a critic can perform. But Byron's admirers (like Wordsworth's) often admire for the wrong reasons and have not felt the better part of his 'vital influence'. More important, and here we come to the aspect of Byron to which Arnold attached the greatest value, his vital influence has not been felt or has been felt but little by the cynically hypocritical aristocracy and the smug, gross, and impregnable Philistines. The penultimate paragraph of Arnold's essay, both in its placement and in the very rhythm of its language, reveals the Byron in whom Arnold believed after all qualifications have been made. This Byron will outlast both fad and detraction:

> As the inevitable break-up of the old order comes, as the English middle-class slowly awakens from its intellectual sleep of two centuries, as our actual present world, to which this sleep has condemned us, shows itself more clearly,—our world of an aristocracy materialised and null, a middle-class purblind and hideous, a lower class crude and brutal,—we shall turn our eyes again, and to more purpose, upon this passionate and dauntless soldier of a forlorn hope, who, ignorant of the future and unconsoled by its promises, nevertheless waged against the conservation of the old impossible world so fiery battle; waged it till he fell,—waged it with such splendid and imperishable excellence of sincerity and strength.

As usual, especially in his late criticism, Arnold is addressing himself to a particular audience; his approach is more rhetorical than critical. Consequently we do not get from him criticism of the particular work, such criticism in this case being virtually precluded by the negative strictures on Byron's artistry.

It is for Byron's importance, then, as a 'soldier in the Liberation war of humanity'[81] rather than for artistic merit that Arnold places him so high in the review of the five leading poets of the first quarter of the century with which he concludes his essay, repeating the evaluations in the first paragraph. Wordsworth, although he will probably never be as popular as Byron and is in some ways his inferior, offers more of lasting value to humanity. But these two are 'pre-eminent in actual performance'. Keats was probably superior to both in innate poetic gift, but died too young to equal them in achievement. Neither Coleridge, 'poet and philosopher wrecked in a mist of opium', nor Shelley, 'beautiful and ineffectual angel, beating in the void his luminous wings in vain', can be considered as rivals. Confidently, perhaps over-confidently, Arnold predicts in the face of contrary opinion that when the new century opens the first names in English poetry for the past one hundred years will be these—Wordsworth and Byron.

One critic has objected that 'the man who never tired of saying that conduct was three-fourths of life, of coupling poetry with "high seriousness" and the grand style' had no legitimate reason for such high prase of Byron while Coleridge and Shelley were airily dismissed. This critic, J. B. Orrick, implies that the alleged inconsistency is the result of Arnold's not knowing his own mind:

> ... fundamentally he neither sympathized very fully with Byron as a man nor admired him greatly as a poet. When he was roused by Professor Dowden's Life of Shelley to the fullest consciousness of himself he gave vent to his real feelings.[82]

But there is really no indication that Arnold possessed a 'fuller consciousness of himself' when he wrote 'Shelley' (January 1888) then when he wrote 'Byron'. The earlier essay does not deny the faults of character expressed with such vehemence in the later but in fact mentions them, although Arnold did put aside in 'Byron' express moral criticism as being not appropriate in that context. It is perfectly clear what that moral criticism would have been if, in Arnold's estimation, it had been called for. In 'Shelley', on the other hand, Arnold is not a literary critic—except of Dowden—but a moral essayist, dealing not with the writings of his subject but his life. Hence in this context moral judgements were appropriate.

This whole matter of conduct and its relevance to Arnold's Byron criticism suggests the question raised by Lionel Trilling: why is it that Arnold, who holds Keats and Shelley so severely accountable for their sexual lives, appears to be so nearly indifferent to Byron's?[83] The question is interesting not so much for what the possible answers may reveal of Arnold's moral principles, as for what they indicate about his pragmatic critical method. As to the non-literary reasons, Trilling suggests an answer to his own question which seems to be borne out by everything we know of Arnold; his leniency toward Byron may be due to the fact that Byron 'did not theorize about love like Shelley nor allow it to "enervate" him like Keats'.[84] For corroboration we may turn to the essay on 'Count Leo Tolstoi' where Arnold expressed himself most fully on sexual matters. Arnold explained why Tolstoi's treatment of 'criminal passion' is superior to that of 'the type of novel now so much in request in France':

> ... there is no fine sentiment, at once tiresome and false. We are not told to believe, for example, that Anna is wonderfully exalted and ennobled by her passion for Wronsky.[85]

So much, the passage implies, for Shelley. As for Keats, again by implication: Tolstoi 'does not seem to feel himself owing any service to the goddess Lubricity'; his novel is free from the taint of sensuality for its own sake, that sensuality which, in the words of the expert witness Burns, 'petrifies feeling'. We may also conjecture, regarding Byron, that Arnold very likely expected little else in the way of sexual behaviour from the pampered Regency peer, and that at any rate he was better than many of his class for not being hypocritical.

But to understand Arnold more fully, and to be fair to him, I think we should also consider the less directly moralistic reasons for these differences of treatment. In spite of his announced definition of the act of criticism as seeing the object as in itself it really is, every one of Arnold's essays in criticism was also a tactic manœuvre in the grand strategy of his apostolate of Culture. Thus each essay aimed not only at its critical goal, but also at some relatively local and temporal purpose, often a kind of setting the record straight. The obtrusion of sexual moralizing in 'Shelley' has already been partly explained; it was a review of the poet's life, not of his poetry. The story of that life as far as it was generally known to the Victorians had become almost a hagiography. Dowden's *Life*, when it appeared in 1886, revealed a great deal which many, including Arnold, found shocking. This material was disruptive of the prevailing angelic legendry, in spite of Dowden's tone of defence and apology, and it required assimilation. Arnold's reaction, severe enough in itself, seems actually temperate alongside the chivalrous Mark Twain's outraged response, *In Defense of Harriet Shelley*. Arnold's essay, then, was an attempt to make this assimilation and adjustment of attitude. The 'Keats' essay, on the other hand, ought to have been primarily literary, having been commissioned for Ward's *English Poets*. But Arnold, always something of a journalist, could not help responding to the recent publication of Keats's letters to Fanny Brawne, and as the essay itself makes clear, he was concerned to establish Keats's reputation on what he considered to be the right grounds, or at least the grounds most relevant at the moment of writing. To accomplish this end he felt it necessary to undercut the basis for much of the specious and sticky adulation of Keats which endangered a true understanding of the poet's virtues. Just as he had tried to preserve Wordsworth from the solemn reverence of the Wordsworthians, he tried to save Keats from the more pawing and sickly of his admirers.

There was no corresponding tactical motivation for dealing with Byron's morality. Those who had caught from him 'the fashion of deranging their hair, or knotting their neck-handkerchief, or of leaving their shirt-collar unbuttoned' were already aged men or were in their graves. There was no need to revise moral judgement of Byron; he had never been considered an angel, soiled, ineffectual, or otherwise. In Arnold's last word on Byron (in 'Shelley'), he speaks of his 'deep grain of coarseness and commonness, his affectation, his brutal selfishness' as common knowledge which need not be argued about or discussed at length. As for Byron's poetry, although it can be vulgar and brutal, it is not sensual. For one thing, Byron's sensibility and his command of language were too coarse to make it so. In *Don Juan*, where sex is most prominent, the sexual episodes are generally comic or satiric. Except for the Haidée idyll, illicit relations are not sentimentalized but the reverse; Byron's satire fully reveals, even exaggerates, the triviality, shallowness, and sordidness of these intrigues. Consequently, Arnold's relative leniency toward Byron need not be considered a special case of indulgence; rather, it was a typical example of his critical pragmatism. There was simply no need to underline the obvious.

The Selections from Byron

Whatever the virtues and deficiencies of Arnold's critical preface on Byron, and I believe the former somewhat outweigh the latter, the accompanying anthology must be considered a failure. The selections do not even adequately represent the outstanding qualities Arnold himself had named: Byron's 'ever-welling force', his 'satire', his 'energy', or his 'agony'. Much less does Byron seem *more* forceful and *more* important in this dress than when he is read in longer and more coherent samples. 'The great art of criticism is to get oneself out of the way and to let humanity decide', Arnold had written in 1864,[86] and again in the Byron preface he called his anthology 'a tribute which consists not in covering the poet with eloquent eulogy of our own, but in letting him, at his best and greatest, speak for himself'. But it cannot be said that he achieved this critical objective in the *Poetry of Byron*, certainly not with as much relative success as in the *Poems of Wordsworth*.

The fact that Wordsworth was allowed to speak in whole poems gave him an enormous advantage; if he does not emerge in Arnold's selections the great philosophical poet Coleridge thought him, he nevertheless remains a great lyric poet with a considerable range of expression, a vigorous and powerful sonneteer, and a substantial and sometimes great narrative poet. But Byron's satisfactory lyrics and short poems are few, and necessarily they make up a very small portion of the selections—twenty-six lyrics and a half dozen brief satirical squibs. Yet in Arnold's hands Byron becomes a writer of short, isolated 'bursts of incident' or 'bursts of sentiment'. Even in the first section of the volume, 'Personal, Lyric, and Elegiac', almost one-third of the pages are given over to excerpts from *Childe Harold* and one or two other long poems. These excerpts are titled by the editor ('The Poet's Curse', 'Nature to the Last', 'Immortality', 'Life', etc.), and presented as short whole poems.

This manner of presentation becomes more obviously damaging in the next section, 'Descriptive and Narrative'. The three longest single excerpts offered consist of twelve and one-half pages from *Mazeppa*, eight pages from *The Siege of Corinth*, and five pages from *The Prisoner of Chillon*. Most of the remaining bits run from one stanza to three pages, presented in an order and with titles provided by the editor. *Childe Harold* again is a major contributor, with eighty-four stanzas and a lyric; Canto IV is the main source, with forty-eight stanzas. Of *Don Juan* there are in this section a total of thirty-four stanzas of which twenty-one are descriptive, eight (Juan's first sight of Haidée) between narrative and descriptive, and only five (the shipwreck) straight narrative.

The third section, 'Dramatic', is highly conventional. It is mostly made up of lengthy excerpts from *Manfred*. For the rest, there is the death speech of Marino Faliero, which Arnold had recited for a prize at school, two other death scenes (*Sardanapalus*,

Act V, sc. i, ll. 88–133, and *The Two Foscari*, Act IV, sc. i. ll. 176–217), and excerpts from two scenes of *Cain* ('Cain and Lucifer in the Abyss of Space', Act II, sc. ii, ll. 26–135, and the scene of connubial and parental love of Cain and Adah, Act III, sc. i, ll. 1–161). This display of Byron's 'rhetoric' shows Arnold's predilection for scenes of death or sentiment, while he avoids passages which might be offensive, even if it means cutting portions out of a speech.

The last section, 'Satiric', is probably the least satisfactory of all. In the first place, it is the shortest section—only forty pages compared with seventy-one for 'Personal, Lyric, and Elegiac', one hundred and three for 'Descriptive and Narrative', and fifty-one even for 'Dramatic'. These statistics alone are sufficient to place this anthology; they form a silent but sufficient commentary upon the true degree of Arnold's sympathy for Byron. But this section fails even more on qualitative than on quantitative grounds. There are a few of the more innocuous short poems, and a few dozen of the tamer lines from *English Bards and Scotch Reviewers*, *The Age of Bronze*, and *Beppo*. And what of Byron's two masterworks, by common critical consensus even of Arnold's contemporaries? *The Vision of Judgment*, undoubtedly Byron's best work of sustained satire, is represented by only eight stanzas, safe stanzas attacking George III, while the far-ranging, complex, and at times almost dazzling *Don Juan* contributes just sixty-nine stanzas in scattered excerpts from eight cantos. In this section, as in fact throughout the volume, Arnold has chosen mostly the safe, familiar, and popular passages. There is nothing to raise a blush to the cheek of the young person; worse yet, there is little to raise a smile to the lips of the grown man. The qualities attributed to Byron in the preface do not appear or are vastly attenuated, while another special quality not mentioned by Arnold, but probably regarded by him as a vice, Byron's mastery of the art of digression and acrobatic change of pace, vanishes utterly. In the words of one reviewer,

> The poet of Haidée and Lucifer has been toned down to the level of Mr. Arnold's enemies the Philistines. In his new guise Byron appears as a very pleasing poet, often capable of short flights of passion and excellent at the composition of *vers de societé*.[87]

The book had best be allowed to rest quietly with its unacknowledged fellows and ancestors, all the 'Beauties' anthologies of the era.

We can only speculate on the reasons for this failure. Certainly Arnold could not have been altogether unaware that the poet he was presenting would never, by these selections alone, have impressed him so strongly as to command the rank of second greatest English poet of the century. Perhaps he assumed, possibly unconsciously, that his readers would be as familiar with Byron's work as he was and would enjoy rereading certain high points mainly as reminders. Other forces too may have been at work. One critic has blamed 'mid-Victorian propriety', perhaps even pusillanimity, for preventing Arnold 'from doing justice to Byron's greatest things'.[88] Another factor may have been Arnold's deficiency of appreciation for the comic and satiric. We know that this accounts for his refusal to grant highest rank to Chaucer, whom he loved dearly. Although he placed Molière among the immortals the judgement seems to be conventional, for he makes the reservation that Molière would have been greater still had he been a tragedian. The reason, he argues, is that 'Tragedy breasts the pressure of life. Comedy eludes it, half liberates itself by irony.'[89] It is by no means obvious that irony must be, although it may be, a form of evasion, and a strong case could be made for a comic 'criticism of life'.[90] Still, Arnold's position is defensible, and if he wished to place Byron's work as a whole in the second or lower rank on these grounds he would be within his rights. But the process of fractional distillation by which Byron's poetry is separated into serious bits and (a few) comic bits does especial violence to what is most essentially Byronic, his characteristic effects of controlled bathos and kaleidoscopic variation of tone.

Whatever the case, whether Victorian propriety or fear of Mrs. Grundy, imperfect sympathy with the comic or an increasing habit of 'touchstone' reading, the selection fails as an act of criticism because it fails to give the essential Byron. Moreover, the *Wordsworth* anthology, whatever its deficiencies, does exemplify and carry out coherently the criticism of its preface; the *Byron* does not. It tends to substantiate the criticism of those who maintain that Arnold did not really care very much for Byron, but ranked him so high only for extra-literary reasons. The last word on this book may as well be Dowden's who cogently summarized the disparity between Byron's work and Arnold's selections:

> ... what interests us in Byron and in Byron's work is precisely this mingling of noble and ignoble, of gold and a base alloy. We do not

thank any one for extracting the gold and presenting it alone. We can get swifter and clearer lyric poetry from Shelley, a truer and finer feeling for nature from Wordsworth, more exquisite satiric art from Pope, dramatic power incomparably wider and deeper from Shakespeare. Seen in elegant extracts, Byron is impoverished, or rather Byron ceases to be Byron. Matthew Arnold's volume of selections, compiled with such excellent intentions, proves at least that his poetry is not of the kind that can be pinned in a specimen case, like preserved butterflies. Line upon line, here a little and there a little, is the way in which such work as his should *not* be read. We must take him or leave him as he is. . . .[91]

IV

THE STRAYED REVELLER:
KEATS

He is; he is with Shakespeare.
What harm he has done in English Poetry.

I. POETIC INFLUENCE

NEXT after Wordsworth and Byron, Keats was the Romantic poet whose impact was most felt by Arnold. This is not to imply that Keats had an important positive influence on Arnold as he had, say, on Tennyson. Indeed, the reverse would be closer to the truth, that Arnold felt Keats's influence as something to be avoided rather than embraced. Keats's richness of language, his symbolic method, his romantic medievalism, and his passionate love of beauty were important elements in shaping the prevailing idea of what poetry could or should be. By the very energy with which Arnold struggled against the Keatsian influence and its derivatives in Tennyson and the Spasmodics, the force of the influence itself is displayed. The story of this struggle has already been sufficiently discussed by others;[1] the net effect of Keats's positive influence may be summed up thus: that echoes of Keats in Arnold's poetry are relatively few, and in general seem to be deliberate importations chosen, or at least admitted, quite consciously for a specific purpose. The major instances of direct influence upon four important poems—*The Scholar-Gipsy, Thyrsis, The Strayed Reveller,* and *Empedocles on Etna*—will be examined below. The remaining minor examples may be dealt with rapidly.

Two passages which seem to echo Keatsian diction or manner occur in *To a Gipsy Child by the Sea-Shore* and in *Sohrab and Rustum.* The first of these is a stanza already mentioned above in connection with Wordsworth [n. 29], for if the first two lines of the stanza are reminiscent of Keats's *Ode to a Nightingale* and *Ode on*

Melancholy, the last two lines and the sentiment of the stanza as a whole appear to allude to the *Ode: Intimations of Immortality* . . .:

> Ah! not the nectarous poppy lovers use,
> Not daily labour's dull, Lethæan spring,
> Oblivion in lost angels can infuse
> Of the soil'd glory, and the trailing wing.

If read carefully in its context, the stanza is extremely obscure. What has sexual love to do with the starveling beggar child, and why is the temporary self-forgetfulness of sensual passion paralleled with the dulling opiate of unsympathetic labour? The 'oblivion-of' formula is awkward, suggesting forgetfulness of a greater past, but the 'soil'd glory' and 'trailing wing' imply that the passage refers to forgetfulness rather of the hopeless and perhaps sordid present. The whole somewhat confused image of a 'lost angel' seeking but not finding forgetfulness of present suffering in a mixture of soporific passion and drudgery seems, as a matter of fact, more appropriate to Arnold's image of Keats than to the subject at hand. The inappropriateness of the imagery here may be an accidental result of a momentary surrender to Keatsian diction. Or, to the psychologically minded critic, it may open curious vistas into Arnold's unconscious attitudes of attraction-repulsion to the world of the senses (Keats) symbolized in class terms (the gipsy urchin, the ill-bred surgeon's apprentice). However, such refinement of speculation need not detain us here, for these latent feelings will become sufficiently apparent as we proceed.

The second passage is less interesting psychologically, but more successful poetically. The description of Rustum mourning his son in *Sohrab and Rustum*, in its monumental, sculptured stability and its richness of vocal orchestration, is reminiscent of the Keats of the opening of *Hyperion*:

> So, on the bloody sand, Sohrab lay dead;
> And the great Rustum drew his horseman's cloak
> Down o'er his face, and sate by his dead son.
> As those black granite pillars, once high-rear'd
> By Jemshid in Persepolis, to bear
> His house, now 'mid their broken flights of steps
> Lie prone, enormous, down the mountain side—
> So in the sand lay Rustum by his son.
>
> [ll. 857–64]

The connection is tenuous, of course, but Keats's description of Saturn, with its combination of stately repose and Miltonic grandeur, is typical of the sort of thing Arnold could admire in Keats as an isolated 'fine thing'.[2]

A few other minor examples of Keatsian elements in Arnold's poetry are perhaps even less decisive. Professors Tinker and Lowry have pointed out that the arras in *Tristram and Iseult* [II, 150 ff.] is similar to that in *The Eve of St. Agnes* in depicting a hunter and his pack, and also to a tapestry in Tennyson's *Palace of Art*.[3] It is possible and even likely that the Keats who helped set the tone of nineteenth-century poetic medievalism provided the source of both Arnold's and Tennyson's image. A tenuous parallel between the verse form of Keats's *La Belle Dame Sans Merci* and Arnold's *A Southern Night* has been pointed out by Tinker and Lowry, who comment on the likeness of elegiac effect in the two poems gained by the use of a short fourth line in each stanza.[4] In general, it may be observed that Arnold's poetic use of medieval material undoubtedly owes something to the fashion to which Keats and Coleridge contributed so much. However, the tradition itself both antedates these poets and stems from sources more diffuse. For this reason, and because in his treatment of medieval subjects Arnold rather avoids than exploits the opportunity to develop the aspects of sensuous richness and pageantry which Keats so dearly loved, it is not possible to infer a very important direct influence. Indeed, although Arnold found poetic 'charm and refreshment' in the Middle Ages, he could take seriously neither the period itself nor its contemporary panegyrists.[5]

Fleeting echoes of the kind just listed, even if multiplied in quantity, would prove little about even the existence of a positive Keatsian influence. As it happens, however, the verse of Keats was of first importance in the making of two of Arnold's major poems, *The Scholar-Gipsy* and *Thyrsis*. H. W. Garrod's excellent technical analysis of Arnold's adaptation of the *Ode to a Nightingale* stanza leaves little to add. He points out the major weakness of Arnold's stanza: its tendency to fall into two five-line units, where Keats with his greater freedom, experience, and virtuosity in handling sonnet forms, had managed a better articulation and smoother development of his ode stanza. Critics have pointed out Keatsian turns of phrase and verbal parallels in Arnold's two great pastorals; they are numerous and the attentive reader may compile his own catalogue.[6] In view of this elaborate and self-conscious borrowing, it is interesting that Arnold did not mention the name of Keats in connection with these poems (so far as surviving correspondence reveals). He indicated direct indebtedness to Theocritus and indirect to Wordsworth in commenting on *Thyrsis*,[7] the more 'classical' of the two poems, but little analysis is required to show that in practice the major stylistic influences on both pastorals were probably Milton and Keats. Although Arnold averred that he meant the diction of *Thyrsis* to be 'artless', or almost 'heedless', it is not, in spite of his naming common country flowers, birds, farm implements, and even 'water-gnats'. These artfully chosen 'artless' words can scarcely de-sophisticate a tone established by the use of rare words or archaisms such as 'coronals', 'sprent', 'engarlanded', 'wends', and others. Aesthetic remoteness from everyday speech is enhanced by such Miltonisms in *The Scholar-Gipsy* as:

> And all his store of sad experience he
> Lays bare of wretched days;
>> [ll. 185–6]

and:

> Still nursing the unconquerable hope,
> Still clutching the inviolable shade,
>> [ll. 211–12]

or in *Thyrsis*, as:

>> yet will I not despair.
> Despair I will not,
>> [ll. 192–3]

while on the other hand the tone, diction, and symbolic method of the poems are, even more than the adoption of verse form, significant evidence of a willing surrender for once to the art of Keats.[8]

Yet Arnold did not achieve in either of these poems, beautiful as they are, the intensity, the perfect subordination of parts to whole, the inevitable ordering of his material—in short, the *architectonicè*—which Keats achieved in his greatest work. Arnold's construction is, comparatively, loose and digressive, while there is a lapidary, decorative quality in his sensuous imagery and nature description which is more reminiscent of the early work of Keats, to which Arnold objected in his 1853 Preface, than it is of the great odes and sonnets. In spite of the classicist strictures in Arnold's withering remarks on Keats's early narratives, it would

seem that it was precisely the self-consciously Romantic medievalism of those poems which was most readily absorbed into Arnold's
narrative poetry, for example, in the fantasy of *The Forsaken
Merman*, or the dreamy mosaic work of *Tristram and Iseult*. But
even in other work, such as the two pastorals under consideration,
when Arnold turned consciously to Keats for inspiration, it seems
to have been the Keats who stood in Arnold's mind for luxurious
sensuousness and Romantic yearning who most influenced him,
and not the constructive and even, in a sense, austere genius of the
great odes.

Perhaps the best clue to Arnold's intention in *The Scholar-
Gipsy*—and consequently to his almost necessary choice of Keats
as mentor—is to be found in the famous purple passage of prose
eulogy to Oxford in the preface to *Essays in Criticism*:

> Beautiful city! so venerable, so lovely, so unravaged by the fierce
> intellectual life of our century, so serene!
>
> 'There are our young barbarians, all at play!'
>
> And yet steeped in sentiment as she lies, spreading her gardens to
> the moonlight, and whispering from her towers the last enchant-
> ments of the Middle Age, who will deny that Oxford, by her
> ineffable charm, keeps ever calling us nearer to the true goal of all
> of us, to the ideal, to perfection,—to beauty, in a word, which is
> only truth seen from another side?—nearer, perhaps, than all the
> science of Tübingen. Adorable dreamer, whose heart has been so
> romantic! who hast given thyself so prodigally, given thyself to
> sides and to lost causes, and forsaken beliefs, and unpopular names,
> and impossible loyalties! . . .

Plainly Oxford, the 'queen of romance', symbolized for Arnold
that dream world of ideal beauty (that beauty which is, by a
Keatsian transformation, only 'truth seen from another side'),
other-worldliness, medieval charm, isolation, and moonlight—the
world of romanticism—toward which Arnold's soul expressed its
yearning in such sternly 'modern' poems as *Stanzas from the Grande
Chartreuse*, and *Dover Beach*, even more clearly than in the medieval
poems themselves. This is the Oxford celebrated in the two great
pastorals. Usually, however, Arnold felt the insistent necessity of a
moral compulsion to stamp out these seeds of romantic rebellion
against the 'despotism of fact'. Typically in his verse, romantic
yearning is firmly if tenderly put aside while the poet, committed

to his rigorous line, returns to the world of reality as he conceived it: pain, duty, and labour in daily life; controversy and science in the world of mind; classical austerity and Wordsworthian simplicity in art. This movement or rhythm from anxiety and weariness, to romantic yearning, followed by a return to stern reality, forms the pattern of inner action or 'plot' in many of Arnold's most characteristic poems, and it is equally characteristic of his inner biography with its tale of moodiness and longing for escape brought under control by strict practical and spiritual discipline.

In *The Scholar-Gipsy*, however, and in *Thyrsis* (that elegy dedicated at least as much to the poet's lost youth as to his dead friend), Arnold deliberately permitted himself to celebrate the Oxford countryside and all that complex of romantic association which it had come to symbolize for him, the complex expressed in his apostrophe quoted above. When he set himself to compose a poem in which richly detailed, sensuous nature description was at the same time to represent the countryside of the spirit of eternal youth pursuing the gleam and drawing its refreshment from moonlight, dew, and nightingales singing to 'enchanted ears', it was inevitable that Arnold should have yielded to the full attractive force of that Keats who, in the words of one recent critic, 'presided over the nineteenth century poetry of the dream-world'.[9] Nevertheless, there are differences of attitude which set even these romantic poems apart from Keats. Arnold's failure to mention Keats's name in connection with them may only mean that he felt it unnecessary to call attention to the obvious, or perhaps that he did not wish to invite too close a comparison between his own efforts and the 'natural magic' of Keats. But possibly a deeper reason than these is that he may have recognized the lack in his own poetry of Keats's intensely affirmative involvement with life, and knew that however akin to Keats these poems were in detail, the prevailing tone of melancholy withdrawal put them, and especially *Thyrsis*, closer to the work of the late Greek pastoralists. His comment to Clough that 'the Gipsy Scholar at best awakens a pleasing melancholy' is evidence of such a recognition.[10] Keats could achieve at least momentary communion with his nightingale, but Arnold's spark from heaven is at two removes: first, not Arnold but the scholar gipsy alone awaits it in hope, and he only because he is 'a truant boy' [l. 198], not a responsible man of the nineteenth century; and second, even flight is not enough to bring success, however momentary, but barely suffices to keep hope alive against some indefinable future.

The puzzling early poem *The Strayed Reveller*, which the poet thought important enough to give the place of honour in his first volume, deserves closer attention than it has received. A key to a reading of this poem may be found in its intimations of profound stirrings of kinship between the youthful Arnold and Keats, whose letters Arnold had found so agitating shortly before the publication of this poem.[11] It deals with the nature of the poet, embodying a blend of two themes common in nineteenth-century romanticism: the apotheosis of the artist (what the gods see 'The wise bards also / Behold and sing', [ll. 208–9]), and the agony of the artist ('But oh, what labour!' cries the reveller-poet to Ulysses, the man of action, 'O prince, what pain!' [ll. 210–11]). The agony stems from the suffering the poet must share with his subjects:

> —such a price
> The Gods exact for song:
> To become what we sing.
> [ll. 232–4]

Nevertheless, the joy of such a communion is so intense that the strayed youth, intoxicated with the Circean wine of imagination, implores the 'wild, thronging train . . . of eddying forms' to sweep faster, faster through his soul. For the moment the vision is overpowering in its profusion. The pain is yet to come, no doubt when the Dionysiac reveller (in the poem he is a worshipper of Iacchus) begins to bring some Apollonian order into his ecstatic visions and seeks to mould meaning out of the chaos of experience.

When Arnold wrote the speeches of the Youth in *The Strayed Reveller*, speeches which Lionel Trilling has aptly characterized as 'an almost barbaric paean to the whole of life, even to pain',[12] he must have had in mind such a poet as Keats. Arnold observed to Clough in a letter of this period that Keats was 'consumed' by the desire for 'movement and fulness', the same desire chanted by the intoxicated reveller.[13] The poem as a whole, however, remains obscure. A main problem is that, as one of Arnold's most 'romantic' poems, *The Strayed Reveller* seems to violate just those critical principles which he was straining to develop at the time he was composing it, principles to be enunciated more fully in the Preface of 1853. Thus, although the poem is written in dramatic form, its central action is slight and heavily overlaid with decoration. Descriptive passages which are supposed to represent examples of the variety of human existence become, because of their length and sensuous elaboration, digressive ornaments:

> Of silk-bales and balsam-drops,
> Of gold and ivory,
> Of turquoise-earth and amethyst,
> Jasper and chalcedony,
> And milk-barr'd onyx stones,
>
> [ll. 193–7]

reminiscent of Keats's 'spiced dainties, every one, / From silken Samarcand to cedar'd Lebanon', but less organically related to their context. Furthermore, the philosophy of poetry the youth expresses, one of the infinite expansion of self through vicarious experience, is closer to Keats's 'negative capability' than to Arnold's view of poetry as making things. Indeed, the reveller comes perilously close to describing poetry as 'a true allegory of the state of one's own mind in a representative history', the view Arnold so sternly reproved in his 1853 Preface. For if the poet becomes what he sings, then he is singing himself in allegorical representation.

Surely it is insufficient to put aside the problems raised by this poem by appealing to Arnold's notorious 'duality', without first attempting other means of clarification. Arnold had expressed himself in 1847 as being fatigued by Tennyson's 'dawdling' with the 'painted shell' of the universe.[14] Could he, as a self-styled 'reformer in poetical matters', give as the title poem of his first volume of poetry a work so seemingly ill-designed to illustrate his principles of reform, so seemingly in the very style of the poets he lumped together contemptuously as 'Keats Tennyson et id genus omne'?[15]

Rather, I am inclined to take as a working hypothesis the premise that Arnold knew what he was about, and that what he was about may be discerned if we accept the possibility that in *The Strayed Reveller* he was using the indirect means of irony and allegory in place of that 'thinking aloud' in verse to which he objected. First, if the poem is to be taken as allegory, the title ought to be carefully considered. It would appear from this point of view that the word *strayed* must convey more meaning than its literal signification in the slender fable of the poem. Moreover, once we have admitted the metaphorical, and pejorative, connotation of *strayed*, Arnold's choice of Circe as the presiding goddess of the reveller's poetic inebriation becomes explicable. Trilling has pointed out that 'This is not the Circe of Homer, for the wine effects no swinish transmogrification; it is the wine of vision and ecstatic madness. . . .'[16] But we may then ask why Arnold chose to use the Circe legend at all, as it was certain to call up a host of undesired associations. The point, it seems to me, is that although this is a modern Circe, refined, subtilized, even spiritualized, she remains essentially the dangerous seducer and debaucher of old. This would be in keeping with Arnold's technique in another poem when he changed Homer's sirens to 'The *New* Sirens', who are, nevertheless, as Arnold explained to Clough, no less dangerous than the old merely because they have become representations of romantic love instead of fierce sensuality.[17]

The reveller, then, a youthful poet driven by his naturally ardent nature and hungering for experience, goes astray and willingly submits to the Circean potation. That her influence is sinister is clear from the accusing questions of Ulysses and Circe's insistence that she did not lead the youth astray, but that he came of his own volition. Under the influence of the 'red, creaming liquor', his brain grows giddy:

> Who can stand still?
> Ye fade, ye swim, ye waver before me—
> The cup again!
> [ll. 289–91]

Through his fiery imagination surges a bright procession of visions, beautiful, but also 'wild', 'thronging', and 'eddying'. So long as he remains astray, drunk with variety and sensation, he can painlessly have these visions of intense but disordered beauty [ll. 270 ff.]. It is the 'wise bards', not drunk on Circean wine, who pay for their visions and insight with labour and pain [ll. 207–11]. But the romantic sensationalist, lacking what Arnold called in a letter 'an idea of the world' and drunk with superficial beauty and variety, finds himself, to quote from the same letter, 'prevailed over by the world's multitudinousness'. Arnold, no doubt with Goethe in mind as a model, complained frequently in his letters of 1847–8 of the pain but also the necessity of dealing with the variety of life in a meaningful manner: 'For me', he wrote, 'you may often hear my sinews cracking under the effort to unite matter.' Even if possessed of the greatest genius, the genius of a Keats, what Arnold called a 'mere recorder of existence' cannot produce 'the truly living and moving'.[18] At the end of the poem, the reveller, as far astray as at the beginning, merely cries out for more wine.

If the reveller is strayed in the sense I have been suggesting, his lyric speeches must be approached with some caution as dramatic utterances. These speeches are indeed rich in description, finely evocative, but they are not unified, they reveal no particular sense of subordination of parts to whole. Though classic in diction, they are the sort of poems a young poet under the influence of Keats and 'dawdling with the painted shell' of the universe would make. Like Keats—and by 'Keats' I mean Arnold's image of Keats—the strayed reveller passionately desires 'movement and fulness', although he seems partly to realize that something more is needed, that great art cannot be all pleasure, all intoxication. The reveller sees the act of creation as one of self-enlargement through vicarious participation—poets become what they sing—and although this may be painful, the pain is a necessary price for partaking of the intense joy of vision, if, at any rate, the vision is to reach fruition, and the bard is to become 'wise' rather than 'strayed'. Arnold seems to have misunderstood Keats's 'negative capability' as a surrender to the flux of phenomena, and hence morally dangerous. He failed to perceive that Keats, not only as a man (as Arnold argued in his late essay) but also in his poetry was no mere sensation seeker; that he, like Arnold, had struggled for a poetic mastery of experience and could not rest content to be its slave. Still, in its time, Arnold's reading of Keats had some justification, for he was right in seeing that the influence of Keats in the middle of the century was not a good one. Moreover, it was destined to become worse before it got better. Arnold's early recognition of this seems almost prophetic of the sensationalism of Rossetti and Wilde and the cult of 'beauty', flying the banner of Keats. Arnold himself, like the reveller and no doubt like most young poets, was powerfully attracted to Circe's wine of sensation.[19] The reveller, unlike Arnold, but like the contemporaries to whose practice he objected, could not resist the attraction. It is interesting to contrast *The Strayed Reveller* with *Resignation*, a poem of the same period. In the latter Arnold uses the first person rather than the dramatic method, and there the speaker is at considerable pains to controvert the reveller's idea of poetry as vicarious experience; instead, he there argues for an aesthetic of detachment. Both because he uses direct utterance in *Resignation*, and because he quotes from that poem in arguing an aesthetic point with Clough,[20] it is reasonable to assume that the views expressed there are far more directly representative of Arnold's own ideas than the wild and whirling lyrics of the drunken reveller.

Certainly this interpretation may not explain all the difficulties in *The Strayed Reveller*, but I believe that the approach adumbrated here has the advantage of accounting for certain rather important matters. First, it provides for a more than literal interpretation of the title. Second, it explains the use and conception of Circe. Third, and most significant, it may solve the rather mystifying question of why the young poetical reformer should have chosen what appears to be one of his most romantic efforts as the title piece of his first volume. (And it is worth observing, as a curious testimony to Arnold's reputation for inconsistency, that this question itself has never been asked.) No reader of the poem, however, can for a moment believe that Arnold's intention was merely parodic. Loving care was lavished upon it, and the descriptions of the floating melon-beds of Cashmeer or of the strange method of crossing the Oxus, in addition to indulging Arnold's taste for Orientalism, are as beautiful as he knew how to make them, for the poem would fail even as allegory if they were not. Furthermore, the parallels with the poetry of Keats and his followers are primarily to be found in overall design, not so much in the style itself.[21] Arnold deplored excesses in the imagery of the Elizabethans and their latter-day imitators, Keats, Shelley, Tennyson, and other, lesser lights. *The Strayed Reveller* is a genuine *tour de force* of 'Greek radiance', rich and exquisitely clear in its realization of objects, but entirely free, as earlier critics have observed, of figures of speech.[22] In Arnold's avoidance of the striking metaphor and the brilliant epithet, we may see the reformer at work. It is as though he were saying, 'Here is the poetry of multitudinousness such as, under the influence of Keats, is now altogether too much in fashion. I can write it too, and with greater purity. But its source is not the wine that makes us "nobly wild, not mad"; it is the liquor of Circe the seductress.' Arnold, both attracted and repelled by the wine of the sensuous, the passionate, the varied, the ornate, has created in *The Strayed*

Reveller not only a dramatic representation of certain romantic attitudes toward art and the self, but also has implied in the structure and diction of the poem a subtle allegorical critique of them.

In *Empedocles on Etna* there is another youthful singer who is enraptured by the beauty of earth and inspired to song by the myths of gods and heroes with which the human imagination has peopled it. The poet is young Callicles; he hopes by his singing to ease the torments of Empedocles who is suffering from the atrophy of the imagination and hypertrophy of the intellect which make up the characteristic nineteenth-century form of acedia. There has been some lively discussion as to whether Empedocles is to be taken as Matthew Arnold's spokesman.[23] Clearly in certain respects he is, but the poet also created Callicles and gave him the last word in the poem—and that a 'yea'. I take it then that Callicles and Empedocles represent, among other things, two aspects of Arnold's divided soul. The tragedy of modern man, according to Joseph Wood Krutch, is that 'try as he may, the two halves of his soul can hardly be made to coalesce, and he cannot either feel as his intelligence tells him that he should feel or think as his emotions would have him think, and thus he is reduced to mocking his own divided soul.'[24] It was Arnold's voice, more clearly and forcibly than any other, which was expressing the sense of this plight eighty years before Krutch's description was written. Nowhere in his poetry has he more successfully dramatized this internal rift than in *Empedocles on Etna* with its exquisite counterpoint between the voices of the despairing old poet turned philosopher and the affirming young singer.

The young Callicles sometimes sounds a bit like Wordsworth, as when he advises Pausanias to lead Empedocles 'through the lovely mountain-paths, / And keep his mind from preying on itself, / And talk to him of things at hand and common' [I, i, 156–8], or rather, perhaps, like that more authentic child of Nature, Dorothy, who applied just such a form of therapy when her brother was suffering from a similar condition. However, the lyrics of Callicles with their static, jewelled landscapes ('One sees one's footprints crush'd in the wet grass' [I, i, 14], their Miltonism ('the pair / Wholly forget their first sad life, and home, / And all that Theban woe' [I, ii, 457–9], and their rapturous but entirely unmystical hymning of a nature peopled by centaurs, Titans,

muses, and fauns, are more reminiscent of Keats than of Wordsworth or any other English poet. Indeed, what Arnold said of
Keats in distinguishing his natural magic from that of Maurice de
Guérin could be applied easily to Callicles: 'Keats has, above all,
a sense of what is pleasurable and open in the life of nature; for
him she is the *Alma Parens*: his expression has, therefore, more
than Guérin's, something genial, outward, and sensuous.'[25]

The resemblance between Keats and the young poets in the
two poems just discussed is one of tone, content, and diction, but
does not generally extend to versification. Both Callicles and the
intoxicated reveller sing for the most part in Arnold's favourite
short lines, irregular in metre and rime scheme; when Callicles
does sing in regular stanzas, in his concluding lyric, the short lines
and frequent anapaests give the poem a tripping lightness and
almost headlong rush rather Shelleyan:

> Where the moon-silver'd inlets
> Send far their light voice
> Up the still vale of Thisbe,
> O speed, and rejoice!
> [ll. 425–8]

Except in *The Scholar-Gipsy* and *Thyrsis*, and in a few occasional
phrases or lines or brief word-pictures elsewhere, Arnold was little
inclined to attempt the 'sweet and easy-slipping movement' that
Keats had inherited from Spenser,[26] although in his blank verse
Arnold sometimes came close to Keats under the pervasive
influence of Milton. But in the dramatic characters of the two young
poets in *The Strayed Reveller* and *Empedocles on Etna*, poets
intoxicated by the beauty of earth, thirsting for experience, and
unmarred by the ravages of the desiccating intellect, Arnold spoke,
though with his own tongue and accent, the language of Keats.

The most striking aspect of Keats's influence on Arnold's
poetry, probably, is the negative one, or what George H. Ford has
admirably analysed as 'his struggle to free his poetry from
Keatsian style'.[27] More than any of his major contemporaries
Arnold tried, although with dubious results, to disburden himself
of the inheritance of romanticism. The world had advanced too
far in knowledge and in the critical attitude, he felt, to be satisfied
with a poetry which contented itself with beautiful expression and
did not meet the intellectual needs of a modern era. If poetry

cannot keep up with the world, the world will leave it behind to the detriment of both. Poetry could survive only if the poet could organize 'the hitherto experience of the world, and his own'; and to perform this 'immense task' only a style 'plain and direct and severe' would serve.[28] The poetry of Keats and Shelley and their Elizabethan progenitors was of no present service to a poet undertaking this challenging task. Yet for all his struggle it cannot be said that Arnold succeeded in evading the influence, or even in understanding it fully. There is no evidence that he ever read Keats's poetry and letters in conjunction, and with careful attention to chronology, and so he seems to have overlooked the prodigiously rapid development of Keats in a few years from a bard of sensuous posies of delight to an intensely serious, mature poet whose goals were similar to Arnold's own. As for Arnold's own poetry, for all his classicism and modernism, it is difficult to avoid Professor Ford's conclusion, that 'the greatest part of his verse is essentially romantic in character'.[29] At least this is true of Arnold's poetic technique, although he was far from being a Romantic in other important ways. His failure to find a new kind of lyrical language except, too often, at the cost of lapsing into metrical prose (sometimes scarcely metrical); the elaborateness of his decorative imagery and the luxuriousness of his symbolic imagery; and, as negative evidence, the museum-piece lifelessness of his most 'classical' showpieces—all testify to the power of just that kind of romantic influence he struggled against. Conversely, some of his most successful poems were written when he abandoned the struggle. The most nearly successful of his 'classical' pieces, *Sohrab and Rustum*, is the nearest in manner to Keats. And when Arnold wanted to hymn the beauties of the countryside of Oxford—the countryside of eternal youth and beauty—or when, and psychologically it amounts to much the same thing, he assumed the character of a young bard hymning the harmonious, imaginary world of mythology, it is Keats to whom for the nonce he surrenders himself.[30]

II. STYLE

Arnold's adverse criticism of Keats has mainly to do with style; hence a brief glance at Arnold's general approach to style will not be out of place here. Almost at once, one is struck by a certain

inconsistency or ambiguity in what he meant by the word itself
I do not refer merely to his often criticized failure to define the
'grand style'; he was well within his rights to suggest what the
great jazz musician Louis Armstrong has said with less elegance but
perhaps more forcefully: 'There's some people that if they don't
know, you just can't tell 'em.' The inconsistency I mean is one
involving Arnold's attitude toward language itself. On the one
hand he often spoke as though he thought there was a definite
split between style and content, an attitude which goes back to
traditional neo-classical theory.[31] On other occasions he seems to
have adopted a more nearly Coleridgean position in which style
is an organic part of the whole, expressing both the character of
the poet and of his subject matter. It is this confusion, I think,
which causes Arnold's most characteristic general utterances on
style to assume the form of a *petitio principii*. For example:
'. . . style is the saying in the best way *what you have to say*'.
Arnold's underscoring does not succeed in rectifying the circularity. But the sentence just quoted was written in private correspondence; here is a public utterance (also, and characteristically,
underscored by Arnold): '. . . the grand style arises in poetry,
*when a noble nature, poetically gifted, treats with simplicity or with
severity a serious subject*'.[32] Here there may be question begging
again, but there also appears to be an attempt at fusion. The
grounding of the grand style in the nature of the poet suggests an
organic notion of style, and is typically Romantic and expres-
sionistic. However, the rest of the sentence, after the word *treats,*
seems to embody a neo-classical concept of style as a quality
separable from the subject.

But in spite of its logical insufficiency, this dichotomy—or is it
merely a confusion?—was made to serve a critical purpose. For
in so far as style is considered as a separable quality of writing,
Arnold was enabled to point out the social value of a literature which
arose from a sound subject matter: '. . . modern poetry can only
subsist by its *contents*: by becoming a complete magister vitae as
the poetry of the ancients did'.[33] This is the moving idea in the
1853 Preface also: 'All depends upon the subject; choose a fitting
action . . . everything else will follow.' On the other hand, in so far
as style may be regarded as an organic part of what is said, the
emphasis changes from social to individual, and style is related
to a man's moral character or lack of it: '. . . in Sophocles what is

valuable is not so much his contributions to psychology and the anatomy of sentiment, as the grand moral effects produced by *style*. For the style is the expression of the nobility of the poet's character, as the matter is the expression of the richness of his mind: but on men character produces as great an effect as mind.'[34] Hence, for example, Francis Newman's eccentric translation of Homer, by lacking nobility, falsifies not only Homer's style but also his thought and matter.

Because Arnold never clarified the distinction between the two approaches, it is not always plain just how much he was including when he spoke of style in any particular context. Often he seems to have meant only diction, imagery, and prosody. However, in the 1853 Preface, which is probably the most central of his critical essays, *style* is used in a way that suggests three fairly distinct meanings. Sometimes it seems to refer to the choice of subject, that is, the death of Agamemnon or of Little Nell, the anguish of Orestes or of Childe Harold. (The poet's theme, on the other hand—the 'what he has to say'—is not so open to conscious choice, for it depends upon the poet's era, his personality, and his 'Idea of the world's multitudinousness.'[35]) A second discernible reference of *style* is to form, organization, or architectonics—the relation of parts to whole and to one another. The third meaning is verbal expression, or style in the narrow sense. As I have said, Arnold's treatment of style even in this last sense is somewhat ambiguous; on the one hand it may be treated as an intrinsic element of form, on the other, as a more or less independent element of the literary composition, as for example when Arnold distinguishes between Shakespeare's architectonics and his 'style'. In Arnold's criticism of Keats all three meanings are operative; for convenience I shall deal with them separately as far as possible.

Arnold's comments on Keats's choice of subject matter are generally incidental, as when he praised the selection of action for *Isabella*, only to point out how much better Boccaccio had handled it. However, Arnold did implicitly praise Keats in this regard by imitating his use of mythological subjects from classical, oriental, and medieval antiquity in his own poems. Still, Arnold's use of medieval material is curiously balanced by his sturdy modernist contempt for the Middle Ages. Indeed, one of his comments in a letter seems almost unconsciously to reveal the breach that had widened during the nineteenth century between thought and poetry even in the attitudes of Arnold himself, the staunch defender of thought in poetry. He, in effect, allows that the fact that something cannot be taken seriously is no objection to it poetically when he writes thus about the Middle Ages: 'I have a strong sense of the irrationality of that period, and of the utter folly of those who take it seriously, and play at restoring it; still, it has poetically the greatest charm and refreshment possible for me.'[36] He not only may be said to have imitated Keats in his choice of subject matter, but when he defended his own practice in the 1853 Preface, he was implicitly defending Keats, too, from such attacks as that of the anonymous reviewer of Monckton Milnes' biography who numbered among Keats's faults 'his mythological subjects, which to be interesting, must call up an audience that have been departed from earth these two thousand years and more'.[37] This sort of criticism was a commonplace of Victorian reviewing: Arnold quotes another sample in his Preface, and in an article on Swinburne, Rossetti, and Morris in the *Quarterly Review* in 1872 a reviewer, deploring the tendency of contemporary poets to ignore current Victorian life and retreat into earlier epochs, explicitly blames the influence of Keats.[38]

In arguing this matter in his Preface, Arnold chose, probably for tactical reasons, not to derogate directly the contemporary scene as a source of poetic subjects. Instead he argued that 'the date of the action signifies nothing'; it is the action itself which is all-important. It is only required that the action be great, the personages noble, and the situation intense. He implied strongly, however, and in his letters and poems stated unequivocally that actions, personages, and situations of this kind are wanting in the present unpoetical age. In February 1849, just before the publication of his first volume of verse, Arnold, then living in the very heart of the great world as Lord Lansdowne's secretary, wrote to Clough: 'Reflect too, as I cannot but do here more and more, in spite of all the nonsense some people talk, how deeply *unpoetical* the age and all one's surroundings are. Not unprofound, not ungrand, not unmoving:—but *unpoetical*.' It is paradoxical that an age 'not unprofound, not ungrand, not unmoving' should be lacking in material for poetry, but other comments on the age in the same correspondence shed light on the paradox. The age for all its grandeur is emotionally sterile; that is the problem. In December 1852 Arnold can do justice to his feelings only with a double negative and emphatic underscoring as he condemns the 'modern situation in its true *blankness* and *barrenness*, and *un-poetrylessness*'. Again, a few months later, he is crying 'for air like my own Empedocles', and praying 'God keep us both from aridity! *Arid*—that is what the times are.'[39]

If Arnold, at least implicitly, defended Keats's choice of subjects remote from the contemporary scene for his narrative poems (and it should be remembered that all Arnold's strictures on subject matter applied to narrative and dramatic, not to lyric poetry), he nevertheless criticized these poems severely on other grounds, which brings us to the second meaning of style. Not Keats's subjects, but his handling of them was at fault. Here, again, Arnold was going against the current of much popular reviewing and even of serious criticism, for if Keats was often blamed for setting or furthering the fashion of choosing remote subjects, he was as often praised, admired, and imitated for his richness of local effects. Arnold admitted Keats's mastery of such effects, but far from considering it a virtue, he felt it was related to the principal defect of Keats's longer poems, their weakness of construction. *Endymion*, he insisted in the Preface of 1853, 'although undoubtedly there blows through it the breath of genius, is yet as a whole so utterly incoherent, as not strictly to merit the name of a poem at all'. *Hyperion*, too, 'fine things as it contains, is not a success'.[40] *Lamia* is ignored and excluded from Arnold's selections for Ward's *English Poets*, and *The Eve of St. Agnes* is not mentioned in the criticism and only the last eighteen stanzas are included in Ward's. Arnold's most extensive comment on a single poem of Keats is his well-known adverse judgement of *Isabella*, the poem he rather unfairly selected in his Preface as an example of deficiency of modern poetry in the prime virtue of *Architectonicé*:

The poem of Isabella, then, is a perfect treasure-house of graceful and felicitous words and images: almost in every stanza there occurs one of those vivid and picturesque turns of expression, by which the object is made to flash upon the eye of the mind, and which thrill the reader with a sudden delight. This one short poem contains, perhaps, a greater number of happy single expressions which one could quote than all the extant tragedies of Sophocles. But the action, the story? The action in itself is an excellent one; but so feebly is it conceived by the Poet, so loosely constructed, that the effect produced by it, in and for itself, is absolutely null. Let the reader, after he has finished the poem of Keats, turn to the same story in the Decameron: he will then feel how pregnant and interesting the same action has become in the hands of a great artist, who above all things delineates his object; who subordinates expression to that which it is designed to express.

The unfairness of this critique lies partly in Arnold's selection of an early work to represent the whole. But, more important, Arnold did not give sufficient credit to Keats for his critical power in moving toward conclusions similar to Arnold's own. Lacking the advantage of a first-hand knowledge of the classics, Keats nevertheless was conscious of the same kind of ailment in modern poetry which Arnold diagnosed; only, he looked to the great Elizabethans, especially Shakespeare, for a tonic to cure it. Anticipating Arnold, he exclaimed in a letter to Reynolds (February 3, 1818): 'Poetry should be great and unobtrusive, a thing which enters into one's soul, and does not startle it or amaze it with itself, but with its subject.' He complained, like Arnold, that modern poets were egotistical, decorative, and private. In the Elizabethans he saw what Arnold saw in the Greeks—a body of central, objective poetry conceived and executed in the grand manner. With this judgement of the Elizabethans Arnold disagreed to be sure, but he underestimated Keats in failing to understand *why* he had turned to them. Yet if Arnold did not fully understand Keats, and if his tactics were not altogether fair, it should be remembered that in the Preface from which the passage on *Isabella* was taken Arnold's main concern was not to pass judgement on Keats, but rather to correct fallacies in contemporary taste. As a poet and poetic reformer, he wanted to diminish in favour of the classics the influence of the Elizabethans and their modern followers. Writing later as a critic and reader in the essay on Keats he could afford somewhat to redress the balance and call Keats a great poet.

If the longer poems of Keats were deficient in form, they were deficient in precisely the *unum necessarium*, and Arnold was enough of a classicist to believe that the longer forms, the narrative and the drama, were inherently greater than the shorter lyrics, sonnets, or odes. Modern poetry, conceived as a replacement for religion or as an agent for intellectual deliverance, would subsist by its contents no doubt, but before it could be poetry at all it needed 'an absolute propriety—of form, as the sole *necessary* of Poetry as such: whereas the greatest wealth and depth of matter is merely a superfluity in the Poet *as such*'.[41] Following Goethe,

Arnold argued in his Preface that 'what distinguishes the artist from the mere amateur . . . is *Architectonicè* in the highest sense; that power of execution which creates, forms, and constitutes: not the profoundness of single thoughts, not the richness of imagery, not the abundance of illustration.' True, he wrote years later, Keats is 'perfect' in his shorter works, but there 'the matured power of moral interpretation, and the high architectonics which go with complete poetic development, are not required'.[42] But whatever his perfection in minor forms, and however great his promise otherwise, Keats, because of his great deficiency in 'absolute propriety of form', remains in his performance a minor poet.

There is more at stake than aesthetic propriety, for Keats's failure in architectonics limits the moral and intellectual relevance of his poetry to modern times. In his inaugural lecture as Professor of Poetry, Arnold expatiated on this relationship between poetry and the age. The greatest poetry must unify knowledge and values in such a way as to render one's own culture intelligible; it must find or create order in the confusion; it must 'enter into possession of the general ideas which are the law of this vast multitude of facts' accumulated from the past and present, an 'immense, moving, confused spectacle' in whose presence we are threatened, confused, excited, and baffled. The man who can find a 'true point of view from which to contemplate this spectacle . . . he who communicates that point of view to his age, he who interprets to it that spectacle, is one of his age's intellectual deliverers'.[43] Such a deliverance, Arnold believed, was the pressing need of his age, and towards carrying it forward Keats and his followers were of no real service for, as he wrote to Clough, 'the language, style and general proceedings of a poetry which has such an immense task to perform must be very plain and direct and severe: and it must not lose itself in parts and episodes and ornamental work, but must press forwards to the whole.'[44] In fact, a poet like Keats was even positively dangerous in exact proportion to the degree of his genius—admittedly of the first rank—and consequently of his attractiveness. Not only does such poetry fail to meet the needs of the time, but by its very beauty it tempts others to stray from their duty into the garden of Circe. After reading the letters of Keats on Clough's recommendation, Arnold wrote: 'What a brute you were to tell me to read Keats' letters. However, it is over now: and reflexion resumes her power over agitation.' He confessed that he too had been tempted to seek fullness and variety, but had been deterred alike by conscience (!) and by 'a great numbness in that direction'. Poets who seek centrality and sanity may fail and yet be 'good citizens enough', but those who follow 'Keats Tennyson et id genus omne . . . yes and those d——d Elizabethans generally . . . go to the dogs failing or succeeding.' Consequently Arnold, recovering from his 'agitation', exclaimed of Keats: 'What harm he has done in English Poetry.'[45]

These vigorous remarks on the 'd——d Elizabethans', and others of similar tenor, form the background against which the famous tribute in the late Keats essay, 'He is; he is with Shakespeare', must be placed, particularly in considering Arnold's criticism of Keats's style in the most restricted sense, his use of language. E. K. Brown has already dealt with this background in his useful article on 'Matthew Arnold and the Elizabethans',[46] so only those opinions most directly relevant to Arnold's criticism of Keats need be mentioned here. Arnold believed that some ages were intrinsically superior to others and that only a coincidence of a first-class poet with a first-class epoch could produce the greatest poetry. The Elizabethan age, however, was a *second class epoch* which happened to be blessed with a great poet in Shakespeare who gave it 'infinitely *more than adequate* expression'.[47] The age itself was 'steeped in humours and fantasticality to its very lips'; revelling in the exercise of its new-found powers, it could 'hardly bring itself to see an object quietly or to describe it temperately'.[48] Shakespeare's gifts then were his own; his vices belonged to his age. These gifts were twofold. First, he shared with the great poets of all ages his fundamental excellence: the ability to choose excellent actions and to develop them with consummate felicity of construction. But also he possessed, and at times over-indulged, a special genius for 'happy, abundant, and ingenious expression', and here is the source of the trouble for later poets. His primary gifts are difficult of mastery, requiring not only genius but the most elevated artistic conscience; however, it is the 'attractive accessories' which he displayed with such virtuosity, and which were tainted by the vices of his age, that are more easily appreciated. These, by their very power and beauty, may overcome the young writer who chooses Shakespeare for his model. Hence his bad influence, to which 'it is in a great degree owing, that of the majority of modern poetical works the details alone are valuable, the composition worthless'.[49] Or, as Arnold had put it in the letter referring to the 'd——d Elizabethans', 'Those who cannot read G[ree]k sh[ou]ld read nothing but Milton and parts of Wordsworth: the state should see to it.'[50]

Of course Arnold knew and was never tired of telling the world that the faults of modern poetry derived from more than merely a bad poetic influence, itself perhaps more a symptom than a cause. If, at the time of most need, poetry was far removed from the high place of responsibility which it ought to occupy, its pathetic inadequacy was certainly owing to causes not exclusively or even primarily literary. But with literature in such a state, the poet's responsibility to choose the right models becomes all the more momentous, in proportion to the effort required to fulfil his supposed obligations to both literature and society. Arnold called Milton and even Shakespeare to witness, avowing that 'had they lived in the atmosphere of modern feeling, had they had the multitude of new thoughts and feelings to deal with a modern has, I think it likely the style of each would have been far less *curious* and exquisite'.[51] But then, as he asks elsewhere, 'What is Keats?' To which he can only reply almost angrily: 'A style and form seeker, and this with an impetuosity that heightens the effect of his style almost painfully.'[52]

Now Keats's diction, imagery, and metrics had repeatedly been criticized as 'bad English' from the time of the opponents of the Cockney school through de Quincey and Clough, before the tide turned in Keats's favour and he came to be ranked after Wordsworth as a great renovator of poetic speech.[53] Arnold seems to have approved, on the whole, Keats's language as such; the tone is all praise where he speaks of Keats's diction and movement in *On Translating Homer*, although the passage only gives full meaning when glossed by other, adverse, comments on the Elizabethans (such as the critique of Chapman's Homer elsewhere in the same lectures). Arnold points to

> the one modern inheritor of Spenser's beautiful gift,—the poet, who evidently caught from Spenser his sweet and easy-slipping movement, and who has exquisitely employed it; a Spenserian genius, nay, a genius by natural endowment richer probably than even Spenser; that light which shines so unexpectedly and without fellow in our century, an Elizabethan born too late, the early lost and admirably gifted Keats.[54]

137

Similar praise can be found in the criticism of Arnold's middle period when he discusses Keats's 'natural magic' in *On the Study of Celtic Literature* and in *Essays in Criticism*; and in the late essay 'The Study of Poetry' Keats is listed with Spenser, Shakespeare, and Milton as one of the great inheritors of 'the tradition of the liquid diction the fluid movement, of Chaucer'.[55]

Hence Keats's rich imagery and his diction, are not in themselves bad, if considered without reference to the needs of the age. But rarely does Arnold, even for a moment, consider verbal style in itself; for the most part he sees in it an index to the character of the poet and of the age. Style itself becomes a moral matter, and it is when Arnold is being most moralistic (see his use of the word *conscience* twice in a single short letter dealing with style[56]) that he seems furthest from the neo-classical concept of style as merely a vehicle for ideas; like Buffon, he sees in the style the man himself. In one of his letters already partially quoted Arnold summed up many of his beliefs about the relations between style and form, style and contents, and style and the culture, morals, religion, and health of modern Europe. The whole passage, complete with its turbidity of expression which must have resulted from the pressure of deeply felt thought, deserves attention:

> More and more I feel that the difference between a mature and a youthful age of the world compels the poetry of the former to use great plainness of speech as compared with that of the latter: and that Keats and Shelley were on a false track when they set themselves to reproduce the exuberance of expression, the charm, the richness of images, and the felicity, of the Elizabethan poets. Yet critics cannot get to learn this, because the Elizabethan poets are our greatest, and our canons of poetry are founded on their works. They still think that the object of poetry is to produce exquisite bits and images—such as Shelley's *clouds shepherded by the slow unwilling wind*, and Keats passim: whereas modern poetry can only subsist by its *contents*: by becoming a complete magister vitae as the poetry of the ancients did: by including, as theirs did, religion with poetry, instead of existing as poetry only, and leaving religious wants to be supplied by the Christian religion, as a power existing independent of the poetical power. But the language, style and general proceedings of a poetry which has such an immense task to perform, must be very plain direct and severe: and it must not lose itself in parts and episodes and ornamental work, but must press fowards to the whole.[57]

'It must not lose itself in parts.' But this is just what Arnold accuses Keats of doing. Hence, Arnold can accept and concur in as high an estimate of Keats's verbal power as anyone might care to make; indeed, the higher the estimate, the stronger is his case against Keats. For the more exquisite the style, the more it distracts the attention of both the poet and the reader away from the all-important *whole*.

III. THE TOTAL ESTIMATE

Natural Magic

How far belief in poetry as a way of knowing had retrogressed between the Romantics and the mid-Victorians can easily be seen in the writings of Matthew Arnold precisely at those points where he attempts to establish poetry's 'interpretative power'. In 'Maurice de Guérin' (1863), he formulated his concept of this power in its twofold aspect, and it was there that he first used the term 'natural magic' as the name for one of these modes of interpretation. But a closer look gives rise to the question whether this interpretation is really interpretation or verbal soothing syrup:

> The grand power of poetry is its interpretative power; by which I mean, not a power of drawing out in black and white an explanation of the mystery of the universe, but the power of so dealing with things as to awaken in us a wonderfully full, new, and intimate sense of them, and our relations with them. When this sense is awakened in us, as to objects without us, we feel ourselves to be in contact with the essential nature of those objects, to be no longer bewildered and oppressed by them, but to have their secret, and to be in harmony with them; and this feeling calms and satisfies us as no other can.[58]

Certainly we have come quite a distance from the impassioned epistemology of Coleridge and Shelley, or from Keats and his 'What the imagination seizes as Beauty must be truth!' Arnold carefully refrains from making any objective statement about knowing or learning. Instead, we find that poetry awakens a 'sense' in us, it makes us 'feel' as though we have something, and this 'feeling' 'calms' and in some vague way 'satisfies' us—this is a most remarkable concession from the critic who wishes to elevate poetry to the position of complete *magister vitae*!

To continue, Arnold anticipates but bluntly evades the question of whether this 'feeling' has any significant connection with reality: 'I will not now inquire whether this sense is illusive, whether it does absolutely make us possess the real nature of things; all I say is, that poetry can awaken it in us, and that to awaken it is one of the highest powers of poetry.' Into these epistemological questions he does not inquire now, nor ever, for philosophical analysis was notoriously not Arnold's métier. But surely before we can trust poetry to be all the things Arnold wants it to be and to give all that he thinks it can give, these are the very questions we most want answered. Yet without attempting to discuss them, without even a persuasive digression to allow us to forget that these questions are not to be answered, Arnold proceeds immediately to beg them: 'The interpretations of science do not give us this intimate sense of objects as the interpretations of poetry give it; they appeal to a limited faculty, and not to the whole man. It is not Linnaeus or Cavendish or Cuvier who gives us the true sense of animals, or water, or plants, who seizes their secret for us, who makes us participate in their life; it is Shakespeare . . . it is Wordsworth . . . it is Keats . . . it is Chateaubriand . . . it is Senancour. . . .' If this 'sense' should be illusive, it would follow that poetry too appeals only to a 'limited faculty', and that a dangerous one. But Arnold simply cannot speak with the conviction of Wordsworth in making his claims. How gently and easily— so much more easily than by the thorny path of analysis or the steep climb of intuition—Arnold slides by verbal trickery from 'intimate sense' to 'true sense', and from there to having us seize now not a 'feeling', but the actual secret of things as we 'participate in their life'.

It is altogether appropriate that Arnold should use the word *magic* to name this mysterious power as applied to nature, since his treatment of it is so magical (magic: influencing natural events by words). But the poetry which does no more than awaken such a 'sense' or 'feeling' is at bottom the merest Celtic recreation; this emerges in the lectures *On the Study of Celtic Literature* (1866) between the lines throughout, and explicitly near the end: 'Magic is just the word for it,—the magic of nature; not merely the beauty of nature,—that the Greeks and Latins had; not merely an honest smack of the soil, a faithful realism,—that the Germans had; but the intimate life of Nature, her weird power and her fairy charm.'[59]

140

'Weird' and 'fairy': these are the key words; natural magic, it seems, has to do with the ethereal and charming in nature, and not with the power and mystery and even terror which Wordsworth could find there and about which Arnold had nothing to say when discussing 'naturalistic interpretation'. Arnold's own true feelings about nature as it is on earth, and not in fairyland, may be found in the speeches of Empedocles and in such poems as *The Youth of Man* and *In Harmony with Nature*: 'Man must begin, know this, where Nature ends.' It is perhaps unconsciously revealed again in his startling misquotation of 'cold' for 'pure' in 'Maurice de Guérin' when he cited Keats's 'moving waters at their priestlike task / Of cold ablution round Earth's human shores'. And if nature itself has become dehumanized, the poetic interpretation of nature can be at best only a secondary matter; the main function and true glory of poetry, especially in modern times, is to interpret the moral world.

To be sure, a poetry of natural magic is worth something; at least it 'calms' and 'satisfies'—rather like tobacco, perhaps. And as with tobacco, there are discriminations to be made:

> *L'Allegro* and *Il Penseroso* are charming, but they are not pure poetry of natural description in the sense in which the *Highland Reaper* is, or the *Ode to Autumn*. The poems do not touch the same chords or belong to the same order. Scott is altogether out of place in the comparison. His natural description in verse has the merits of his natural description in prose, which are very considerable. But it never has the grace and felicity of Milton, or the natural magic of Wordsworth and Keats. As poetical work it is not to be even named with theirs.[60]

Nature poetry may be discriminated not only in quality but also in variety. German realism and Greek radiance have their place as well as Celtic magic; Keats, like Shakespeare, is counted a master of both the Greek and Celtic modes.[61] Nevertheless, the whole business of nature interpretation in poetry is of secondary importance. True, the very greatest poets combine the power of natural magic with the powers of moral and intellectual interpretation (and with the good fortune of living in a first-class epoch). But of these three powers, the one most easily dispensed with is that of natural magic. Wordsworth had it combined with that of moral interpretation, but his greatness really rests upon the latter.

Goethe lacked it but his powers of moral and intellectual interpretation were so highly developed that he created the most nearly
adequate poetry of the nineteenth century.[62] But where is Keats,
who is lacking in all but natural magic, albeit of Shakespearean
intensity? He is far from the mainstream, and his work remains,
in spite of his genius, one of the minor currents of modern poetry;
after all, 'It is a moral interpretation, from an independent point
of view, of man and the world' which is the 'grand business' and
'immense serious task' of modern poetry. Poor Keats not only
failed stylistically in his major compositions to come up to classical
standards; by devoting his great gifts to naturalistic interpretation,
he failed equally in his contents to 'apply modern ideas to life'.[63]

Dangers of the Senses

But Keats's poetry failed in more than social utility. There is also
the matter of morality. When Matthew Arnold wrote 'dangerous'
in the margin beside Keats's phrase 'loading every rift of a subject
with ore'[64] he was undoubtedly thinking of more than the dangers
to the verse itself. In 'Maurice de Guérin' Arnold gave his most
thorough analysis of the temperament belonging to the poet whose
main faculty is that of naturalistic interpretation. Although Arnold
is speaking of Guérin, the same observations may be applied to
Keats, for the two are compared throughout the essay, and in both
men 'the faculty of naturalistic interpretation is overpoweringly
predominant'.[65]

> This faculty has for its basis a peculiar temperament, an extra-
> ordinary delicacy of organisation and susceptibility to impressions;
> in exercising it the poet is in a great degree passive (Wordsworth
> thus speaks of a *wise passiveness*); he aspires to be a sort of human
> Æolian harp, catching and rendering every rustle of Nature. To
> assist at the evolution of the whole life of the world is his craving,
> and intimately to feel it all:
>
> > ... 'the glow, the thrill of life,
> > Where, where do these abound?'
>
> is what he asks: he resists being riveted and held stationary by any
> single impression, but would be borne on for ever down an en-
> chanted stream. ... He is thus hardly a moral agent, and, like the
> passive and ineffectual Uranus of Keats's poem, he may say:

   ... 'I am but a voice;
My life is but the life of winds and tides;
No more than winds and tides can I avail.'

He hovers over the tumult of life, but does not really put his hand to it.

This passage and the one following are significant to the student of Arnold's psychology, recapitulating the inner struggle of his earlier years, as the quotation from his own *Obermann* in the passage above indicates. Arnold seems to have identified the romanticism of a Keats or Guérin with those tendencies in himself which he considered irresponsible or morbid, and consequently the passage is probably more accurate as thinly disguised autobiography than as a portrayal of John Keats. As Arnold is carried away by his own melodramatic rendering of the effects, if unchecked, of such a temperament on its possessor, he conveys a lurid stereotype of decadence, prophetic of the *fin de siècle*:

> Assuredly it is not in this temperament that the active virtues have their rise. On the contrary, this temperament, considered in itself alone, indisposes for the discharge of them. Something morbid and excessive, as manifested in Guérin, it undoubtedly has. In him, as in Keats, ... the temperament, the talent itself, is deeply influenced by their mysterious malady; the temperament is *devouring*; it uses vital power too hard and fast, paying the penalty in long hours of unutterable exhaustion and in premature death.[66]

Both of the modern historians of Keats's fame have agreed in wishing that Arnold had written his estimate of Keats before the publication in 1878 of the letters to Fanny Brawne, those letters he found so offensive. George H. Ford believes it to be 'likely that the tone of his comments would have been considerably different. The sympathetic analysis which he made of Keats's personality in the *Maurice de Guérin* essay gives us some clue to what he might have written. . . .' J. R. MacGillivray argues that Arnold was more appreciative of romantic art in the 1860's when he wrote the essays on Guérin, Heine, and Celtic literature, but was so shocked and angered both at the publication of the letters and at Keats for having written them that he 'turned vindictive and unjust'.[67] I cannot agree, however, that the difference would have been considerable, for it seems to me that the critic who wrote the analysis just quoted from 'Maurice de Guérin', and who in 'Heinrich

Heine' summed up the genius and work of Keats in the following words, has revealed his bias quite clearly: 'Keats passionately gave himself up to a sensuous genius, to his faculty for interpreting nature; and he died of consumption at twenty-five.'[68]

Indeed, Arnold's estimate of Keats, even in the 'romantic' 60's, is indicated by the fact that he linked him with Guérin at all. I cannot pretend to judge here with authority, but at least two critics who, whatever their faults, knew French literature as Arnold never did have found the comparison inexplicable and wrong-headed. George Saintsbury called Guérin 'a mere nobody', and felt that there was nothing to do about such a comparison but pass with averted face. Swinburne was no idolator of Keats, but as early as 1867, when he was still an ardent admirer of Arnold, he censured both Arnold's judgements on French literature and his preference for 'poëtes manqués' to true craftsmen. Keats was 'above all Greece and all Italy and all England in his own line and field of work', while Guérin 'could not as much as prove himself a poet by writing passable verse at all'.[69] Even if allowance is made for Swinburne's characteristic hyperbole, his relative estimate surely comes closer to the truth than Arnold's. Not, it should be noted, that Arnold greatly exaggerated the importance of Guérin; the point is rather that in the 1860's Arnold did not seem to see much difference between him and Keats in stature and personality.

Consequently I cannot believe that his critical estimate of Keats would have differed much in substance at any time, although the letters to Fanny Brawne influenced the tone and tendency of the late essay. Conversely, it is even possible that if Arnold had not been stimulated by his irritation with the love letters, he would not have felt so powerfully impelled to take his stand against the 'Johnny Keats' legend. He might possibly then not have been so diligent to search out and establish the manly Keats with flint and iron in his character. An earlier portrait might have highlighted the morbid, sensuous, and irresponsible, and more nearly resembled the one he painted of Guérin's 'elusive, undulating, impalpable nature'.

The fact is that Arnold was always somewhat embarrassed by the frank sensuousness and passionate love of experience he found in such writers as Keats and Shakespeare; even as a young man he found Keats's letters agitating, and called Clough a brute for telling him to read them. Later, when he read Haydon's autobiography, he was so struck by the tale of Keats spreading pepper on his tongue in order to appreciate more richly the delicious coldness of claret, that, although he thought Haydon a 'false *butcher*—revolting',[70] he repeated the anecdote in his essay on Keats twenty-seven years later. And in 'Pagan and Medieval Religious Sentiment' (1864), a line from Keats—'What pipes and timbrels! What wild ecstasy!'—finds its way as though automatically into a discussion of hedonism, the 'religion of pleasure'. Arnold's 'Puritanism' has often enough been held accountable for some of his less judicious critical performances such as the essays on Keats and Shelley, but I think it is necessary to go further and attempt to define a specific, unfortunate quality in his Puritanism. There was in Arnold a certain strain of vulgarity of feeling which must be taken into account to explain the snobbish acerbity and want of amenity in the opening pages of the Keats essay.[71]

Even in the Marguerite poems, I confess, I find something of this tone, something cold and hard as of a Puritan Lord Byron, which tends to make their cries of love-longing as embarrassing as moving. (These love poems will be discussed more fully below in connection with Shelley; see pp. 159-62.) A similar snobbish lack of delicacy may be seen elsewhere in Arnold's praise of the love letters of the roué Alfred de Musset as those of a 'gentleman', while those expressing the monogamous passion of Keats are called the letters of a surgeon's apprentice.[72] Apparently Arnold, respectable and devoted family man, believed with the rake Byron that love was—or ought to be—of man's life a thing apart. Thus he has little to say about Byron's sexual irregularities and nothing about George Sand's, but Keats, who knew what it was to be consumed by a single, overwhelming passion, was thereby unmanned. The social snobbery that has already been hinted at may also account for Arnold's peculiar judgement that Guérin's talent, 'exquisite as that of Keats', although it has 'much less of sunlight, abundance, inventiveness, and facility in it than that of Keats', does have 'more of *distinction* and power'. [My italics.] But perhaps the particular tone I am trying to isolate may best be seen by comparing a passage from one of Arnold's letters with another from one of Keats's, by which Arnold must have been struck for he copied it into his General Notebook. Arnold wrote Clough on September 29, 1848, that he had grown tired of Béranger:

I am glad to be tired of an author: one link in the immense series
of cognoscenda et indagenda despatched. More particularly is this
my feeling with regard to (I hate the word) women. We know
beforehand all they can teach us: yet we are obliged to learn it
directly from them. Why here is a marvellous thing. The following
is curious—

> 'Say this of her:
> The day was, thou wert not: the day will be,
> Thou wilt be most unlovely: shall I chuse
> Thy little moment life of loveliness
> Betwixt blank nothing and abhorred decay
> To glue my fruitless gaze on, and to pine,
> Sooner than those twin reaches of great time,
> When thou art either nought, and so not loved,
> Or somewhat, but that most unloveable,
> That preface and post-scribe thee ?'—[73]

This astounding attitude toward love might seem a mere foppish
youthful affectation, or part of a reaction to romantic difficulties
with 'Marguerite', and so be passed over lightly, were it not for
the later criticism of Keats. But here is Keats writing on Burns,
likewise considering the problem of suffering and experience,
especially in love:

> Poor, unfortunate fellow! His disposition was southern. How sad it
> is when a luxurious imagination is obliged, in self-defence, to deaden
> its delicacy in vulgarity and in things that are not! No man, in such
> matters, will be content with the experience of others. It is true
> that, out of suffering there is no dignity, no greatness; that in the
> most abstracted pleasure there is no lasting happiness. Yet who
> would not like to discover over again that Cleopatra was a gipsy,
> Helen a rogue, and Ruth a deep one ?[74]

This surely is the expression of not only a richer but a finer
sensibility than Arnold's.

As Arnold grew older his preoccupation with the dangers of the
senses seemed to grow stronger, almost obsessive. 'Congruere cum
cogitatione magna voluptas corporis non potest', he copied out
four different times in his notebooks. Twice he there reminded
himself of Paul's words, 'To be carnally minded is death.'[75] Other
maxims expressing similar sentiments abound. We find him regarding France's defeat by Prussia as, in part, a retribution for
French lubricity, French worship of the Goddess Aselgeia. He
divides the whole matter of conduct into two portions, chastity

and charity, and the sexual concern becomes the greater of the two. He is deeply disturbed by the declining veneration for chastity, and, as Lionel Trilling has put it, his 'whole and final comment on all speculations about love and marriage is the sentence from *Proverbs* on the "Strange Woman": "He knows not that the dead are there, and that her guests are in the depths of hell"—to be repeated like a litanic charm to banish whoredom.'[76] He is repelled by Shelley's sexuality, and Keats must be defended as being more of a man than his sensualist devotees imagine. It is understandable, then, even though Arnold's view of the Keatsian temperament was already formed before the publication of the letters to Fanny Brawne, that these letters and their presumed effect upon society should have loomed large enough in Arnold's consciousness to affect the emphasis, if not the basic attitudes, in his notice of Keats for Ward's *English Poets*.[77]

The Keats Essay

Nevertheless, the intention of the essay on Keats will be misunderstood if we see it merely as a specimen of moralizing. For Arnold, of course, criticism and moralizing could not be far apart; in 'Wordsworth', discussing poetry as a criticism of life, he applies even to Keats for a moral idea.[78] In the Keats essay, however, the moralizing is thoroughly fused with a critical purpose. That purpose is not the purely literary one of reaching a 'real' estimate of the poet John Keats; it is rather to clear away certain fallacies in contemporary taste and put Keats's fame on what Arnold considered a healthier and sounder basis. Thus, the essay is linked in rhetorical intention with 'Wordsworth' and 'Byron'; it is polemical, popular, and in a certain sense parochial.

The clue to this purpose appears in a passage about one-fifth of the way into the essay. Arnold has cited all the most damaging evidence against Keats, and made his ungenerous and gratuitous sneers about surgeon's apprentices, breach of promise suits, and the Divorce Court, and is just about to turn to the main body of the essay (almost two-thirds) which will be devoted to a rehabilitation of Keats's character. At this rhetorically crucial point, Arnold, referring to one of the love letters, says:

> The sensuous man speaks in it, and the sensuous man of a badly bred and badly trained sort. That many who are themselves also

badly bred and badly trained should enjoy it, and should even think it a beautiful and characteristic production of him whom they call their 'lovely and beloved Keats', does not make it better. These are the admirers whose pawing and fondness does not good but harm to the fame of Keats; who concentrate attention upon what in him is least wholesome and most questionable; who worship him, and would have the world worship him too, as the poet of

> 'Light feet, dark violet eyes, and parted hair,
> Soft dimpled hands, white neck, and creamy breast.'

Here was the real object of criticism, the real audience for the character study in 'John Keats'. In this essay designed for a popular anthology, as in so much of Arnold's later prose, problems of taste not only involve but have become matters of morality, and Arnold is using literature as a central battleground with *l'homme sensuel moyen*. To this average sensual man—and woman—Arnold insisted that their idol was something other and better than they knew: he was a true man, and within limits a true poet. Let them, if they could, admire what was truly admirable in Keats. But if 'they' could not, then there was still a 'we' who believe 'Keats to have been by his promise, at any rate, if not fully by his performance, one of the greatest of English poets, and who believe also that a merely sensuous man cannot either by promise or by performance be a very great poet. . .'. Hence 'we cannot but look for signs in him of something more than sensuousness, for signs of character and virtue'. This is certainly not a lower estimate of Keats than that in the first *Essays in Criticism*. It will be recalled that in 'Wordsworth' and in 'Byron' there was also a 'we' and a 'they'; Wordsworth was to be rescued from the narrow sectaries, the Wordsworthians, and Byron from the 'passionate admirers' who 'never got beyond the theatrical Byron'. And now Keats is likewise to be rescued from the sicklier kind of admiration, and made respectably available for a guarded but more wholesome kind of acceptance. By implication, modern poetry is simultaneously warned to free itself from the influence of the merely sensuous which regrettably makes up a large portion of Keats's poetry, a large but not the ultimately valuable and significant portion.

Arnold then proceeds with an examination of Keats's letters. He is not, however, seeking to study the literary thought and philosophical development of a poet, but rather is intent upon making up a catalogue of 'signs of character and virtue'. Whether this

catalogue is sufficient to offset the depreciation and innuendo of
the opening pages is a question only the individual reader can
answer. It is true that the long catalogue of virtues, almost because
of its length, has something of an apologetic tone: would a true
man need so much defending? Furthermore, the opening characterization of the underbred, sensuous man, though relatively brief,
has a quality of wit and epigram that makes it memorable, while
its placement at the opening of the essay tends also to emphasize
its importance. Some readers feel that the tone of the opening
negative part of the criticism, and even of the praise itself, is
enough to destroy the balance.[79] Other readers, forcibly impressed
by the placement of Keats with Shakespeare toward the end of
the essay (and possibly ignoring Arnold's anti-climactic qualifications), may feel that despite the tone of the opening, the total
weight of the essay is in Keats's favour. Whatever the reader
concludes, it cannot be denied that the catalogue itself is impressive.

Keats, we are told, displayed a wholesome attitude toward the
virtues and vices of men and a sound understanding of friendship,
as well as shrewdness and clear-sightedness in estimating the
character of other poets (Milton, Byron), and his own. Moreover,
in spite of his sensuousness, he was a man capable of detachment
and even coldness in his attitude toward women. He showed
'wholesome resolve' in respect to financial independence and the
necessity of work, and did not exaggerate the importance of poetry.
His attitudes towards fame, towards the general public, and towards
criticism and the literary world are faultless. He could show both
character and 'strength and clearness of judgment' in criticizing
his own work; he was completely devoted to the 'best sort of
poetry', and his attachment to the Beautiful, his master passion,
was not 'sensuous or sentimental', but was truly an 'intellectual
and spiritual passion'. The relation between beauty, truth, and joy
is a truth we have deep need to know, although it is not all we
need to know, and Keats was a great spirit because of his 'just and
high perception' of this 'necessary relation'. Finally, Keats did
recognize that 'place must be found for "the ardours rather than
the pleasures of song"' in his own poetry. I have given this point
last, although that is not its placement in Arnold's essay, because
it is made in the shortest paragraph in the whole piece. As I
argued above (p. 134), Arnold never sufficiently recognized this
element in Keats, and seems to have mentioned it here only in

passing. The 'high seriousness' of Keats hardly needs further emphasizing today, but it is regrettable that the spiritual son of Wordsworth, the critic who agreed with Hesiod that the Muses were born 'that they might be "a forgetfulness of evils, and a truce from cares"',[80] did not do greater justice to the poet who wrote even in the early *Sleep and Poetry* of 'the great end / Of poesy, that it should be a friend / To sooth the cares, and lift the thoughts of man' [ll. 245-7]. Yet it must be remembered that Arnold, writing after the Spasmodics and Tennyson, and at the time of the Pre-Raphaelites, was more concerned with Keats's influence than with his intentions, and this was not, for the most part, an influence calculated to provide those things which Arnold thought the age needed. Needless to say, Arnold's essay suffers as literary criticism from his social concern, but then literary criticism is not its purpose. Seven-eighths of the essay is devoted to Keats's character, and only a few paragraphs at the end to his poetry.

Judging by Keats's actual poetic accomplishment and not by his promise, and assuming the inherent superiority of the drama and long narrative as poetic forms, Arnold necessarily could not rank Keats with the greatest poets. In that lesser branch of poetic interpretation that Arnold called naturalistic, and in his gusto and gift of language, Keats is with Shakespeare. But although more consummately gifted than Wordsworth or Byron or any other English poet since Milton, Keats 'died having produced too little and being as yet too immature to rival' his two great contemporaries. 'For the second great half of poetic interpretation, for that faculty of moral interpretation which is in Shakespeare, ... Keats was not ripe', nor was he sufficiently mature as an artist to produce great wholes like the *Agamemnon* or *King Lear*. In his shorter works, though, 'he is perfect', and since perfection presumably defies analysis, Arnold does not discuss them further, but lets the poems he has selected prove his assertion.[81] 'To show such work', he says, 'is to praise it.'

If for the moment we put aside our modern Keats of the letters, the hero of thought, the courageous, afflicted bard, and the nascent Shakespeare,[82] and judge him only by what he produced as a poet and not by what he might have produced, can we say that Arnold was, in his final estimate, so very wrong?

V

THE INTENSE INANE:
SHELLEY AND COLERIDGE

What a set! what a world!
Coleridge took to opium.

I. WHY SHELLEY WITH COLERIDGE?

TODAY, when Coleridge's stock in the literary market place is so high, and Shelley's, though rising sharply, remains generally rather lower, some justification may be due for linking them in a single chapter of a study such as this. An argument might indeed be based on intrinsic likenesses between them. For one thing, it has been observed that Wordsworth, Keats, Burns, Blake, and Byron have been denied the title 'romantic poet' by one critic or another, while Shelley and Coleridge share 'the distinction of an unchallenged romanticism'.[1] A Belgian critic, Albert Gérard, has suggested in *L'Idée Romantique de la Poésie en Angleterre* that the conventional division of the Romantic poets by generations— Wordsworth and Coleridge, Shelley and Keats—is largely accidental, and that it would be more useful to emphasize the correspondences between Keats and Wordsworth on the one hand, and Shelley and Coleridge on the other.[2] Actually, the view that Shelley and Coleridge belong together in any such grouping is not a new one. A. C. Bradley believed Coleridge to have had a significant stylistic influence upon Shelley, and drew up a considerable and by no means exhaustive catalogue of Coleridgean echoes in Shelley's poetry. Perhaps the most notable, and certainly the most insistent of those who coupled these poets during Arnold's own time, was Swinburne, who repeatedly referred to the relationship as one of master and disciple.[3]

Matthew Arnold had so little to say about Coleridge's poetry (but one remark in all his works, letters, and notebooks) that it is difficult to make out where he would have placed him as a poet. In the one place where he acknowledged Coleridge's poetic genius, he paired him with Keats as the composer of a very few pieces of surpassing worth, his remaining poetry being of inferior quality. As for Shelley, Arnold sometimes associated him with Keats and the Elizabethans, and sometimes with Byron as a modernist. However, Arnold did think of Coleridge and Shelley as similar in some ways. In the first place, they were apparent exceptions to his dictum that the Romantics did not know enough: 'Shelley had plenty of reading', he admitted; 'Coleridge had immense reading.'[4] Secondly, Shelley and Coleridge, in spite of their book learning, were the two greatest failures among the grander names of the Romantic movement. In a famous summary Arnold said: 'I for my part can never even think of equalling with [Wordsworth and Byron] any other of their contemporaries [but Keats];—either Coleridge, poet and philosopher wrecked in a mist of opium; or Shelley, beautiful and ineffectual angel, beating in the void his luminous wings in vain.'[5]

Finally, and this is my conclusive reason for treating them together, Arnold had very little to say about the poetry of either, while the personal element played a great part in his estimate of both. Indeed, all of Arnold's literary comments on both men could easily be put on one page. Consequently, although it will not be possible completely to fuse the discussion of the two poets, consideration of proportion dictates relative brevity and, as far as possible, unity in dealing with them.

II. POETIC INFLUENCE

Arnold never considered either Shelley or Coleridge very important as poets, although in his later years he did begin to have a somewhat more sympathetic attitude toward Shelley's verse, to judge from his reading lists.[6] However, it would have been virtually impossible for a young poet in England at Arnold's time to avoid totally the influence of these poets who had contributed so decisively to what the rest of the century would consider the very nature of poetic utterance to be. Some critics have, as a matter of fact, insisted that Shelley was a strong poetic influence on Arnold, but these are invariably the same critics who are most interested in defending Shelley against him. The typical line of argument is that Arnold the poet was more sensitive and honest than Arnold the critic; if, then, it can be established that Arnold the poet borrowed from Shelley, Shelley's poetic worth is proved albeit at the expense (willingly paid by most Shelleyites) of labelling Arnold the critic as mistaken, biased, or downright ungrateful.

Each generation has possessed at least one spokesman for this point of view. Swinburne came close to it in the last century. He did not actually assert that Shelley was an important influence on Arnold's verse, but he did argue that Arnold as a good poet himself had no excuse for not appreciating Shelley's art, especially since he shared it to a limited degree, and had written at least one poem 'so exactly after the manner of Shelley that both in style and in spirit it is not unworthy of the honour to be mistaken for a genuine lyric of the second order among the minor poems of our greatest lyric poet'.[7] Representing the next generation is Sir Arthur Quiller-Couch, who believed that the poet of *The Strayed Reveller* and of the songs in *Empedocles* 'must . . . have loved Shelley in his time, and with a whole heart'. For 'proof' Quiller-Couch points to *The Scholar-Gipsy* and *Thyrsis*, where 'the very accent is Shelley's', and quotes a passage from the former [ll. 211–14, 221–30] along with stanza xxx of *Adonais*. Commenting on the parallel passages, he concludes that 'Arnold had at some time drunk thirstily of Shelley's magic potion', although later the potion had soured.[8] This argument might have been more convincing if the passage chosen from *Thyrsis* did not seem so very decidedly in the tone and even language of Keats's *Ode to a Nightingale*. Finally, the most modern commentator to take this point of view is also the one who pushes it furthest. Mrs. Olwen Campbell in her able book *Shelley and the Unromantics* is no less ardent than Swinburne but much less shrill in her defence of Shelley. She repeats and amplifies the charge against Arnold of ungrateful inconsistency, and quotes numerous passages from Arnold's lyrics illustrative of 'passion aged into melancholy', 'a heart longing like Shelley's for love, and for calm and power within', and an exhortation to his own 'fainting soul' in support of her argument that Matthew Arnold is Shelley's most formidable adversary because they agreed on the purposes of poetry and were 'spiritually akin . . . in many ways'. They are alike not only in spirit, she says, but in subject:

Both might be called 'philosophical' poets. Both were mainly concerned with expressing the longing of man's spiritual nature, and
his discontent with earthly life. Both wrote some very personal,
almost one might say egotistical poems. Both were inspired by
Greek models and wrote dramas based on the Greek, with choruses
and lyrical passages, and between *Empedocles* and *Prometheus
Unbound* there is more than a superficial resemblance. Both wrote
love poems—mainly of restless and unhappy love. Each wrote a
famous elegy.

'And yet', she exclaims passionately, 'Arnold turned and rent
Shelley.'[9] Mrs. Campbell's list of points is impressive, and
undoubtedly she has seen deeper into a true emotional similarity
between the two poets than any previous critic. It would be easier,
though, to accept her argument that Shelley really had an important influence on Arnold if one were not aware that the whole
list of similarities in the passage quoted above could be applied
with only the slightest of changes to a comparison between Shelley
and T. S. Eliot, who would fulfil all the items but the last; he has
not yet composed a formal elegy.

Such are the strong claims that have been made for Shelley as an
influence on Arnold, but no one at all has spoken up for Coleridge,
not even Swinburne, who was almost as angry about Arnold's
low ranking of Coleridge as he was about Shelley. And yet, by
methods of argument similar to Mrs. Campbell's, it would not be
difficult to establish Coleridge's 'influence'. One could point to
Arnold's versification and use of medieval legends and magical
imagery in such poems as *Saint Brandan*, *The Neckan*, and *The
Forsaken Merman*; to his frequent use of poetry in a conversa-
tional key for discursive purposes; to his employment of ballad
measure; and to some verbal echoes as evidence of Coleridgean
influence. The too easy possibility of such 'proof' by internal
evidence is of course one of the dangers of influence tracing. With
Wordsworth we were on safe ground; Arnold's well-known and
self-confessed discipleship, coupled with frequent specific allusions to Wordsworth in Arnold's poetry, gave us a firm basis for
proceeding. For Byron we have Arnold's own word that he deeply
felt the impact of his personality. Since Arnold's own attitude
towards Keats was mixed, it was necessary there to move with
caution, but there is at least the evidence of frank imitation in
two of Arnold's major poems. When dealing with Shelley and

Coleridge, however, we are lacking totally in any such solid under-pinning. Arnold certainly knew their works, but never admitted that he found them in any way useful to him in composing his own poems.

Of the two poets, Coleridge is certainly the less important in this connection, and may be dealt with first. There is little in Arnold which would need have been decidedly different if Coleridge had never written. Undoubtedly *The Rime of the Ancient Mariner* and *Christabel*, with their aura of the supernatural, their verbal and metrical felicity, and their rich sensuous and symbolic imagery, opened for the nineteenth century new possibilities in the literary ballad and lyrical narrative. Such poems as *Saint Brandan, The Forsaken Merman*, and some parts of *Tristram and Iseult* may be said to be partly in the tradition fostered by Coleridge. *The Forsaken Merman*, especially, seems to indicate that Arnold had studied the metrics of *Christabel* and the sea-imagery of *The Rime of the Ancient Mariner*. But we can really infer no necessary direct influence from such evidence, for on the one hand Arnold was familiar with the similar work of German poets, and on the other Coleridge's poems had so fully entered into the main stream of Victorian verse through Keats, Scott, Byron, and Tennyson that they almost may be considered for Arnold's time linguistic facts rather than specific influences. They were a part of the poetic atmosphere he breathed.

Specific echoes of Coleridge are exceedingly rare in Arnold's poetry. The mood of *Dejection: An Ode* certainly is to be felt in *Empedocles on Etna* and elsewhere.[10] But the same malaise was as much a part of nineteenth-century sensibility as the spleen had been of the eighteenth, and, to name a few of Arnold's well-established sources, may be found expressed in Senancour, de Musset, and Wordsworth. Arnold's friend John Duke Coleridge claimed for his grand-uncle the image of 'the unplumb'd, salt, estranging sea' from Arnold's poem beginning 'Yes! in the sea of life', but Mrs. Kathleen Tillotson has convincingly argued that of the numerous possible and likely sources for the image, *Christabel* is one of the less significant. One or two other faint possibilities are worth mention only in a note.[11] In truth, there seems to have been too great a temperamental difference between the poets to allow of a decisive influence. This difference may be seen in Arnold's treatment of the Saint Brandan legend. In contrast with

The Ancient Mariner, Arnold's poem is bare and sparse; oppor-
tunities for picturesque elaboration latent in the saint's magical
sea voyage seem to have been willingly sacrificed to the moral
intention.[12]

Coleridge's poetic influence on Matthew Arnold then was
merely general and diffuse, if not trivial, but that of Shelley was
somewhat more marked. However, because of Arnold's fixed
attitude of depreciation during his poetic years at least, it is a
rather difficult influence to assess. At any rate, Arnold did read
Shelley and discussed him frequently in his correspondence. He
thought him important enough even as a failure to be linked with
Byron as one who was groping toward a sense of poetic responsibility to the modern world, and he even expressed an interest in
doing the Shelley volume for the English Men of Letters Series in
which he had declined to do the Shakespeare.[13] Some years later,
after reading Dowden, Arnold must have felt great relief that the
plan had fallen through, but we must regret losing what would
have been his considered critique of Shelley as a poet. This
continuing interest, then, offers some basis for examining Arnold's
poetry and his beliefs about poetry for traces of Shelleyan influence.

Arnold's beliefs about poetry do indeed show some marked
similarities to Shelley's. There is little or nothing in Shelley's
'Defence of Poetry' from which Arnold would have to dissent, and
we must bear in mind Arnold's praise of Shelley as an essayist
although he referred to no specific work. Shelley's belief in poetry
as the expressor and even creator of values, and as an instrument
of moral good working by indirection on the emotions and the
imagination, is good orthodox Arnold. However, in the absence of
more concrete evidence, no critical influence may be inferred, for
two reasons. First, this belief in the high calling of poetry was not
uniquely Shelleyan, for it coincides with much that Coleridge had
said, too, and is not far from the faith of Wordsworth who had
influenced both Shelley and Arnold. Second, Arnold was never
able consistently to maintain the romantic faith in poetry; this has
already been indicated in the analysis above of Arnold's passages
on the interpretative power of poetry and in his curious praise of
Keats for not taking poetry too seriously, and will be discussed
more fully in my concluding chapter. If we turn to Arnold's
poetry itself we may be on somewhat surer ground.

Here I think we shall find that Shelley was a minor but genuine influence, affecting in particular a handful of Arnold's lyrical poems, mainly those dealing with the Shelleyan subject of the melancholy mutability of things, with love, and with nature. In a few instances the blend of Arnold's sad lucidity with Shelley's airy, musical versification is successful; on the other hand, in some of the love poems, where Arnold is more like Shelley in tone, the effect is likely to be most offensive. Even in his metrical imitations, Arnold's ear was not fine enough always to sustain the music without grievous lapses.

Two early lyrics, *The Voice* and *A Question*, are among Arnold's more successful poems in irregular stanzas. Both are rich in the music of Shelley's 'lovely wail'. Of the two, *The Voice* is somewhat more ambitious, obscure, and unsuccessful. Much of its imagery is of the most conventionally 'romantic' variety—the moon on sleepless waters, mothers weeping for dead children (metonymized as flowers), throbbing brows, burning breasts, a wild rose climbing a mouldering wall, a 'gush' of sunbeams, a ruined hall, and lute-like tones. Metrically the poem is more successful, containing such lovely passages as the opening lines, reminiscent of Shelley's 'When the lamp is shattered':

> As the kindling glances,
>   Queen-like and clear,
> Which the bright moon lances
>   From her tranquil sphere
> At the sleepless waters
>   Of a lonely mere,
> On the wild whirling waves, mournfully, mournfully,
>   Shiver and die.

On the other hand, we also find a tongue-twister like the following, a monstrosity Shelley could never have fathered[14]:

> When the flower they flow for
> Lies frozen and dead—

A Question, the poem which received Swinburne's equivocal praise as worthy of Shelley when Shelley wasn't doing his best, is simpler, and in Arnold's best vein of lyrical melancholy; it resembles in mood and theme Shelley's late lyric *Mutability*. The imagery, though often abstract, is delicately evocative, and the poem never falls metrically far below the exquisite opening:

> Joy comes and goes, hope ebbs and flows
>   Like the wave.

Shelley's influence, if any, on Arnold's longer poems is faint. For his part, Arnold seems to have paid little attention to Shelley's longer poems, at least until fairly late in his life, accepting instead the view of Shelley as mainly a singer of delicate, sweet lyrics, a view fostered even by so impassioned an admirer as Swinburne. It is a reasonable certainty, though, that the section of *Obermann Once More* [ll. 283–96] depicting the dawn of the new world, and containing the line 'The world's great order dawns in sheen', was influenced by the final chorus of *Hellas* and possibly by the conclusion of *Prometheus Unbound*. Moreover, Shelley set an example which may have encouraged Arnold to use a variety of lyric forms within a single narrative, as in *Tristram and Iseult* and *The Church of Brou*, but the same device had been used by others including Goethe. Incidentally, it is curious that one of Shelley's most ardent defenders, Sir Arthur Quiller-Couch, criticized Arnold for not choosing a single metre for each long poem and managing to make it express all the needed moods by his handling.[15] I fail to find the resemblance between *Empedocles on Etna* and *Prometheus Unbound* which Mrs. Campbell saw there; even the songs seem for the most part more reminiscent of Keats than Shelley. However, the concluding lyric with its shimmering forms, kinetic imagery, and metrical rapidity is undoubtedly more in the manner of Shelley:

> Through the black, rushing smoke-burst,
> Thick breaks the red flame;
> All Etna heaves fiercely
> Her forest-clothed frame.

Empedocles's long philosophical soliloquy [Act I, Scene ii] is in a stanza slightly modified from Shelley's 'Skylark' stanza, but its movement is very different. Arnold's stanza is intentionally slower, rather ruminant and discursive, partly because of his shifting the metre of the short lines from Shelley's dominantly trochaic to a dominantly iambic, partly because of his syntax, and very noticeably because of his characteristic use of a much higher proportion of long syllables than Shelley (sometimes as many as six in a six-syllable line: 'Once read thy own breast right'). The long line at the end of the stanza is nominally the same as Shelley's, iambic hexameter. Its effect, however, is quite different from Shelley's, partly because of the metrical differences in the preceding four

trimeter lines, but also because Arnold lacked Shelley's delicacy in
handling the caesura; Arnold's long lines too often tend to break
sharply into a pair of trimeters. Sometimes, too, Arnold's metre
in the long line is too thumpy and regular, while at other times it
stumbles (e.g., 'And believes Nature outraged if his will's gain-
said', where in context *his* requires a rhetorical stress). However,
even the singer Callicles in this poem occasionally coughs; the
following lines are supposed to be a rhymed couplet:

> For he taught him how to sing
> And he taught him flute-playing. [Act II, ll. 169–70]

I have put Arnold's love poems last for separate consideration,
for in them as a group I find a similarity of a regrettable sort to a
certain side of Shelley. In the discussion of Keats I indicated that
my sympathy with these poems of Arnold's is imperfect because of
a quality of posturing self-dramatization, of shrillness, and of
insensitivity I find marring at least some part of each lyric in the
Switzerland group, except the one called *Absence*. In *Meeting*, for
example, it is not necessary to accept the flippant psychologizing
of 'Hugh Kingsmill' about Dr. Arnold as the 'God'[16] to find something of what Matthew Arnold called *le faux* in such lines as

> I hear a God's tremendous voice:
> 'Be counsell'd, and retire.'

This meddling deity who takes so personal an interest in Matthew
Arnold's love affairs appears again in the last stanza of *To
Marguerite—Continued* ('Yes! in the sea of life'):

> Who order'd, that their longing's fire
> Should be, as soon as kindled, cool'd?
> Who renders vain their deep desire?—
> A God, a God their severance ruled!
> And bade betwixt their shores to be
> The unplumb'd, salt, estranging sea.

Truly, in spite of the fine last line, I cannot help thinking that this
poem as a whole would be better if the last stanza, with its futile
questioning and its answer that is no answer, were cancelled. The
preceding poem in the series, *Isolation. To Marguerite*, is even more
embarrassing; here Arnold compares his lonely heart to the moon-
goddess experiencing a 'conscious thrill of shame' when she
descended 'To hang over Endymion's sleep', and he advises it to
return to its own 'remote and spheréd course'. This posture is

consistent, however, with the preachiness of two stanzas in *A Farewell*:

> But in the world I learnt, what there
> Thou too wilt surely one day prove,
> That will, that energy, though rare,
> Are yet far, far less rare than love.
>
> Go, then!—till time and fate impress
> This truth on thee, be mine no more!
> They will!—for thou, I feel, not less
> Than I, wast destined to this lore.

This in turn seems to me of a piece with the later, harder tone of gratuitous superiority in *The Terrace at Berne*:

> Or hast thou long since wander'd back,
> Daughter of France! to France thy home;
> And flitted down the flowery track
> Where feet like thine too lightly come?
>
> Doth riotous laughter now replace
> Thy smile; and rouge, with stony glare,
> Thy cheek's soft hue; and fluttering lace
> The kerchief that enwound thy hair?

Of course, there is nothing in all this for which we can blame Shelley. However, if there is an unfortunate self-regarding tone, at once smug and shrill, to which Arnold is temperamentally predisposed, then it should not be surprising to find him uncritical of a similar tone which is sometimes found in Shelley. Let us examine *Parting*, the second of the *Switzerland* group, which Professor Bonnerot calls the most romantic piece Arnold wrote, and which he perceptively relates to Shelley's *Ode to the West Wind* and *Mont Blanc*.[17] Now it is striking that in all Arnold's animadversions on Shelley's poetry, he always censured Shelley for vaporousness and incoherence, but had nothing to say about the tone of exaggeration, shrillness, or self-pity which occasionally mars even Shelley's better poems. (It is true that in his review of Dowden's *Life of Shelley*, Arnold accused Shelley of a want of humour and hinted that this defect could be felt in his poetry; nevertheless, the bulk of Arnold's comment adds up to making Shelley an incoherent Keats.) Apparently deaf to this tone when it occurs in Shelley, Arnold might not be expected to hear it in his own verse, as in the following passages of *Parting*:

> Blow, ye winds! lift me with you!
> I come to the wild.
> Fold closely, O Nature!
> Thine arms round thy child.

and

> —I come, O ye mountains!
> Ye torrents, I come![18]

and the almost parodic

> Ah! calm me, restore me;
> And dry up my tears.

It should be added, though, that mingled with this insistent rhetoric there are in *Parting* some finely realized images of mountain scenery and, if one does not listen too closely to the words, a decided lyrical grace.

Underlying this occasional similarity of tone seems to be a certain similarity between Arnold and Shelley in their attitudes toward love, although not, to be sure, in their consciously held philosophies nor in the practical consequences in their lives. The likeness, rather, is in a tendency both poets reveal towards passivity and a correlative tendency to seek escape from the storms of passion by casting the loved one in the role of sister or mother, as in Arnold's *A Farewell*:

> How sweet, unreach'd by earthly jars,
> My sister! to maintain with thee
> The hush among the shining stars,
> The calm upon the moonlit sea!

and Shelley's *Epipsychidion* [ll. 45–8]. In fairness to Shelley, it should be recognized that his treatment of this relationship is charged with philosophic and symbolic significance, whereas in Arnold it is difficult to see much beyond the psychological. This attitude towards love makes itself felt not only in the Marguerite poems, but also, if less insistently, in *The River*, one of the group called *Faded Leaves* traditionally associated with Arnold's wooing of Miss Wightman:

> My pent-up tears oppress my brain,
> My heart is swoln with love unsaid.
> Ah, let me weep, and tell my pain,
> And on thy shoulder rest my head!
>
> Before I die . . .

We know that the outcome of this wooing was, after some difficulties, successful, but if we had only the poetry to judge from, it would seem almost fair to retort upon Arnold his comment on Keats's love letters, that a man who writes love-poems in this strain is probably predestined to misfortune in his love-affairs. Of these love poems, then, we may conclude, and we have the judgement of many of Shelley's admirers to support us, that if Shelley did not directly influence them, at least he helped to naturalize in the English love poetry of the nineteenth century a certain posture and tone which was by no means uncongenial to Matthew Arnold.

III. GENERAL INFLUENCE

In considering the general influence of Shelley and Coleridge on Arnold, we shall find that here it is Shelley who may be dealt with rapidly, while the influence of Coleridge will require more careful attention. Unfortunately, the nature of the evidence in the latter case is such that the more careful the attention, the more confusing and tentative the conclusions tend to become. Nevertheless, Coleridge was in some measure a significant influence on Arnold, as he was on almost all thinking minds of the century. But first it will be convenient to dispose of Shelley.

Since a man has, after all, some choice among available teachers, Arnold's well-known low opinion of Shelley's mentality might altogether discourage further search. However, Arnold's peculiar judgement that Shelley would live longer as the author of the essays and letters than as a poet, even if it was intended as reductive irony, ought to make us take another look. We shall then recall that one of the few good words Arnold had for Shelley was the passage in 'Heinrich Heine' where he praised him and Byron for having at any rate attempted, alone in their generation, 'to apply freely the modern spirit' in poetry; although they failed in their work, he predicted that their names would be remembered. What Arnold apparently meant by this limited praise was that Byron had expressed some religious heresies and had challenged, in a rather loose and crude way, all existing configurations of political power, and that Shelley had gone still further in his rebellion against accepted religious and political forms and ideas and in his sensitivity to social injustice. Since Arnold seems to have approved of Shelley's modernness, we may expect to find in

Shelley's prose certain ideas congenial to Arnold, especially in the writings on religion, since for Arnold, the outstanding 'modern idea' consisted of a rationalistic historical approach, coloured by emotional sympathy, to the literature and events of the Christian religion.

Most of Shelley's ideas on Christianity might have come out of Arnold's *Literature and Dogma*. For the character of Jesus Shelley consistently expressed during his late years a sincere admiration; particularly, he praised Him for His moral teachings, His 'extraordinary genius', and His 'invincible gentleness and benignity' (cf. Arnold's 'sweet reasonableness').[19] According to Thomas Medwin, Shelley wrote a treatise on the life of Jesus which (like Arnold's religious writings) differed from the work of the German Rationalists only in treating the subject with more respect.[20] On the *function* of popular religion, Arnold and Shelley differed totally, of course. What was for Shelley a mere device for the enslavement of the masses was for Arnold a force basically good and necessary, both for the happiness of the people and for the moral and political welfare of the state. But in their views of the *nature* of popular religion, Arnold and Shelley were not far apart. Shelley scorned, Arnold deprecated what Shelley called (in Arnoldian diction) 'the gross imaginings of the vulgar'. Shelley's God, conceived of as 'something mysteriously and illimitably pervading the frame of things, ... the overruling Spirit of the collective energy of the moral and material world', is remarkably similar to Arnold's 'stream of tendency by which all things fulfil the law of their being' or his 'power not ourselves that makes for righteousness' ('righteousness' being at least three-quarters of the proper end of man, and hence the law of *our* being). Arnold certainly would have agreed with Shelley's belief that the vagueness and imprecision of this conception is a virtue, for, in Shelley's words, 'where indefiniteness ends idolatry and anthropomorphism begin'. Finally, Arnold's Jesus is like Shelley's in showing a remarkable tendency to be misrepresented by all, or almost all, previous interpreters, a lamentable state of affairs which He would surely deplore, like Shelley's 'mild and gentle ghost / Wailing for the faith he kindled' [*Prometheus Unbound*, I, i, 554–5].

However, it is absurd to think of Arnold going to Shelley to learn religion, even if he might condescendingly approve of much he found there. The true key to the similarity in their ideas and language is undoubtedly to be found in a common interest in the teachings of Baruch Spinoza, or a romanticized version thereof. Professor Fairchild finds that 'Spinoza was a bridge over which Shelley could pass from Holbach to Plotinus.' Arnold's indebtedness was at least as great, as he himself confessed; his own metaphor for Spinoza was 'life-preserver'. 'To him', Arnold wrote to Huxley, 'I owe more than I can say.' It was Spinoza who had saved him from drowning in the German Biblical critics with whom it angered Arnold to be associated.[21] Consequently, it is impossible to conclude that Arnold's religious ideas, any more than his theory of poetry, owe anything to Shelley. He did find in Shelley certain congenial ideas and attitudes which had been held by only a few rare spirits in Shelley's time, but which formed a sizeable part of the intellectual ambience in which Arnold came to maturity. On the whole, the personalities of the two men and the operations of their minds were so different—the one radical, speculative, and romantically impatient of empirical reality, the other melioristic, journalistic, and stoically pragmatic—that any greater degree of influence, such as Shelley had on Swinburne and later rebels, would have been almost a psychological impossibility.

Coleridge, too, was of a temperament vastly different from, and in the main repugnant to, Arnold's, and in part for similar reasons; nor do we find the mature Arnold seeking to learn from him. But where Shelley's peculiarity made of him an influence which could be chosen or rejected, Coleridge's centrality and his many-sided brilliance made of his teachings a force in nineteenth-century thought which could have been avoided only by strenuous conscious effort. That his place as one of the two seminal minds of the age should have been defined by the utilitarian John Stuart Mill is evidence enough of his pervasive, all but inescapable influence. But it is just for that reason that it becomes extraordinarily difficult to define with any precision the nature and limits of his influence on Arnold. An inordinately lengthy survey might be made of the parallels in Arnold's and Coleridge's literary theory and criticism, their religious thought, and social-political ideas.[22] But if it made any pretence to completeness, such a survey would be decidedly out of proportion to its importance here for two reasons: first, it would lead far from Arnold as a poet and literary critic, and second, it would suggest that Coleridge's writings were much more directly and consciously in Arnold's thoughts

than they probably were. Moreover, it was as poets that Wordsworth and Byron and Keats exerted their power over Arnold. But
in Arnold's estimation, Coleridge as a poetic force was negligible.

That some sort of intellectual influence existed, nevertheless, is
indubitable, as most of Arnold's critics have assumed. Lionel
Trilling says, for example, that in Bible interpretation Arnold's
guides 'were the two men who had in many other ways influenced
his thought: Spinoza and Coleridge'. Again, J. D. Jump comments
that in making education 'a responsibility of the state . . . [Arnold]
was following his own father and Coleridge and Burke.'[23] Although
these generalizations and others of similar tenor are certainly true,
there is a real problem of substantiation since Arnold himself, so
frank generally in naming the 'rigorous teachers' who seized his
youth, nowhere gives such credit to Coleridge. Here, then, it might
be useful to list the available evidence of direct contact between
Coleridge and Matthew Arnold, and attempt to infer from it just
when and how much Arnold read Coleridge; later I shall sum-
marily indicate something of the nature of the ideas they held in
common. Coleridge must have exerted some indirect influence
through Dr. Arnold, his great admirer, but to attempt to sort out
definitively the tangled streams of influence on Arnold's religious,
ecclesiastical, political, and educational thought emanating from
Dr. Arnold, Wordsworth, Coleridge, Emerson, Newman, Spinoza,
and Burke, would be a difficult and dubious proceeding. As for
personal contact, the Arnold boys seem never to have met the
great man their father referred to with mingled respect and pity
as 'old Sam'.[24] By the time the Arnold family had begun to
frequent the North, Coleridge was firmly ensconced at Highgate,
and he died when Matthew was twelve. The Arnolds were well
acquainted, however, with Derwent and the elfin, ravaged Hartley.
Coleridge's nephew, Judge Coleridge as the Arnold boys called
him, was one of Dr. Arnold's best friends, and the friendship was
continued in the next generation when Matthew Arnold and John
Duke, later Lord Coleridge and Lord Chief Justice, were class-
mates and friends at Balliol; after Arnold's death it was Lord
Coleridge who saw through the press and contributed a prefatory
note to *Essays in Criticism: Second Series*.

A principal source of knowledge about Arnold's reading is his
notebooks and reading lists, and it is striking to discover there a
total absence of direct quotation from Coleridge's writings. The

greatest source of quotation is, out of all comparison, the Bible; the *Imitation of Christ* appears frequently, and, of secular authors, Goethe is most heavily drawn upon. Others who contribute considerably are Renan, Sainte-Beuve, George Sand, Bishop Wilson, and Joubert, the 'French Coleridge'; none of this is surprising to the reader of Arnold's prose, of course. But there are only three references to Coleridge throughout, and all are taken from secondary sources. The first, a definition of faith, and the second, a definition of an approving conscience, are copied out of an essay on Coleridge in the *North British Review* for December 1865, written by Arnold's friend from college days, J. C. Shairp, Principal of St. Andrews College.[25] The definition of faith as 'the allegiance of the moral nature to Universal Reason, or the will of God' must have struck home in 1866 when Arnold was already no doubt considering the material that was to become *Culture and Anarchy*, in which Bishop Wilson's 'reason and the will of God' play so large a part. The second quotation, 'An approving conscience is the sense of harmony of the personal will of man with that impersonal light which is in him, representative of the will of God', is also reminiscent of Arnold's use in *Culture and Anarchy* of Bishop Wilson's maxim: 'Firstly, never go against the best light you have; secondly, take care that your light be not darkness.'[26] The third and final Coleridge entry is in one of the undated general notebooks. Under the heading 'The Great Coleridgian Position' Arnold copied out: 'That Christianity, rightly understood, is identical with the highest philosophy, and that, apart from all question of historical evidence, the essential doctrines of Christianity are necessary and eternal truths of reason—truths which man, by the vouchsafed light of Nature and without aid from documents or tradition, may always and anywhere discover for himself.'[27] Although the extremely Deistic implications of this 'position' may go beyond what Coleridge would wish, there is little doubt that Arnold found it highly sympathetic. What is interesting about this entry, however, is the question of date. The editors of the *Note-Books* have traced the passage to John Simon's prefatory memoir in J. H. Green's *Spiritual Philosophy*, and they have given this as Arnold's source. Since Green's work was published in 1865, the implication would be that Arnold had read it and was familiar with it during his 'ecclesiastical decade'. And yet it is perfectly incredible that anyone with Arnold's temperament would have

ploughed through this treatise by Coleridge's disciple. The answer
to the puzzle is to be found in one of Arnold's uncollected periodical essays, his last public utterance on religious matters, called
'A Comment on Christmas'. There he refers to H. D. Traill's
Coleridge which had been published in 1884 in the English Men of
Letters Series. Arnold in this essay takes from Traill not only the
passage from Simon, but the heading 'the great Coleridgian position', and he also approvingly cites Traill's judgement that Green
had failed in his self-appointed task of establishing and elucidating
that position, although Arnold then gives his own reasons for the
failure.[28] (In spite of this, says Arnold, the position itself is true
and deeply important, 'and by virtue of it Coleridge takes rank, so
far as English thought is concerned, as an initiator and founder'.)
This dating, then, as well as the total absence of Coleridge entries
in Arnold's notebooks between 1866 and 1885 (except that the
second quotation from Shairp was copied over into the 1867 and
again into the 1868 notebooks), is fairly strong evidence that
Coleridge, whatever his importance as an initiator, was not
actively in Arnold's thought during the years when Coleridge's
doctrines might have been of most direct use to him.

Arnold's reading lists, which we possess from 1852 to 1888,
although they are not exhaustive and hence give no final evidence,
tend also to corroborate this negative conclusion. They contain
only three entries related to Coleridge: 'Shairp on Coleridge',
1866, struck out (indicating that the entry had been read), 'Traill's
Coleridge', 1885, struck out, and 'Coleridge—Course of Lectures—', 1888, not struck out and therefore probably unread. The
last probably refers to the *Lectures and Notes on Shakespeare*, ed.
T. Ashe, London, Bell, 1885 (Bohn's Popular Library); this entry,
along with some others, indicates that Arnold was contemplating
some criticism of Shakespeare before he died. Coleridge's works,
it would seem, were almost defiantly absent from Arnold's direct
cognizance during his mature years. Moreover, Coleridge's name
occurs rarely in letters. That it was generally not present in his
thoughts until Traill's biography reminded him of it is indicated
by its glaring omission in a letter to his mother on Christmas Day,
1867. He says that with respect to carrying forward the work of
modernizing Christianity, Dr. Arnold 'was perhaps the only
powerful Englishman of his day who did so. In fact, he was the
only deeply religious man who had the necessary culture for it.'[29]

If this omission is not merely an act of filial piety (piety of a rather dubious sort from Mrs. Arnold's religious point of view), it is an interesting oversight, the clue to which may lie in the adjective 'powerful'. Where Dr. Arnold's direct and personal as well as literary influence had manifested itself in the careers of Dean Stanley, Matthew Arnold, and a whole generation of Rugbeians—future teachers, clergymen, substantial businessmen—the sage of Highgate may have been seen as wasting himself in gushes of brilliance, like a Roman candle, and influencing such ineffectuals as the mystagogue Joseph Green and the intellectually cloudy Maurice, the most 'popular and eminent' of Coleridge's disciples.[30]

Nevertheless, we are justified in assuming that Arnold did absorb some, perhaps many, of his Coleridgean ideas at first hand, that he had at some time read or read in most of Coleridge's principal prose works and absorbed much from them. His few overt references to Coleridge do cover a wide range: *Aids to Reflection, Confessions of an Inquiring Spirit, Biographia Literaria, On the Constitution of the Church and State, The Friend,* and perhaps the *Literary Remains.*[31] These references are not only relatively few, however, by comparison say with those to Wordsworth, but they are for the most part incidental and even inaccurate, like something dimly remembered. For example, in his preface to Johnson's *Lives of the Poets,* Arnold appeals to Coleridge's authority: 'Poetry has a different logic, as Coleridge said, from prose; poetical style follows another law of evolution than the style of prose.' In fact, Coleridge was not talking about style but about ways of thinking, and he had opposed poetry and science, not poetry and prose. The remaining handful of explicit references do not merit detailed consideration; they are listed in a note.[32]

More important are the many ideas, sometimes expressed in phrasing very similar to Coleridge's, scattered through Arnold's prose works on social, ecclesiastical, and religious matters, which seem to parallel Coleridge. Here, however, we discover that Arnold has given us no clue to follow. This reticence might be attributed to questionable motives in another man, but as I have said, Matthew Arnold was usually scrupulous in letting the reader know the source of his material. Moreover, the evidence from letters, notebooks, and direct reference supports the conclusion that Coleridge was little in Arnold's conscious thought; even in the essay on Joubert (1864) in which Coleridge is discussed, most of the references to him are extremely general while those to Joubert are highly explicit, indicating that Arnold had not freshly studied Coleridge.

The hypothesis which I think best accounts for this peculiar combination of positive and negative evidence is that Arnold, like most of the more serious and talented young men at the Universities around 1840, had hearkened to the voice of Coleridge along with those of Newman, Emerson, and Carlyle; that he had read or read in and discussed with his friends in the Decade[33] the works of Coleridge and other prominent thinkers, ancient and modern; that this collegiate influence may have been reinforced by Dr. Arnold's admiration for 'old Sam'; and that consequently many of Coleridge's ideas and phrases had passed into the texture of Arnold's thought during this highly formative period.[34] Coleridge did not become, as Goethe did, a source of intellectual stimulation to be revisited regularly through later years; very likely Arnold never again did more than look up occasionally some reference in Coleridge's works, if, indeed, his typical inaccuracies permit us to think he went so far. His impression of Coleridge as an important but rambling, disorganized, eccentric, and even premature initiator of modern ideas was probably formed early and he never saw need to return to chaos and old night for the sort of stimulation which lay nearer and more attractively to hand elsewhere. Towards the end of his life, Traill's biography and Arnold's apparent intention to do some critical work on the earlier English writers[35] re-awakened his interest in Coleridge as a critic, and in 1888 he planned to read over Coleridge's lectures. The result might have been an interesting revaluation of the 'd——d Elizabethans', but on Sunday, the 15th of April, 1888, Arnold, in Liverpool to greet his daughter and granddaughter arriving on a visit from America, ignored his hereditary weak heart and in joyful anticipation skipped over a low fence, fell, and died at once.

There remains only to sketch some of the parallels of thought alluded to above. But first we must observe a basic similarity in intellectual temperament which probably underlies many of the similarities in particular areas. The one quality which Arnold and Coleridge most strikingly have in common is the need to see variety reconciled and unified; that 'self-surrender of the mind to the disconnected impresssion of sense' which Shawcross says 'was foreign to Coleridge from the first'[36] was equally foreign to Arnold. Even in a passing comment on a new botany book, Arnold sounds a note which may be heard again and again in his letters, early and late, and in his public writings: 'Hooker's new book ... is delightful. He tends to unify varieties, while Babington tends to multiply them; so to me he is a much more satisfactory man.'[37] This sentiment is echoed over and over in the notebooks in quotations in the ancient and modern languages. In his youth Arnold had felt the attraction to the 'movement and fulness' he associated with Keats, Shelley, Browning, Tennyson, and the Elizabethans, but even then the urge towards unifying varieties, towards organization, centrality, balance, and subordination of parts to whole was a powerful check; perhaps, however, his early attraction to romantic disorder accounts for the vehemence with which he cries, as late as 1865, 'I hate all over-preponderance of single elements.'[38]

This drive toward unity, reconciliation, and balance manifests itself, as he himself said, in everything he did. It may be seen, for example, in his use of the comparative method in literary criticism, a method which Coleridge, too, thought the best way to proceed. It is plainly visible in his attempts to balance and blend Celtic, German, and Latin; Hebraism and Hellenism; religion and science; Christianity and stoicism; Liberalism and Conservatism; and in his religious efforts to preserve the old piety and morality and use them to cement the old institutions and the new learning. Like Coleridge and Dr. Arnold, he saw in the Established Church the unifying principle at least potentially embodied in a living institution.[39] But did the Church in fact represent merely one sect of many? The answer then was not disestablishment, but to broaden the base of the establishment to include perhaps even Catholics and Jews. Did the State in fact represent the interests of a ruling class rather than an abstract principle of unity among all classes? Then do not weaken the State and thereby intensify class warfare, but rather strengthen and broaden the functions of the State as leader and educator, so that it may truly come to represent the whole nation's 'best self'. Similarly, man himself required for his true happiness and fulfilment the balanced and orderly development of all his faculties—moral, intellectual, aesthetic, spiritual, physical—subordinate to an organizing principle; he needed what Arnold summed up in the word 'culture', or what Coleridge had called 'cultivation' defined (in language later echoed by Arnold) as 'the harmonious development of those qualities and faculties that characterize humanity'.[40] Both men looked to the development of a minority of leaders and teachers owing primary allegiance not to a single class of the existing polity, but to the State as a whole, and beyond that to the highest ideals and aspirations of all mankind; this elite group was Coleridge's 'clerisy', and Arnold's 'remnant' of the cultured.

To balance this similarity of intellectual temperament, however, there is an equally striking dissimilarity; if the two men shared the need to seek principles of unity in variety, their approach to the implementation of the principles was quite different. If all men are indeed born either Platonists or Aristotelians, it would be hard to find better examples of the dichotomy than Coleridge and Matthew Arnold. For Coleridge, the unifying principle of phenomena was to be found in the transcendental realm of pure idea; for Arnold, it resided in the Aristotelian mean between extremes, or in a judicious blending of disparate elements. Coleridge distrusted all conclusions not derivable from first principles of speculative metaphysics; he worshipped, though he never succeeded in possessing, system. Arnold, on the contrary, distrusted speculative metaphysics and logic; for systematic thought he had neither capacity nor admiration. Coleridge's passion for metaphysics, based on his faith in the ability of the intuitive reason to know Truth, is countered by Arnold's profound scepticism about ultimate Truth or man's ability to grasp it; in the real world, he believed, its manifestations were always historically and culturally conditioned, and so could be approached only by a discreet balancing and selection of possibilities.

And yet it is one of those characteristic and even trite ironies of human nature that Coleridge was far more a creature *ondoyant et divers* than Matthew Arnold, who copied over and over in his notebooks two maxims from the *De Imitatione Christi* which he seems successfully to have made the guiding principles of his active life: 'Secundum propositum nostrum est cursus profectûs nostri' and 'Semper aliquid certi proponendum est.' This temperamental difference was certainly influential in the formation of Arnold's contemptuous total estimate of Coleridge to be discussed later, but here let us observe how the combination of differences, philosophical and personal, affected the work of each. Coleridge was for ever proposing works of the most gigantic scope. With an almost painful lack of humour or common sense he would envision his encyclopedic Summa, in which all knowledge, mundane and divine, was to be incorporated into one tremendous philosophical system based upon ineluctable first principles. But what he has actually left, though sufficient in bulk to stand as a respectable life's work, is a collection of fragments. That these fragments are often of unexampled brilliance, depth, and scope is of course indisputable, but for all the power of his almost unique genius, he never was able to compose one complete book capable of even slightly satisfying his own conception of wholeness. Arnold, on the other hand, always proposed to himself projects which were strictly limited in scope and directly relevant to a particular situation, and his individual works may consequently suffer from historical obsolescence or from narrowness of approach. Where Coleridge read prodigiously, and had to know everything bearing on a subject before he could say the first word on it, Arnold was prepared for limited conquests with limited means. His characteristic form was the essay, not the multi-volume treatise, although his essays sometimes grew into books, as Coleridge's proposed treatises typically remained essays. With the rarest exceptions, whatever job Arnold proposed to undertake he completed, sometimes brilliantly but almost always at least with distinction.

It would not be fair to Coleridge's gigantic inclusiveness, however, to conclude this brief comparison without recalling that he was no mere visionary. For him, as C. R. Sanders has said,

> Philosophy . . . was not to content itself with flights of speculation having nothing to do with man's practical needs. A true philosophy was 'the power of contemplating particulars in the unit and frontal mirror of the idea'. The ideal philosopher thus brought the light of heaven to bear upon the simplest problems of everyday life. It was the 'two-fold function of philosophy to reconcile religion with common sense, and to elevate common sense into reason'.[41]

In spite of the difference in philosophic approach between Arnold and Coleridge, the latter's concern for the Absolute did not make him forget the pragmatic aspects of religion, and it is here, in fact, that we find the deepest grounds of similarity between the two men. So insistently did Coleridge, like Arnold, base the sanction of religion on the needs of man that Oliver Elton wrote: 'Coleridge might now be termed a kind of "pragmatist", justifying

Christianity by its meetness, as shown by centuries of experience, for the inward needs of mankind.' Similarly, H. N. Fairchild, a less sympathetic critic of Coleridge's religious thought, has wittily remarked: 'For a religion supposed to be in perfect agreement with eternal metaphysical principles, his Christianity is strangely pharmacological—a prescription compounded for a personal disease.'[42] From his position as an orthodox Anglo-Catholic, Fairchild presumably has in mind the two principal objections to the pragmatic 'proof' of the truth of Christianity independent of external verities: that it may too easily be subverted to make man the measure of all things; while on the other side, the argument that a religion perfectly meets man's needs may also be urged as the strongest reason for denying rather than affirming its objective validity. Also it is logically inadmissible to hold, as William James seems to, that since what is true is useful, what is useful must be true, unless, like him, we employ persuasive redefinition to make the terms interchangeable; but then the inference becomes, though valid, tautological and vacuous. Although Coleridge was also aware of these possible objections and tried to meet them head-on by simply denying final jurisdiction in these realms to logic and the 'Understanding', the critic may observe that with respect to the truths of religion, Coleridge's 'Reason' is not always far from James's 'Will to Believe'.[43]

For his part, Arnold met—or avoided—the objections to pragmatism in his own way. Like Coleridge, he believed that the proof by miracles was vain, that it was 'much more safe, . . . as well as much more fruitful, to look for the main confirmation of a religion in its intrinsic correspondence with urgent wants of human nature, in its profound necessity!'[44] Religion, like food, was necessary, hence inevitably good. 'Truth', that is, scientific truth, is here irrelevant; and in the poetic sense, isn't 'true' somehow the same as 'good'? The 'Truths' of religion were, for Arnold, purely and solely emotional truths, to be verified by introspection and experience:

> But if . . . [the masses] ask: 'How are we to verify that there rules an enduring Power, not ourselves, which makes for righteousness?'—we may answer at once: 'How? why, as you verify that fire burns,—by experience! It is so; try it!'[45]

Since these truths assert nothing about the nature of the universe, except by metaphorical projection (I. A. Richards's 'pseudo-statement', or in Arnold's words, language 'thrown out' at moral phenomena which are but dimly apprehended by the intellect), they are susceptible to neither proof nor disproof but only to belief or unbelief. Thus, Arnold did not attempt the metaphysical leap from 'useful' to 'true'; religion is useful. profoundly so, because it is useful, and there is an end of the matter. In areas of fact, where criteria of objective truth may properly be applied, religion was to step aside, fraternally bowing to science. In this way, purifying itself of materialistic, anthropomorphic contamination, religion would not only be behaving decently to the intellect but, more important, would be protecting itself against the conquests of science. This in turn would save religion from obsolescence and neglect, and make its virtues again available to those modern spirits who could no longer accept it on the old terms. A noble reconstructive effort, no doubt, on Arnold's part. But by giving up its claims to absolute and objective truth, surely religion loses its appeal to the multitude who cannot pray to something that they do not believe exists apart from their own feelings and wishes. It becomes, as Arnold said, poetry, and most would add, mere poetry.[46]

Coleridge, in spite of his rejection of the understanding as a final judge, did not by any means wish to adopt the obscurantist posture of excluding it from religious matters altogether. On the contrary, he said, 'Most readily do I admit, that there can be no contrariety between revelation and the understanding.'[47] He was in agreement with Dr. Arnold's position, that 'the understanding has its proper work to do with respect to the Bible, because the Bible consists of human writings and contains human history',[48] and believed that on the highest level the truths of the understanding could not conflict with the truths of Reason. This, indeed, is the cornerstone of his entire system. However, he insisted on the will as the primary fact of consciousness, and like Newman argued that assent was antecedent to understanding in religious matters: '*Unless ye believe*, says the prophet, *ye can not understand*. Suppose (what is at least possible) that the facts should be consequent on the belief, it is clear that without the belief the materials, on which the understanding is to exert itself, would be wanting.' Consequently, he tests doctrine by asking of it, 'Will the belief tend to the improvement of my moral or intellectual faculties?' Or he exclaims, 'evidences of Christianity! I am weary of the word. Make a man feel the want of it; rouse him, if you can, to the self-know-ledge of the need of it; and you may safely trust to its own evidence. . . .' Imagining a troubled reader of unformed faith asking of the tenets of Christianity, 'How can I comprehend this? How is this to be proved?' Coleridge replies: 'To the first question I should answer: Christianity is not a theory, or a speculation; but a life; not a philosophy of life, but a life and a living process. To the second: TRY IT.'[49] Coleridge had too profound a sense of sin and was too much an orthodox theologian to rest on this pragmatic level; it was impossible for him not to make the leap to the super-natural.[50] But in so far as he is dealing with religion as it operates in the world of man, his pragmatic attitudes, and even their expression, are very similar to Arnold's.

Like Coleridge, Arnold argued that Christianity proved its value and what he called its deep human truth in practice. He agreed with Coleridge, who argued that stoicism was inadequate because it ignored or suppressed feelings, while the 'especial aim' and 'characteristic operation' of Christianity 'is to moralize the affec-tions'. But Arnold turned this phrase of Coleridge's upside down in his characterization of religion as 'Morality touched [or: lighted up] by emotion'.[51] Christianity was more than mere morality for Arnold because it not only taught righteousness, it inculcated the *love* of righteousness; it appealed not only to the intellect but to the whole man. Coleridge's quotation from St. Augustine:

> 'In Cicero, and Plato, and other such writers', says he, 'I meet with many things that excite a certain warmth of emotion, but in none of them do I find these words, *Come unto me, all ye that labor, and are heavy laden, and I will give you rest.*'[52]

may be put beside such passages from Arnold as his comparison of the Spinozistic ideal and the Christian:

> Between the two conditions there is all the difference which there is between the being in love, and the following, with delighted comprehension, a reasoning of Plato.[53]

Observing in passing that Coleridge is far more nearly exempt than Arnold from the criticism of F. H. Bradley that 'it is not *any* emotion that touches morality and translates it into religion', but only a specifically *religious* emotion,[54] I here remind myself of the limitations I have imposed on this discussion. Perhaps enough has been presented to indicate how Matthew Arnold, while ignoring or rejecting the metaphysical foundation of Coleridge's thought (but Arnold would probably have called it a superstructure), was able to absorb probably by both conscious and unconscious selection much that was useful to him. This was particularly true with respect to Bible interpretation and the pragmatic aspects of religion.[55] It is likely, as I have suggested, that Arnold's failure to give more credit to Coleridge was due to his having absorbed Coleridge's teachings early in life, so that they became quite interfused with his own thought. Another possible reason, however, was his feeling of repugnance to Coleridge as a man. Like Coleridge, he believed that by their moral fruits shall religious teachings be known: 'He that saith, I know him, and keepeth not his commandments, is a liar, and the truth is not in him.'[56] But whatever the reason or combination of reasons for Arnold's putting Coleridge out of his consciousness, the fact remains that for him as for all English thought and letters in the nineteenth century, Coleridge was a significant and fructifying influence.

IV. LITERARY CRITICISM

If, by comparison with corresponding portions of the other chapters, this discussion of Arnold's literary criticism of Coleridge and Shelley seems disproportionately small, the defect is inherent in the materials. In the first place, Arnold's most widely remembered comments on these poets are personal rather than literary. Secondly, he never attempted a solid critical study of either. His total criticism of Coleridge's poetry amounts to nothing more than an almost reluctant recognition that he had written a few brilliant poems, and that he had the reputation of an eminent poet. But Arnold had no sympathy with the cult of isolated and limited perfectionism which was one aspect of Victorian aestheticism; he demanded of any poet who was to claim serious attention and high rank a large, solid, and varied body of work. Shelley, of course, offered or was thought to offer such a body of work, and in spite of his belief that Shelley had failed, Arnold recognized his claim to critical attention. Towards the end of his life Arnold planned to write an essay on Shelley's poetry, but although the project was prevented by death, he has left enough

incidental comment in his letters and essays for us to recon-
struct generally what his overall critical judgement might have
been.

Arnold's one specific comment on Coleridge's poetry occurs in
his Byron preface. There he bowed to the conventional reputation
of *Christabel, Kubla Khan, The Rime of the Ancient Mariner*, and
perhaps *Lewti* and the two famous odes on France and Dejection,
by admitting that 'There are poems of Coleridge and of Keats
equal, if not superior, to anything of Byron or Wordsworth; but a
dozen pages or two will contain them, and the remaining poetry is
of a quality much inferior.'[57] Arnold's demand for a substantial
body of work may be contrasted with Swinburne's view. In his
angry rebuttal, Swinburne did not disagree with the factual part
of Arnold's remark, except that he would have been unequivocal
in using the word 'superior'. For him, however, the implications
were completely different. He believed that the chief task of a
singer was to sing, and that if Coleridge had made only one poem
in his life, but that one of finer quality than anything of Wordsworth's, he would not have hesitated to give Coleridge the higher
rank. The same similarity in factual judgement but opposition of
taste and tendency may be seen in Arnold's and Swinburne's
opinions of Shelley.[58] Both agreed on the primacy of music in
Shelley's verse, but where this is a principal factor of his greatness
for Swinburne, to Arnold it was evidence that Shelley was on the
wrong track. This comparison perhaps illustrates, incidentally,
that however much Arnold struggled against his age in his views
of the function of poetry, he was very much of his time in his
apprehension of its stuff, its texture. If he differed strenuously
with, say, Swinburne on the value of what they found, he never-
the less tended to look for and find the same things in what he
read, except that Swinburne showed, if anything, a greater
catholicity of taste and appreciation for kinds of poetry not his
own. This conventional side of Arnold's taste is shown in the
drawing-room-table-anthology flavour of his list in 'Wordsworth'
of 'our chief poetical names', in which list Coleridge is included.
Aside from Chaucer, Shakespeare, and Milton, these names are:
Spenser, Dryden, Pope, Gray, Goldsmith, Cowper, Burns,
Coleridge, Scott, Campbell, Moore, Byron, Shelley, Keats, and
above all these, Wordsworth. The inclusion of such names as
those of Cowper, Scott, Campbell, and Moore, or even Dryden,

Pope, and Gray, makes it clear that we are not to take very seriously the presence of Coleridge's.

It is notable that in Arnold's nearest approach to a critique of Coleridge, in 'Joubert', he mentions only once in passing that Coleridge was a poet, but this incidental fact was evidently not important enough to count as a differentiating factor between him and his French counterpart. Like Joubert, Coleridge is praised for maintaining as a religious philosopher his 'perfect independence of mind'. Outwardly they were similar—both renowned talkers, desultory and incomplete writers. Their inward and true likenesses were these: both were passionately devoted to reading and thinking 'out of the beaten line' of their day; both studied ardently 'old literature, poetry, and the metaphysics of religion'; both were students of language; and both were conservative in religion and politics, in reaction to a narrow, shallow, and vulgar sort of liberalism. The essence of their similarity is 'that they both had from nature an ardent impulse for seeking the genuine truth on all matters they thought about, and a gift for finding it and recognising it when it was found'.

Here, indeed, seems to be high praise. But what did Coleridge do with his priceless gift? His work, though 'abundant and varied', is finally so full of defects that Arnold exclaims, in one of his weaker moments of prophecy, 'How little either of his poetry, or of his criticism, or of his philosophy, can we expect permanently to stand!' What will stand is the stimulus of his example, an example of continual effort 'to get at and lay bare the real truth of the matter in hand, whether that matter were literary or philosophical, or political, or religious', at a time when such an effort of intellectual liberation, such a critical effort ('to see the thing as in itself it really is') was practically unknown in England. Although the works will not last, the stimulus of this example will 'as long as the need for it continues'. But somehow, although Arnold does not say as much, his tone implies that the need may not continue much longer now that the muse of criticism has put aside Coleridge's 'smoke and turbid vehemence' in favour of Arnold's urbanity and unction.

The substance of Arnold's criticism of Coleridge, then, consists of high praise for his gifts and for the relevance of his way of working, but a very moderate estimate of the tangible results. Coleridge at last falls behind in the comparison with Joubert for several reasons. If Coleridge had more 'power and richness', Joubert had more 'tact and penetration. He was more *possible* than Coleridge; his doctrine was more intelligible than Coleridge's, more receivable.' Partly this was due to Joubert's greater clarity of expression, partly to his greater clarity of thought and a 'keener sense of what was absurd'. (One imagines Arnold writing an essay on Coleridge's prose style, deftly quoting Coleridge's maxim 'Let distinctness in expression advance side by side with distinctness in thought' and juxtaposing it to some particularly turgid passage bristling with subject, object, pentad, etc.) Partly, too, perhaps even mainly, Coleridge's succcess was limited by personal faults, and Arnold takes pains to emphasize in 'Joubert' his moral disapproval of Coleridge. But at least some of the fault lay in his environment; he had the disadvantage of living at Highgate instead of Paris, of being a pioneer 'voyaging through strange seas of thought, alone', while Joubert lived and worked in the city that had not yet for Arnold degenerated from the capital of light to the capital of lubricity. Because Coleridge had attempted in his prose to move in the main stream of modern thought, as Byron and Shelley had attempted to do in their poetry, Coleridge, like them, is at least valuable as example, stimulus, and object lesson. But the permanent value of his work, like theirs, was impaired both by personal defect and (the theme of *Essays in Criticism*) by the want of an adequate national intellectual environment.

Arnold's literary criticism of Shelley was more considerable, although his opinion of Shelley as a literary man was more devastatingly negative even than his judgement of Coleridge. Two general views of Shelley competed during the nineteenth century, and for that matter still do. Some readers emphasized his moral and didactic side; they saw in him a poet of liberty, a teacher, or a prophet-seer-mythopoet. Those who held this view were inclined to be contemptuous of another group who found intoxication in Shelley's word magic and insisted that his music and colour were more important than his ideas in just the proportion that consummate poets were vastly more rare than men of ideas. The first view has two characteristic dangers. First, the poet may be appreciated for those works whose doctrine is most pleasing to the reader, and the result may be such critical curiosities as G. B. Shaw's opinion that *Queen Mab* is a great poem, while *Prometheus Unbound* is a 'boyish indiscretion'.[59] The correlative danger is that the critic who finds Shelley's ideas repugnant may, like T. S. Eliot, reject him out of hand as a poet on these grounds alone. Those who hold the second view, on the other hand—for example, Swinburne and an anonymous reviewer Arnold quoted in his notebooks[60]—risk delivering their poet into the hands of critics of the high seriousness persuasion who, like Arnold, demand of poetry solid substance related to the real world, and are unsympathetic to sheer lyricism of whatever quality. There has been an increasing tendency in modern criticism to fuse the two points of view and, as Yeats did, consider Shelley's poetic techniques and his thought in intimate relation. Nevertheless, examination of specific critiques usually reveals a leaning more or less distinct in one direction or the other. Matthew Arnold never quite settled on either side, or to be more accurate, he argued that Shelley had tried to be both prophet and singer, and had failed at both. On the side of ideas, or what corresponds roughly to Arnold's category of 'moral interpretation', Shelley was incoherent himself, and like his contemporaries he lacked an adequate cultural milieu. On the side of expression, which corresponds more or less with 'naturalistic interpretation', he lacked the intellectual force to master the medium of words apart from their sounds.[61]

Arnold's earliest public utterance on Shelley was the well-known passage in *Stanzas from the Grande Chartreuse*:

> What boots it, Shelley! that the breeze
> Carried thy lovely wail away,
> Musical through Italian trees
> Which fringe the soft blue Spezzian bay?
> Inheritors of thy distress
> Have restless hearts one throb the less?

As is so often true of Arnold's criticism in verse, this stanza is a remarkably complete summary of all his later views on the same subject. Arnold conveys here his notion of Shelley's poetry as (1) sad, (2) evanescent, (3) lovely (hence, not powerful), (4) musical, inarticulate, infantile ('wail'),[62] and (5) ineffectual. The words of the stanza emphasize Shelley's lyricism, but the question in the last two lines, and the general context of the passage, indicate Arnold's awareness of Shelley's claim to recognition as a prophet-teacher. Consequently, these lines offer a convenient entry to Arnold's opinions on this aspect of Shelley.

The lines in *Stanzas from the Grande Chartreuse,* and the corresponding remark in 'Heinrich Heine' about Shelley's modernity, do not imply any serious criticism of Shelley's ideas as such. Certainly Arnold thought many of them naïve, shallow ('nonsense about tyrants and priests' is the phrase Arnold used in 'Shelley'), even repugnant. But at least on his rationalist side Shelley's intentions were good; he was 'modern'. Furthermore, in two specific areas he was, if extreme, on the side of the angels from Arnold's point of view: socially, in his belief in eventual democracy, the abolition of tyranny, and the ultimate enlightenment of mankind; and religiously, in his belief that the dogmas of the old supernatural religion were no longer viable and must be replaced or reinterpreted. But if Arnold approved of some of the substance of Shelley's thought, with his modes of thought Arnold was quite unsympathetic. Arnold's intellectual temper was too pragmatic for him to accept either the methods or the conclusions of radical rationalism. He trusted the experience of mankind more than he trusted its reason. Arnold, schooled by Burke, Coleridge, and his father, believed in the value and significance of history, while Shelley did not; Shelley shared the typical utopian radical's view that the lesson of history was a long tale of error and wickedness on the part of the rich and powerful, the ecclesiastical and secular lords of the earth. Especially Arnold felt the inadequacy of the substitutes offered by modern liberalism for traditional religion. The ideas it offered to take the place of moribund Christianity were either vague ('Justice', 'Revolution') or jejune and mere machinery ('unit of administration', 'gradual suppression of privilege', 'equal taxation').[63] Like Coleridge, Arnold in both politics and religion liked to think of himself as feeling 'sincere sympathy with the good which is at the bottom of ... received opinions'.[64] Unless new ideas could be reconciled with traditional values, they were worse than useless: 'It is one of the hardest tasks in the world to make new intellectual ideas harmonise truly with the religious life, to place them in their right light for that life.'[65] Shelley, although possessed of the 'new intellectual ideas', was, as a rationalist, too radical in his manner of working to please Matthew Arnold.

With the transcendental aspect of Shelley's thought, however, Arnold was even less sympathetic. Much of my demonstration will have to be based on inference from general comments or remarks Arnold made on other writers, using these to gloss the few brief sentences on Shelley. We know that in general Arnold's way of striving for unity was the way of simplification, mediation, and reconciliation, not the way of transcendence. In the infinite he saw only confusion. His impatience with Amiel indicates something of what he might have said of Shelley in the critique he did not live to write:

> The desire for the all, the impatience with what is partial and limited, the fascination of the infinite, are the topics of page after page in [Amiel's] Journal. It is a prosaic mind which has never been in contact with ideas of this sort, never felt their charm. They lend themselves well to poetry, but what are we to say of their value as ideas to be lived with, dilated on, made the governing ideas of life? Except for use in passing, and with the power to dismiss them again, they are unprofitable. Shelley's
>
> > 'Life like a dome of many-coloured glass
> > Stains the white radiance of eternity
> > Until death tramples it to fragments'
>
> has value as a splendid image nobly introduced in a beautiful and impassioned poem. But Amiel's 'coloured air-bubble', as a positive piece of 'speculative intuition', has no value whatever. Nay, the thoughts which have positive truth and value, the thoughts to be lived with and dwelt upon, the thoughts which are a real acquisition for our minds, are precisely thoughts which counteract the 'vague aspiration and indeterminate desire' possessing Amiel and filling his Journal.[66]

Arnold's own notebooks are full of such schoolmasterish 'ideas to live with' as 'Semper aliquid certi proponendum est', ideas (in his own words a page later in the essay on Amiel) 'staunchly counteracting and reducing the power of the infinite and indeterminate, not paralysing us with it'. A similar attitude may be found in the much earlier essay on Joubert, and in the letters to Clough, *passim*; it was one of Arnold's most deeply rooted attitudes and certainly contributed to his impression of Shelley's ineffectuality. In 'Joubert', Arnold admitted that one may enjoy visit to the infinite, but insisted that it was not a healthy home-site. He approvingly quotes Joubert on Plato: 'Plato loses himself in the void . . . but one sees the play of his wings, one hears their rustle. . . . It is good to breathe his air, but not to live upon him.' The language, of course, anticipates Arnold's famous line on Shelley, 'beautiful and ineffectual angel, beating in the void his luminous wings in vain'.[67] Arnold had little understanding of Plato, and certainly no realization of how richly saturated Shelley's poetry was with his philosophy. Even if Arnold could have known how profound a Platonist Shelley was, it is doubtful that he would have been favourably impressed. His temperamental anti-Platonism probably made him incapable of being a very sympathetic reader of Shelley.

I have already commented in several places upon how far even Arnold, the apostle of poetry-as-religion, was from possessing the high faith in the imagination shown by all the major Romantics but Byron, and so will not dwell here upon the obvious implications of the passage on Amiel quoted above. However, even though Arnold is inconsistent in seeming to imply that untrue ideas may be poetically valid and attractive without necessarily damaging the poetry, he nevertheless believed that the habit of indulging one's yearning towards the infinite would certainly harm a poet's work. True, such a yearning might co-operate with a striving for richness of language and imagery to help produce, as in Shelley, 'snatches and fragments' of great value.[68] But although one might enjoy, even love, these fragmentary spoils of raids on the infinite, no one of mature mind should confuse them with the great works of abiding value; as Arnold said of John Tauler, 'I love the mystics, but what I find best in them is their golden single sentences, not the whole conduct of their argument and the result of their work.'[69] In modern times especially, great poetry demands the fusion of true feeling with true thought; the imagination must be disciplined by the intellect's understanding of things as they are. Arnold found, for example, that 'the *Hang zum Unbegrenztem*, the straining after the unlimited, . . . made it impossible for Byron to produce poetic wholes such as the *Tempest* or *Lear*'.[70] German poetry, Goethe's poetry, by 'going near the ground', has been most successful in speaking to and for the modern world. Just as Arnold failed to understand that Keats had not merely given 'himself up to a sensuous genius', but had been groping as a poet towards philosophic truth, so he seems to have misunderstood Shelley. 'No one', he wrote to his mother in 1865, 'has a stronger and more abiding sense than I have of the "daemonic" element—as Goethe called it—which underlies and encompasses our life; but I think, as Goethe thought, that the right thing is, while conscious of this element, and of all that there is inexplicable round one, to keep pushing on one's posts into the darkness, and to establish no post that is not perfectly in light and firm. One gains nothing on the darkness by being, like Shelley, as incoherent as the darkness itself.'[71] Arnold may have apprehended something of the importance of the 'daemonic' element in Shelley, but he probably did not know of Shelley's own devotion to Goethe, nor did he grasp that, whatever Shelley's success, his whole life was a quest for philosophic reality, not a surrender to darkness.

In spite of a certain amount of praise for Shelley's modernity, then, Arnold did not really admire any aspect of Shelley's thought. He found Shelley not only deficient in command of thought, but also in command of language. Indeed, Arnold never really liked Shelley the writer much in any way, but he shared much of the going Victorian attitude of reverence and love for Shelley's personality and hence was all the more disappointed to learn finally that Shelley also lacked command of self. Arnold's low opinion of Shelley as an artist is expressed repeatedly in his letters; his basic attitude toward Shelley is very well summed up in one of 1854. In that year Mme. Blaze de Bury, under the pen name 'Arthur Dudley', published a review of the poems of Matthew Arnold and Alexander Smith as the second of a series of three articles entitled 'Du Mouvement poétique en Angleterre depuis Shelley'. In a rather confused and arbitrary way she seemed to find that all modern English poetry stemmed from Shelley, with Matthew Arnold as his principal disciple. Arnold protested in a letter to Sainte-Beuve that he hoped the authoress' English origin (she was Scottish, née Rose Stuart) would not abuse her French readers about the strength of Shelley's influence or his true rank among English poets. By way of setting the record straight Arnold gives his own evaluation of Shelley:

> Shelley était, sans doute, un homme très remarquable: mais c'était plutôt un homme, un être, extrêmement intéressant, qu'un grand artiste: et jamais il n'a commandé ni l'attention ni la sympathie du grand nombre des lecteurs. D'ailleurs il est mort très jeune, et sans être (*sic*) atteint à la pleine maturité de son talent. Parler de lui comme d'un *maître* et le préférer hautement à Byron (que M. Arthur Dudley, du reste, traite un peu sans façon, en le qualifiant du titre d' '*esprit léger*')—c'est simplement ridicule.[72]

Nine years later, in 'Maurice de Guérin', Arnold explained a little more amply what made Shelley so interesting as a man, so weak as a poet. Discussing the two kinds of poetic interpretation, moral and naturalistic, Arnold comments that in those poets who unite both powers—Lucretius, Wordsworth, Shakespeare—the moral 'usually ends by making itself the master'. In Shelley, however,

> there is not a balance of the two gifts, nor even a co-existence of them, but there is a passionate straining after them both, and this is what makes Shelley, as a man, so interesting: I will not now inquire how much Shelley achieves as a poet, but whatever he achieves, he in general fails to achieve natural magic in his expression; in Mr. Palgrave's charming *Treasury* may be seen a gallery of his failures.[73]

So much for poor Shelley as a poet; as incoherent as he is in thought, if he does not achieve natural magic in his expression, then his case is indeed a desperate one. In his lyric poetry, where his musical gift might be expected to carry him through, Arnold will not allow that he was sufficiently master of his own mind to be a master of words; in a footnote Arnold manages to turn even praise of Shelley's musical ability into utter damnation of his poetry:

> Compare, for example, his 'Lines Written in the Euganean Hills', with Keats's 'Ode to Autumn'. . . . The latter piece *renders* Nature; the former *tries to render her*. I will not deny, however, that Shelley has natural magic in his rhythm; what I deny is, that he has it in his language. It always seems to me that the right sphere for Shelley's genius was the sphere of music, not of poetry; the medium of sounds he can master, but to master the more difficult medium of words he has neither intellectual force enough nor sanity enough.[74]

Arnold's language may be a little strong, but it cannot be denied that there sometimes occur in Shelley's verse shocking examples of divorce between sound and meaning. Even *Prometheus Unbound*, which is generally recognized as Shelley's masterwork of both philosophy and poetry, is occasionally defaced by passages like

> Years after years
> Through blood and tears,
> And a thick hell of hatreds, and hopes, and fears.
> [Act IV, ll. 117–19]

Admittedly the lines are taken out of context, but the metrical portrayal of pretty little girls dancing in a ring submerges whatever the words are trying to say.

It will be observed that most of Arnold's animadversions on Shelley's verse have a strikingly modern ring—incoherence of thought and imagery, divorce between music and meaning, and general vaporousness. His remark in a letter to Alfred Austin that the lines in *Prometheus Unbound* beginning 'My soul is an enchanted boat' are 'little more than musical verbiage' is characteristic, and may be compared with a recent writer's calling the same lyric 'at the most, perhaps, a pretty piece of flummery' belonging to 'a faded world of album verse'.[75] Reviewing Stopford Brooke's *Primer of English Literature* in 1877, Arnold again called Shelley 'a most interesting and attractive personage', but regretted that so much space was given him in a small book. With approval he quoted Brooke on Shelley's lyrics: 'They form together the most sensitive, the most imaginative, and the most musical, but the least tangible lyrical poetry we possess',[76] and we can almost see Arnold mentally underlining *least tangible*. In 'The Study of Poetry' Arnold recommended Burns as an antidote to the vaporousness of 'that beautiful spirit building his many coloured haze of words and images

"Pinnacled dim in the intense inane." '[77]

On the other hand, except for a vague suggestion in 'Shelley' that Shelley's poetry was injured by his lack of humour and his power of self-delusion, Arnold did not complain of Shelley's lapses of tone, especially into self-dramatizing shrillness or self-pity. Perhaps this omission was merely intended as charitable restraint (who breaks a butterfly upon a wheel?), or perhaps, as I have suggested above, it represents an actual deaf-spot in Arnold which accounts for similar lapses in his own poetry. At any rate, this is the only important way in which Arnold failed to anticipate what modern hostile critics of Shelley have had to say.

In 1881, in his 'Byron' preface, Arnold wrote what turned out to be his last words of literary criticism of Shelley. Since these few sentences make up the most nearly complete critique Arnold was to write, and also contain his most famous remarks on Shelley, I shall quote them fully:

... I cannot think that Shelley's poetry, except by snatches and fragments, has the value of the good work of Wordsworth and

Byron; or that it is possible for even Mr. Stopford Brooke to make up a volume of selections from him which, for real substance, power, and worth, can at all take rank with a like volume from Byron or Wordsworth.

Shelley knew quite well the difference between the achievement of such a poet as Byron and his own. He praises Byron too unreservedly, but he sincerely felt, and he was right in feeling, that Byron was a greater poetical power than himself. As a man, Shelley is at a number of points immeasurably superior; he is a beautiful and enchanting spirit, whose vision, when we call it up, has far more loveliness, more charm for our soul, than the vision of Byron. But all the personal charm of Shelley cannot hinder us from at last discovering in his poetry the incurable want, in general, of a sound subject-matter, and the incurable fault, in consequence, of unsubstantiality.

(Later in the essay we learn that Byron's topics, by contrast, 'were not Queen Mab, and the Witch of Atlas, and the Sensitive Plant—they were the upholders of the old order, George the Third and Lord Castlereagh and the Duke of Wellington and Southey, and they were the canters and tramplers of the great world, and they were his enemies and himself.') To continue with Shelley:

Those who extol him as the poet of clouds, the poet of sunsets, are only saying that he did not, in fact, lay hold upon the poet's right subject-matter; and in honest truth, with all his charm of soul and spirit, and with all his gift of musical diction and movement, he never, or hardly ever, did. Except, as I have said, for a few short things and single stanzas, his original poetry is less satisfactory than his translations, for in these the subject-matter was found for him. Nay, I doubt whether his delightful Essays and Letters, which deserve to be far more read than they are now, will not resist the wear and tear of time better, and finally come to stand higher, than his poetry.

In concluding the essay, Arnold says of Wordsworth, Byron, and Keats: 'I for my part can never think of equalling with them any other of their contemporaries;—either Coleridge, poet and philosopher wrecked in a mist of opium; or Shelley, beautiful and ineffectual angel, beating in the void his luminous wings in vain.'[78]

Swinburne, in his lengthy essay 'Wordsworth and Byron', has performed so slashing and thorough a dissection of Arnold's criticism in his essays on Keats, Wordsworth, and Byron, that there is really nothing to add in the way of destructive analysis.[79] However, a few of Arnold's more striking inconsistencies may be summarized here. First, the passages quoted above from 'Byron' show Arnold's continued affection for Shelley the man, an affection seriously damaged later but not totally vitiated even by Dowden's biography. He admits that Shelley is 'at a number of points immeasurably Byron's superior' as a man. Yet, he insists that Byron is a better poet than any of his contemporaries but Wordsworth and the basis of Byron's superiority turns out to be his personality, for he is neither artist nor thinker. Apparently, then, Arnold's admiration for force is enough to overcome his moralism, so that the dynamic Satan becomes as a poet more important than the beautiful angel. Secondly, the comments on subject-matter seem almost wilfully wrong-headed. Surely the poet of the New Sirens, Empedocles, Balder, and the Forsaken Merman, and the author of the 1853 Preface, had no call to praise Byron for writing about such up-to-the-minute-subjects as Wellington and Castlereagh, and to disparage Shelley for choosing to embody his themes in mythic subjects. Furthermore, Arnold seems to contradict his earlier tribute to Shelley as a poet who, like Byron, had at least tried seriously to cope with modern problems; perhaps to strengthen his case for Byron, he was willing to forget that Shelley was at least as interested in the modern world as Byron, and was certainly more profound in his thinking about it. If Shelley is ineffectual as a poet, it is surely not because he chose subjects that were not out of the newspapers, but because of whatever he did or failed to do with the subjects he did choose. Arnold's earlier criticism, as usual, seems more accurate in his recognition there that Shelley was not a mere aesthetic Ariel, but a man 'passionately straining' after the two gifts of naturalistic and moral interpretation. Another and related objectionable feature of Arnold's critique is his device of setting up a lay figure for demolition, one of his favourite rhetorical tricks. Swinburne compares Arnold to Jeffrey in this, and impugns Arnold's sincerity, since surely he cannot

affect to imagine that 'those who extol him as the poet of clouds, the poet of sunsets,'—if any there be whose estimate of his poetry is based exclusively or mainly on their value for such attributes of his genius—are in any truer or fitter sense to be accepted as representatives of Shelley's real admirers, than are those sickly

drivellers over the name of another great poet, the fulsome worshippers of weakness whose nauseous adoration Mr. Arnold has so
justly rebuked, to be fairly accepted as representatives of those
who share his admiration for the genius of Keats.[80]

Equally ridiculous and unjust, says Swinburne, is Arnold's citation
of *Queen Mab* as an adequate and representative specimen of
Shelley's work. Indeed, there is no sentence of Arnold's Shelley
criticism that has not been subjected to controversion, usually
exacerbated, by Swinburne and later defenders of Shelley—Alfred
Austin, Quiller-Couch, Saintsbury, A. C. Bradley, and Mrs.
Campbell, to name some of the more prominent. But probably
enough has already been said to convince even the reader who
agrees with Arnold's conclusions that, as so regrettably often in
his late criticism, he did not have his eye very certainly on the
object in the details of his argument. It would be a thankless
operation to complete the examination microscopically.

Bearing in mind that Arnold himself felt in his last years that
he had been unjust to Shelley, let us excise the elements of praise
we find in his various comments on Shelley and imagine how they
would have been developed to redress the balance. It is unlikely
that Arnold would have revised his estimate very greatly; he was
not much given to changing his mind, and his criticism of Shelley
as we have it is remarkably consistent from first to last. However,
if we imagine the emphasis somewhat shifted in favour of Shelley,
we should probably still find that it is as a man—or rather spirit—
that Shelley exerts his greatest appeal, in spite of Dowden's
revelations. Instead of harping on Shelley's faults, Arnold would
have dwelt on the elements of 'loveliness' and 'charm' and
'enchantment' in Shelley's personality—his generosity, his
modesty, his moral and physical courage, and even, in spite of his
'inflammability', his distaste for impure thought and language; but
over and above these mundane virtues, his soaring idealism and
visionary hopes for mankind. Arnold might have recalled his own
earlier criticism and given some praise to Shelley's passionate
devotion to modern ideas, especially in the areas of religion and
politics. His evaluation of Shelley as a poetical craftsman would
probably not have been much altered, although Mrs. Iris Sells
tells of a letter from Arnold to a nephew in Tasmania in which
he revised his verdict on Shelley.[81] With mixed admiration and
antipathy he might have brought out Shelley's exuberance of

imagination, and very likely would have too unreservedly praised Shelley's metrical capabilities. Shelley's architectonics he could not have said much for, but among the longer poems he probably would have had some praise for *Adonais* and, to judge from its recurrence on the late reading lists, *Prometheus Unbound*; here he might have remarked upon the advantages of following classical models while regretting that, at least in the case of *Prometheus Unbound*, Shelley had not stayed closer to them. My imagination boggles at the vision of Arnold, by now the arch-foe of sexual irregularity, trying to cope with *The Cenci*. He probably would have ignored this play, or at most animadverted upon Shelley's defection from the classics because of the unfortunate influence of the Elizabethans and Jacobeans upon modern poets. We could expect skilful quotation of some of Shelley's isolated felicities, perhaps along with some lapses from the same works to illustrate both Shelley's genius and its failure to endure sustained flight. Shelley's poetic translations would be praised but with the reservation probably that in their richness they are un-Greek; the prose translations from Plato Arnold would have praised more enthusiastically (he quoted Shelley's translation of the *Symposium* in his notebooks), and this might have provided the opportunity for a graceful excursus on Plato which would have infuriated followers of that philosopher for ever after, since Arnold would probably with some condescension have confessed to enjoying the beauty of Plato's ideas, but refused to give them serious consideration as true philosophy. Finally, he might have expanded his good word for Shelley's essays and letters. Some of the latter he did quote approvingly in 'Shelley'; they were at least, unlike Keats's, the letters of a gentleman. Of the essays, Arnold might be expected to find most interesting and satisfying the 'Defence of Poetry' and the fragmentary 'Essay on Christianity'. Somewhere near the end of our imaginary critique we should probably find Arnold quoting with approval Shelley's line that 'poets are the unacknowledged legislators of the world'. He would have remarked regretfully that Shelley, because of his temperamental and intellectual limitations, and because of the wretched state of early nineteenth-century English culture, was unable to live up to his own high vision of the prophetic calling of the poet, but he would have concluded that nevertheless, even in his failure, Shelley had provided an instructive and inspiring example.

V. THE PERSONAL ESTIMATE

It would be pleasant to end this chapter on the note of reconciliation struck at the close of the preceding section. But Arnold did not live to write his essay on Shelley's poetry, and the last word he did write was an angry and disgusted review of Shelley's *Life*—and life. Like the essay on Keats of six years earlier, it was stimulated mainly by the recent revelation of unpleasant aspects of the subject's personality, in the one case, by the letters to Fanny Brawne, in the other, by Dowden's *Life of Shelley*. But where Arnold had made a serious attempt to achieve judicial balance on Keats, in the Shelley essay he gave himself almost entirely to making an angry and unbalanced delineation of the cracks in the fallen idol, with only a brief and half-hearted attempt at rehabilitation. In spite of the assertion near the end of the piece that 'we have come back again, at last, to our original Shelley', we obviously have not, and the very last word is depreciatory. Because Arnold's moral judgements on their personalities played so important a part in his criticism of both Shelley and Coleridge, and because these judgements are so well-remembered, I have reserved this subject for separate discussion here.

Arnold's basic objection to both Coleridge and Shelley was that they were irresponsible. On Coleridge, there was never the least equivocation; but also this attitude toward Shelley emerges even from Arnold's praise, in his evocation of Shelley as 'an enchanting spirit', an angel too beautiful for real life, and this even before Dowden had set his teeth on edge. At best, Shelley was for Arnold an Ariel, no more substantial or accountable than Shakespeare's or Pope's sprites, and his song was as lovely and meaningless as, in Pope's description of the sylphs, the 'colours that change whene'er they wave their wings'. He was a charming figure, and on the whole a trivial one. But triviality takes on a more sombre hue when this airy creature is confronted with real life problems, especially in the relations between the sexes, and he behaves not like Arnold's conception of an English gentleman, but rather as one of the little people might indeed be expected to behave. As for Coleridge, Arnold never showed signs of anything but contempt for a man who could live on others, leave his family's support to his friends, and escape from both the responsibilities and the guilt, while simultaneously destroying his talents, by drowning himself in a sodden mist of opium. And as the last indignity, both Shelley and Coleridge compounded their irresponsibility by self-delusion. Coleridge constantly proposed in all seriousness grandiose literary schemes, impossible even were he a healthy and disciplined worker; immersing himself in religion, his genius could become a very fountain of truths, but he could not amend his life. Shelley, for his part, could always convince himself that what he did or what he wanted was right, because he did it or because he wanted it. Especially as regards women, he could convince himself that each new attachment was true love, and with equal ease put aside the old, but with not even the honesty of a libertine like Byron, who neither apologized nor extenuated but callously took what was offered him. No, Shelley could and did convince himself that what he did was right, and was in accord with true morality and true philosophy. These, in summary, seem to have been Arnold's views, and whatever their degree of accuracy, they undoubtedly were instrumental in causing him to depreciate unduly the literary accomplishments of Shelley and Coleridge. Like Milton, and indeed like Shelley himself, it seems, Arnold believed that a poet's life should be a perfect poem—and moreover a poem which would have been acceptable to the moral standards of Dr. Arnold and 'clerical and respectable Oxford'.[82]

As for Coleridge, Arnold's opinion was by no means unusual in the nineteenth century; in fact, only in slighting Coleridge's poetry does Arnold seem to differ from the general attitude. His picture of the 'poet and philosopher wrecked in a mist of opium' was like Leslie Stephen's, and must not have seemed unusually harsh when even Coleridge's disciples were likely to see in him mainly the excess of glory obscured. Julius Hare, for example, while defending his master against De Quincey's attacks, seemed to admire Coleridge's intellect in what C. R. Sanders calls 'an antenatal state'; typically he described it as 'a wreck', 'dark', 'extinct', and 'burnt out'.[83] Carlyle's views were similar but much harsher, and his influence on Matthew Arnold should not be underestimated in spite of Arnold's eventual revulsion against him. Another view of Coleridge with which Arnold was certainly familiar was that he had degenerated from poetry into metaphysical speculation, and this interpretation would have been so congenial to Arnold that the only probable reason for his not having expressed it himself is that he devoted so little space or attention to Coleridge at all.[84] The even more hostile belief that philosophy and opium were about the same in both function and effect in Coleridge's life, being what a modern critic has called 'avenues of escape from fear', was supported by Coleridge's own words and was not unknown to nineteenth-century criticism.[85]

Arnold's most extensive comment on Coleridge's character, or want of it, is in the essay on Joubert, but his most dramatic utterance occurs in his review of the Romantic movement in 'Heinrich Heine', where he divided the principal authors of the period into those who attempted to confront the modern spirit (Byron, Shelley) and those who withdrew (Scott, Wordsworth, Keats, Coleridge). Of the latter group, his comments on Scott, Wordsworth, and Keats are literary or partly literary, but Coleridge, one of the greatest geniuses of the age and one of the profoundest literary thinkers of any age, is sufficiently accounted for in four words: 'Coleridge took to opium.' This summation, amounting to a total dismissal, is more concrete and specific at any rate than most of the moral criticism in 'Joubert', where Arnold inclined to a certain vagueness, although his distaste is plain. For example, in the latter essay Arnold referred to the stimulus to other thinkers of Coleridge's continual effort to get at the truth of things, but he was constrained to interrupt himself with the qualification: '—not a moral effort, for he has no morals'.[86] Again, at the end of the same paragraph, Arnold somewhat irrelevantly had to interrupt a sentence of praise to express this adverse opinion in subjective language [my italics]: 'His action will be felt as long as the need for it continues. When, with the cessation of the need, the action too has ceased, Coleridge's memory, *in spite of the disesteem—nay, repugnance—which his character may and must inspire*, will yet for ever remain invested with that interest and gratitude which invests the memory of founders.'[87] It seems that Arnold could scarcely mention Coleridge's name without some outburst of disgust.

He did not discuss Coleridge's faults in any detail, as he was to do with Keats, Shelley, and Byron, perhaps because the matter was both too well known and too painfully sordid. But a few specific points emerge. The first is self-indulgence. Joubert, we are informed, was extremely fragile and sickly in his physical constitution, and was subject to constant suffering and pain; he faced the situation and accomplished as much as he did in spite of his condition because 'he lived by rule, and was as abstemious as a Hindoo'. Arnold makes no invidious comparisons at this point, but of course the point makes itself, and is underlined by the sentence less than one hundred pages earlier in *Essays in Criticism*, 'Coleridge took to opium'. The second fault in Coleridge which inspires repugnance is his lack of moral consistency. Like Joubert, he 'sincerely loved light'. But Joubert was not only 'full of light, he was also full of happiness . . . his life was as charming as his thoughts'. This is as it should be, 'For certainly it is natural that the love of light, which is already, in some measure, the possession of light, should irradiate and beautify the whole life of him who has it. There is something unnatural and shocking where, as in the case of Coleridge, it does not. Joubert pains us by no such contradiction. . . .' With Aristotle, Arnold believed that the intellectual virtues were the crown of the moral life. To be sure it was possible to possess the moral virtues and still be incapable of the life of the intellect, but the reverse, to be possessed of the intellectual virtues in a high degree, and to have 'no morals'—this was an almost unthinkable *saltus naturae*. There is a third failing about which we may infer that Arnold had strong feelings, but which he never mentioned directly. This is financial irresponsibility. Certainly Arnold was aware of Coleridge's defects in this regard, and such a failing could only have seemed very grave to him, with his own high sense of honour in money matters. H. D. Traill, in his biography which Arnold read in later years, discussed the matter and quoted some of Coleridge's own self-questionings about the propriety or honourableness of certain financial arrangements. The biographer declines to answer these questions, averring that 'The reply to be given to them must depend upon the judgment which each individual student of this remarkable but unhappy career may pass upon it as a whole. . . .'[88] What Arnold's answers would have been, however, we may infer not only from the facts of his own hard-working life, but also from a significant item he chose to set down of a 'proof of character' in Keats:

> . . . Charles Brown, whose kindness, willingly exerted whenever Keats chose to avail himself of it, seemed to free him from any pressing necessity of earning his own living. Keats felt that he must not allow this state of things to continue. He determined to set himself to 'fag on as others do' at periodical literature, rather than to endanger his independence and his self-respect. . . .[89]

Arnold's judgement of Coleridge may seem harsh, but this method, using implication for the most part, must be considered delicacy itself when compared with his attack on Shelley in the review of Dowden's *Life* that has done so much to injure Arnold's reputation for urbanity and amenity. It is not difficult to account for the difference. As with Byron, Arnold and his contemporaries had never been under any illusion about Coleridge. His faults were for the most part well known, and he had never been sanctified by legend. Shelley, on the other hand, had been a vision full of beauty and charm; the belief in the existence of such a creature (whatever his lack of merit as a poet) had brought joy and refreshment to the spirit in the arid later times. That myth, consequently, had been far more valuable than any number of facts which could bring nothing but weariness and vexation of spirit. In spite of his emphasis on 'knowing', and his often-praised unflinching realism, Matthew Arnold still partly believed in the value of benevolent fictions. Perhaps he absorbed some of this attitude from his father, from whom he had, paradoxically, also learned respect for the scientific method in history. In any case, the words of Professor Sanders about Dr. Arnold apply equally to his son: 'Arnold did not identify the true with the good. Not all truth, he said, needed to be insisted upon; but only "essential" truth, truth related to right conduct.'[90]

In Matthew Arnold's treatment of Bishop Colenso, in his attitude towards the publication of Keats's letters to Fanny Brawne, and most emphatically in his response to Dowden's *Life of Shelley* is this trait to be seen—the desire for Swift's 'sublime and refined point of felicity, called, the possession of being well deceived'. Truths which did not inspirit, refresh, or improve us either in themselves or in the way they could be used were of no value, and might be positively harmful. A sentence quoted by Arnold from Joubert is enlightening: 'With the fever of the senses, the delirium of the passions, the weakness of the spirit; with the storms of the passing time and with the great scourges of human life,—hunger, thirst, dishonour, diseases, and death,—authors may as long as they like go on making novels which shall harrow our hearts; but the soul says all the while, "You hurt me".' Arnold admired this statement and called it, rather unaccountably, worthy of Goethe, saying that it clears the air at one's entrance into the region of literature. It could also, of course, clear the library shelves of most of the great literature of the world if applied too literally, but Arnold had in mind the modern realistic novels, those 'monstrosities' which reveal truth in such a way as to do the very opposite of composing and elevating the soul. With full approval Arnold quoted from Joubert on the novel another passage which begins: 'Fiction has no business to exist unless it is more beautiful than reality', and ends: 'in literature the one aim of art is the beautiful. Once lose sight of that, and you have the mere frightful reality.'[91]

Apparently biography, too, has little business to exist if it cannot be more beautiful than 'the mere frightful reality' which Professor Dowden came so near to substituting for the beautiful fiction called Shelley. Arnold's essay on Shelley is well known and contains little of relevance to his literary criticism which has not already been absorbed into the foregoing discussion; moreover, it has been repeatedly discussed, corrected, and attacked by those who could speak more authoritatively of Shelley's life than I.[92] The essay itself is one of Arnold's poorer ones, and scarcely deserves the amount of attention it has received. Hence I shall review it only briefly. Arnold opened by expressing regret over the publication of the book, because it impaired the 'picture of Shelley to be desired'.[93] He then criticized Dowden on two counts—he was too much the advocate for Shelley, and his style was verbose and florid —and praised him for having produced all the documents so that the reader might form his own judgement, and also for having provided an excellent index. The earlier, beautiful picture of Shelley, based upon Hogg's description, Shelley's own writings, and Mary Shelley's notes, 'one would gladly have kept unimpaired.' It has been badly damaged, and although it still subsists, it is only 'so as by fire'. Arnold then proposed to deal first with the 'ridiculous and odious' in Shelley's character, in order to show later 'that our former beautiful and lovable Shelley nevertheless survives'. Next follow twenty-three pages of mainly factual summary of Shelley's life up to his marriage to Mary in December 1816. Along the way, however, Arnold makes some incidental comment on Dowden's absurdities and (referring to Shelley's letter inviting Harriet to join him and Mary) on one of Shelley's allegedly besetting weaknesses, his 'disastrous want ... his utter deficiency in humour'.

Here ends the factual summary. The next eight pages are a

prolonged, disgusted outburst, beginning with a description of Shelley's world. To this *sale* world, as Lionel Trilling says, 'only amazement (and French) can do justice'. The description itself is indeed worthy of a novelist for vividness, but its critical value is nil. Arnold's own sense of humour and his memory as well must have been dozing when he chose to compare Shelley's 'set' with the 'clerical and respectable Oxford' of Keble and Copleston and Hawkins and Newman; it is amusing to compare this evocation from Arnold's old age with his outburst to Clough in 1850: 'What a miserable place Oxford and the society of the serious middle classes must have been 20 years ago.'[94] Also, Arnold ignored Shelley's own disapproval of or outright hostility towards most of the people Arnold lumped together as his 'set'. Next, Arnold took up Dowden's unsubstantiated innuendoes against Harriet's character,[95] then developed his idea of Shelley's other cardinal weakness—his power of self-delusion—and concluded with another outburst of disgust at Shelley's sexual 'inflammability' and the loose conduct of the members of his 'set'. But now the time has come to return to 'our ideal Shelley'. 'Unhappily', says Arnold, and this is at the centre of his angry reactions, 'the data for this Shelley we had and knew long ago, while the data for the unattractive Shelley are fresh; and what is fresh is likely to fix our attention more than what is familiar.'

The last few pages of the essay discuss Shelley's virtues—his generosity and charity, his gentleness, refinement and delicacy of mind and manner, and even his possession of a sort of nobility which, if extravagant, is extravagant in a 'beautiful and rare' way. In his treatment of Godwin, Shelley showed forbearance and dignity, and although he was humourless, he could sometimes judge character with as 'quick and sharp a tact as the most practised man of the world'. Finally, as the climax of praise, we are given testimonials male and female to Shelley's beauty of face and bearing. Now at last Trelawney's Shelley 'blushing like a girl' has been reconstituted, not with an unblemished reputation to be sure, but as pretty as ever. No wonder that admirers of Shelley have often been angrier at Arnold's praise than at his censure! Deliver any man from such praise, but above all a man who is thought to have a serious claim to an important place as a poet; for him charges of immorality are far less damaging in the long run than such patronizing and belittling affection.

Early in the essay Arnold had referred to the 'charm' of Shelley's poems, and in the last paragraph occurs the only other reference to them. This charm, he allowed, must be added to his personal charms, for 'It is his poetry, above everything else, which for many people establishes that he is an angel.' But what the first half-paragraph seems to give (the phrase 'for many people' is ominous), the last half takes away. There, after regretting that he had not the space to speak of Shelley's poetry, Arnold did proceed to speak of it for four sentences in terms which, if valid, would be enough to consign Shelley's works once for all to the lunar sphere, along with Pope's

> Cages for gnats, and chains to yoke a flea,
> Dried butterflies, and tomes of casuistry.

Though familiar, the passage is brief enough to be worth quoting whole:

> But let no one suppose that a want of humour and a self-delusion such as Shelley's have no effect upon a man's poetry. The man Shelley, in very truth, is not entirely sane, and Shelley's poetry is not entirely sane either. The Shelley of actual life is a vision of beauty and radiance, indeed, but availing nothing, effecting nothing. And in poetry, no less than in life, he is 'a beautiful and *ineffectual angel*, beating in the void his luminous wings in vain'.

Just what Shelley ought, as a man, to have effected is not clear; moreover, the bulk of the essay rather shows all that Shelley did accomplish both for good and evil. At any rate, the penultimate sentence not only serves as preparation for Arnold's self-quoted (from 'Byron') poetic judgement in the last sentence; it also perhaps suggests to what an extent the Ariel concept of Shelley (sullied or unsullied) influenced Arnold's reading of his poetry.

As remote as 'Shelley' is from Arnold's literary criticism when he is at his best, or even second best, it still exemplifies one feature of his criticism that I have pointed out before: his desire to clear away the claptrap and clutter that obscures the clear view of the subject, and particularly that kind of claptrap which is the result of an inappropriate or indiscreet attachment to the wrong things in the subject. This purpose was dominant in the essays on Wordsworth and Keats; it is present in the lectures on Homer; there is at least a trace of it in 'Byron'; and it forms the whole basis of Arnold's religious and political writings. Arnold wrote to his friend Lady de Rothschild, 'In this article on Shelley I have spoken of his life, not his poetry. Professor Dowden was too much for my patience.'[96] Quiller-Couch, though completely out of sympathy with Arnold's opinions of Shelley, put his finger on this motive: 'If you read between the lines, you will detect that nine-tenths of Arnold's apparent disparagement of Shelley, when it is not actually directed upon Shelley's indiscreet admirers, springs out of irritation with them.'[97]

Anger with Shelley's indiscreet admirers, though, does not fully account for the animus of the essay, because after all, as Quiller-Couch also takes notice, conduct was for Arnold three-quarters of life. It was impossible for him to avoid mixing his personal with his literary estimates. In an essay on Spinoza Arnold observed: 'The power of imagining, the power of telling what goodness is and the habit of practising goodness, were therefore the sole essential qualifications of a true prophet.' Later in the same essay he says that what a philosopher does for human thought is only enough to make him noteworthy, not great. 'To be great, he must have something in him which can influence character, which is edifying; he must, in short, have a noble and lofty character himself, a character,—to recur to that much-criticized expression of mine,—*in the grand style*.'[98] Since, for Arnold, the poet was to combine the offices of prophet and philosopher, we may infer that these qualities are equally demanded of him. But both Shelley, even at his most angelic, and Coleridge were so far from satisfying the demands of character, that Arnold was never able to put aside his own personal estimates enough to render an adequate literary appraisal of either one.

BETWEEN TWO WORLDS: MATTHEW ARNOLD AND ROMANTICISM

Il y a dans la poésie toujours un peu de mensonge. L'esprit philo-sophique nous habitue à le discerner; et adieu l'illusion et l'effet.

DIDEROT

I. ARNOLD AND ENGLISH POETIC TRADITION

IN turning from specific discussions of Wordsworth, Byron, Keats, Coleridge, and Shelley to consider the general relations between Arnold and Romanticism, we may well feel like Milton's Satan, pondering a voyage into a wild abyss where questions and answers swarm and jostle like embryon atoms. Arnold himself did occa-sionally use the word *romantic*, but not when specifically speaking of the five poets named above. There is no way to know just how far he would have gone in applying it to any of them, and indeed, there is no way to be sure what the word meant to him except as a generally pejorative antonym for *classical*. Then there is the difficult question of whether Arnold himself was a Romantic. We have, for example, E. K. Brown's assurance that he was, Ludwig Lewisohn's that he was not, and George H. Ford's argument that he was 'something of a romantic', but was extremely wary of the dangers of romanticism.[1] This question leads in turn to others even more terrifying: What is Romanticism? Classicism? Finally there is the question of the usefulness and validity of Arnold's judgements on the Romantics and on Romanticism. While some critics agree more or less totally with his overall judgement, various defenders of Romanticism believe that Arnold badly underestimated and mis-represented the Romantic poets.[2] As for Arnold's opinions on the individual poets, the foregoing chapters have indicated some of the diversity of response which they called forth. I propose to consider here Arnold's relations with Romanticism first in connection with the poetic tradition available to him, secondly in terms of his own ambivalence of feeling towards Romanticism, then by discussing changing attitudes towards the relationship between truth and poetry in the nineteenth century, and finally by reviewing the judgement he passed on the English poetry of the first quarter of the nineteenth century.

In the chapters above I have tried to delineate the nature and extent to which Arnold's poetry reveals the specific influence of the major Romantics. Here I should like to consider more generally Arnold in his relation to a poetic tradition. Let me say at the outset that I do not believe that a 'tradition' has any real existence in the same sense that particular poets and particular poems have. Moreover, it is clear by the middle of the twentieth century that there is not one major poetic tradition, but rather there are many traditions, almost as many one might say rashly as there are important modern poets seeking to relate themselves to the literature of the past. For in any discussion of influence and tradition it is salutary to remember that a poet certainly is free to exercise some choice in his reading and studies, constructing, if he wishes, a 'tradition' out of the most heterogeneous elements; Ezra Pound with his amalgam of Browning, Whitman, Propertius, Old English, Provençal, early Italian, and classical Chinese is a sufficient example. Nevertheless, a poet is born at a certain time and place; he goes to certain schools and reads certain books; and both his society and the very language he speaks are historically conditioned. This means that his personal choice, however free, is still not completely unlimited in its field of operation. There are limits to the 'usable past' available to him.

What was this 'usable past' for Matthew Arnold about the middle of the last century? I refer especially to English poetry and the English language, because it is my conviction that, except perhaps for true bilingual poets like Milton or Tagore, foreign influence, however strong, must always be in some sense secondary. The poet's raw material is his own language; foreign influence is only significant to the extent that the poet can transmute it, recreating and validating its effects in his own living language. The multi-faceted problems of poetic translation are enough evidence for this, I believe. Arnold himself, though deeply affected by German and French writers, for example, was primarily concerned as a practising poet with what he felt were the inadequacies of English poetry, and his major purpose was to put English poetry on the right path. To answer the question put at the beginning of this paragraph might require a book in itself, but some generalizations may be hazarded.

We may best approach the make-up of Arnold's 'tradition' by seeing first what is omitted. Arnold's list of 'our Chief poetical names' from the age of Elizabeth downwards includes Shakespeare and Milton, Spenser, Dryden, Pope, Gray, Goldsmith, Cowper, Burns, Coleridge, Scott, Campbell, Moore, Byron, Shelley, Keats, and Wordsworth. It is indeed strange, as Lionel Trilling comments, 'that a roll of the great English poets does not include such names as Marlowe, Jonson, Donne, Marvell, Herbert, Vaughan, and Blake'.[3] And these are not all the significant omissions, while even among the names included by Arnold are several whose presence was merely conventional. Thus, Arnold could include Dryden and Pope in 'a large and liberal first class among English writers', but he had no real sympathy with them as poets though he could treat them respectfully as men of letters. It is significant that in his essay on Johnson, he urged the reading of Pope, Addison, Dryden, and Swift for their historical interest. If we re-examine Arnold's list of 'chief poetical names' with our attention on Arnold's own views of their usefulness to him, we shall get a fairly clear picture of his available tradition. Chaucer he excluded as 'anterior' and for 'other' reasons; that is, I suppose, because of linguistic and cultural differences and because of his alleged lack of high seriousness. Spenser's 'fluid movement and liquid diction' he praised in passing, but there is no evidence that he took Spenser seriously, or thought he had much to offer a modern poet beyond some lessons in refinement of craft, already overemphasized by Keats, Tennyson, and their followers. Dryden and Pope are 'classics of our prose', indispensable in their time and place but no longer useful, and Arnold praised the Romantics for rejecting the poetry between Milton and Wordsworth.[4] Such lesser lights as Goldsmith, Cowper, Campbell, and Moore named in his list may be put aside without comment. Scott's true glory was as a novelist; his verse, Arnold thought, was competent and enjoyable but unimportant. We are left, then, from the original list, with

Shakespeare and Milton, Gray, Burns, Wordsworth, Coleridge, Byron, Shelley, and Keats. But Shakespeare, though an unparalleled genius, is dangerous as an influence. The Gray in whom Arnold is interested is essentially a minor Romantic, in spite of Arnold's opinion that Gray was saved from the worst poetic excesses of his time by his thorough knowledge of the Greeks.[5] Burns is at his best when he writes in Scottish of Scottish life—a foreign poet, and also a minor one. What remains is Milton and the great Romantics as the living tradition of read and reread poets who could form his attitudes towards the stuff of English poetry. These are the English poets, selected partly by the taste of the age and partly by conscious choice, whose work created the linguistic milieu in which Arnold formed his image of what had been successfully and relevantly accomplished in English verse; it is against this background that his own poetry should be placed.

Hence, we can see that Arnold was cut off by taste, opinion, and conditioning from most of the English poetry outside the Romantic tradition. The line of Shakespeare, Milton, and the Romantics was for him, as for most of his contemporaries, *the* tradition in English poetry, and even Shakespeare is suspect in proportion as he becomes subtle and 'conceited'. This background is an important limitation to the possibility of Arnold's rebellion against Romanticism and to the possible scope of his reform of English poetry. Recognizing this, Arnold sought help by turning to contemporary Europe and to the literature of the past. In modern Europe he found Goethe and Senancour valuable above all, but was also interested in George Sand, Maurice de Guérin, and Joubert; what is such a list but a roll call of Romantics, great and small? German critics, to be sure, do not regard Goethe as a Romantic. We must not underestimate his broad rationality and his humane classicism, but it still seems, from a modern and cosmopolitan point of view such as Santayana's, that Goethe's classicism is but one facet of his immensely energetic, many-sided, and limitless development of the self. His hero Faust is the very epitome of that restless, expansive individualism which we associate on the economic side with the bourgeois revolution, on the scientific with the human conquest of brute matter, and on the literary with Romanticism. It is true that Faust marries Helena, but their offspring Euphorion bears a striking resemblance to Lord Byron.

As for the literature of the past, Arnold tended to see that too, in part, through the filtering lens of Romanticism, although it was primarily in that literature that he sought an antidote for modern subjectivism and excessive richness and refinement of artistry. Medieval Europe offered such an antidote in Dante, whom Arnold greatly admired. True, Dante's civilization was second-rate from Arnold's point of view, but then so was Homer's,[6] and, after all, Dante's accomplishment was enormous. In the clear and precise use of language Dante is unsurpassed; there is no clutter, no bombast, no decoration. His verse possesses all the virtues of great prose, combined with that fusion of symbol, object, and idea at the greatest intensity of imaginative power which marks the greatest poetry. Moreover, this power of fusion, this intensity, coupled with clarity in the texture of his verse, is amplified in the completeness of his architectonics. Perhaps more than any other work one can think of, Dante's *Divine Comedy* possesses the magisterial qualities of depth, comprehensiveness, grandeur, seriousness, and organization which Arnold demanded. In spite of all this, when we look at what Arnold had to say about Dante, we do not find that he selects his work as an example of the 'literatures which in their day and for their own nation have adequately comprehended, have adequately represented, the spectacle before them'. Instead, wearing the twin blinders of the Enlightenment's contempt for the age of jarring monks, and Romantic sentimentalizing of medieval spirituality, Arnold saw only a Romantic version of Dante as an other-worldly visionary: 'the vital impulse of Dante's soul is towards reverie and spiritual vision. . .'. Dante, that is—and the whole tenor of the essay on 'Dante and Beatrice' bears this out—is a more impassioned Senancour, a Senancour living at a time when belief in a spiritual order was still possible:

> . . . the task Dante sets himself is not the task of reconciling poetry and reality, of giving to each its due part, of supplementing the one by the other; but the task of sacrificing the world to the spirit, of making the spirit all in all, of effacing the world in presence of the spirit. . . .[7]

Arnold seems quite to overlook Dante's attitude of tough-minded, Christian realism, an attitude which brings Dante in some ways nearer than Arnold to the spirit of classical literature. In fact, Arnold's whole essay on Dante is a remarkable example of romanticizing under the guise of correcting another critic for doing so. In its lack of historic insight, its unconscious employment of contemporaneous assumptions, it smacks more of the Romanticism of the eighteenth century, however, than of the nineteenth. Arnold was too much a child of the Enlightenment to take the Middle Ages seriously; that epoch was too irrational, too un-modern.

In Athens during the age of Pericles he found what he wanted— a *modern* epoch with an *adequate* literature. There he found the wholeness, simplicity, order, and objectivity of the highest art for the moment achieving perfect balance with the critical intellect and profound moral insight. Yet even in his praise of classic art there is to be detected something of the tone of Wordsworth's 'old, unhappy, far-off things, / And battles long ago' and of Keats's 'a billowy main, / A sun, a shadow of a magnitude'; that is, he tends to be Romantic about the Classic. The tone is audible in Arnold's Preface to *Merope*:

> . . . I am convinced, even in England, even in this stronghold of the romantic school, a wide though an ill-informed curiosity [exists] on the subject of the so-called classical school, meriting a more complete satisfaction than it has hitherto obtained. Greek art—the antique—classical beauty—a nameless hope and interest attaches, I can often see, to these words, even in the minds of those who have been brought up among the productions of the romantic school; of those who have been taught to consider classicalism as inseparable from coldness, and the antique as another phrase for the unreal. So immortal, so indestructible is the power of true beauty, of consummate form: it may be submerged, but the tradition of it survives: nations arise which know it not, which hardly believe in the report of it; but they, too, are haunted with an indefinable interest in its name, with an inexplicable curiosity as to its nature.

Arnold was capable of a different sort of perception of classical art when dealing with its 'criticism of life' (see his comment on the *Iliad* below, p. 217), but in his nostalgic yearning towards Greece, a yearning to be felt in the very rhythms of the passage just quoted, there is a definite Romantic element. And consequently the usefulness to him of Classicism as an antidote to Romanticism was limited.[8]

II. ARNOLD'S AMBIVALENCE

So far we have seen two kinds of limitations in Arnold which may justifiably be related to his derivation from the Romantic movement—first, a narrowness of taste that cut him off from a sizeable body of work in English of potential usefulness in his effort to reinstate the social utility of poetry, and second, a certain tendency to romanticize and hence to limit the medicinal effectiveness of the literatures of the past. Two further limitations which have already been discussed in various places in the chapters above are perhaps the practical consequences of the foregoing: namely, Arnold's narrowing concept of the permissible emotional range of poetry to the exalted, the solemn, the melancholy, or the pathetic, and his inability to construct a new style adequate to his demands on poetry. These limitations, representing the negative side of Arnold's inheritance from the giants of the preceding generation, were particularly effective in preventing him from fulfilling his very highest ambitions for poetry because he was at the same time lacking in many of the positive attributes of Romanticism. He was deeply mistrustful of the craving for the infinite which Muirhead sees as the essential quality of Romanticism.[9] Above all he lacked the energy of the Romantics; he lacked their robust, expansive ego;[10] he lacked their faith in the imagination as the highest, truest, and the most creative way of knowing; he did not share in the slightest degree their nature animism; and he did not, consequently, believe in a special system of correspondence between nature and the mind of man. Of course, the five major Romantic poets did not all possess all these attitudes, or possess them all at once, or for ever. But in so far as we call them 'romantic' (with Byron always the doubtful case in certain respects), we have in mind, among lesser things, some combination of them.

Arnold could not sustain the Wordsworthian faith in

> How exquisitely the individual Mind
> (And the progressive powers perhaps no less
> Of the whole species) to the external World
> Is fitted:—and how exquisitely too—
>
> .   .   .
>
> The external World is fitted to the Mind.

In its expression of this loss of faith and of regret for the loss, Arnold's poetry reveals both his derivation from the Romantics and his reaction against them. As an anti-romantic, he harped continually on the limitations imposed by a lawful but inscrutable universe upon the subjective demands and expectations of the self. But while Arnold's thought in his poetry is naturalistic, his feeling is thoroughly unclassical. Classical art recognized that the world was not made for man, but showed that man could achieve dignity in that world. In accepting with total clarity of vision this view of the relationship between man's aspirations and the rigorous limitations imposed by circumstance and natural law, classic art rises to tragic grandeur. Arnold, more than any other leading poet of his day, participated in such a vision of man. But his feeling, instead of rising to tragic clarity, is one of disillusionment, and since this implies anterior illusionment, and unresolved regret, it is at the opposite pole from the tragic emotion. Arnold's disillusionment seems romantic when contrasted with the stern realism (Santayana's 'naturalism') of pagan antiquity. Perhaps it would not be too much of a distortion to suggest that if Arnold was not a Romanticist, he nevertheless wished he could be, and that his melancholy attitude of lost and yearning disenchantment defined the nature of his own Romanticism.

Arnold's negative Romanticism, his self-pitying sense of the rigorous subjection of the ego to natural law, is reflected in his work and thought by a split between the reason and the imagination, symbolized by the characters of Empedocles and Callicles in *Empedocles on Etna*; this subjective split is complemented on the objective side by an equally firm division between man and Nature. Both dichotomies are caught up in the loss of faith in the imagination, the faith that had been so powerful a force in stimulating the creativeness of the Romantics. It is true that in the essay 'Pagan and Medieval Religious Sentiment', Arnold, like the Romantics before him, urged the necessity of the 'imaginative reason' in poetry, but the general drift of the essay is toward favouring the reason over the imagination. He nowhere shows interest in, or even awareness of, the profound and complex theories of Wordsworth and Coleridge on the imagination, or of their distinctions between imagination and fancy or between primary and secondary imagination. In short, for Arnold the concept of the imagination, in spite of a few instances of his using the word honorifically, has been stripped of most of the prestige it enjoyed among the Romantics, and has become almost synonymous with emotion, superstition, wish, and self-will.[11] Lacking the Romantic faith in man's ability to create reality, Arnold, like Aristotle, divides man's higher impulses between the intellectual and the moral—'the effort to see things as they really are and the effort to win peace by self-conquest'.[12] The imagination, in turn, seems at times to have shrunk in Arnold's usage to the 'false secondary power', not by which we multiply distinctions, but by which we invent mechanisms of escape from stern reality. Certainly Arnold was not always conscious of the extent to which he was depreciating the imagination, as I have tried to show in discussing his description of poetry's 'interpretative power' (p. 139), but it is visible there and in the turn at the end of *Celtic Literature*, amounting almost to a sleight of hand, by which he decisively elevates German intellectualism in poetry over the Celtic imagination of the great English geniuses.

The obverse side of Arnold's elevation of reason at the expense of the imagination may be seen in his atitude towards Nature; the latter attitude may indeed be the cause of the former. Defending what another critic had called Arnold's 'week-end' attitude towards Nature, J. D. Jump points out that

> Arnold was not protected by private income, personal gift, sinecure, or legacy from the obligation of working for a living in the ordinary Philistine sense of the phrase. Because he knew it in his own life, Arnold presents in his verse the dilemma of many who in the modern world are compelled to live their lives in circumstances which fail to satisfy their natures, which distract them indeed from learning what those natures are, and which they must for their own well-being periodically elude. If Arnold's landscapes are commonly those of a week-ender—and the Goergian poets are indeed his enfeebled successors—at least he also knew and gave utterance to that unease which drives the week-ender to the countryside.[13]

This economic explanation merits consideration, but it does not go deep enough. Arnold could not feel 'at home' in Nature for reasons more profound than this, and, given his temperament and beliefs, we cannot imagine that a well-timed legacy of £1000 a year would have substantially altered the situation. The main point to consider is that for Arnold, Nature was irrevocably *other* than man and limited him; its rigorous laws were firm barriers against man's egocentric, expansive tendencies. Hence, man can never be more than a 'week-ender' in the physical universe. Here Arnold differs most profoundly from Wordsworth, Coleridge, Shelley, and Keats, who all, in their various ways, saw in the imagination a power creative of reality. True, Arnold reveals some kinship with them in the feeling of disillusion that accompanies his belief, and he is like them in deriving a philosophy from Nature. But his philosophy as expounded by Empedocles, and by Arnold speaking for himself in other poems, is a doctrine of discipline, limitation, self-control, and stoic resignation. Hence he is more in accord with Senancour and other continental Romantics who, in the words of a French critic, were 'emmurés en eux-mêmes; le monde extérieur ne leur apporte ni réconfort ni chaleur'.[14] It has been argued that science can fulfil a religious function by 'enforcing belief in a real world which imposes limits upon human self-will'.[15] Empedocles-Arnold would have agreed that science in fact fulfilled such a function, but from his position at the bleak terminus of Romantic faith he would not have thought of calling it religious. Starting from this dead end, there would seem to have been two paths open to him—that of Christianity or that of a thorough-going naturalism. Unable to choose, he bent his mightiest efforts towards a reconciliation of the two, and so ended his years impaled, but with a minimum of discomfort, upon both horns of the dilemma.

How did these conflicts affect his poetry? Arnold's critics are in substantial agreement that he was at his best when he was most romantic. Indeed, if Arnold was situated in relation to the Romantic tradition in the way I have described above, how should it have been otherwise? Caught in the conflict between rationalism and Romanticism, and expressing the emotional effect of this conflict with deep honesty, it was inevitable that his poetry should be most moving when it deals with the alienation and incompleteness of modern man in such poems as *Dover Beach, Obermann, Stanzas from the Grande Chartreuse, The Scholar-Gipsy*, and *Empedocles on Etna*. It was in this work, and not in his academic efforts to achieve classical serenity, that his poems truly represent, as in 1869 he said they did, 'the main movement of mind of the last quarter of a century'.[16] But also, since he recognized the inadequacy of disillusion as a philosophy for either life or art, it was inevitable that he should have agreed with Goethe, that 'Klassisch ist das Gesunde, romantisch das Kranke'.

III. TRUTH AND POETRY

It was almost a necessary consequence that Arnold should have been unable to take poetry itself as seriously as most of the Romantics had done, in spite of his extravagant claims on its behalf. For in his feelings there was as deep a split between 'truth 'and 'poetry' as there was between 'science' and 'religion', or 'reason' and 'imagination'. To explore this hypostatization, we shall have to examine various meanings of 'truth' in Arnold's thought.

In his 1865 preface to *Essays in Criticism*, Arnold personified truth as a mysterious Goddess 'whom we shall never see except in outline', but even in outline only by supple and dialectical processes. Although he had learned much from such systematic thinkers as Aristotle and Coleridge, he had never acquired their passion for careful definition and for the rigours of logic; on the contrary, he frequently asserted his radical mistrust of abstract speculation and of systematic thought. We shall not expect to find, therefore, and do not find any consistent set of ideas in Arnold about so complex a concept as 'truth', either as to its own nature or concerning the faculties and means by which we may gain apprehension of it. For this reason, any attempt to reduce his ideas and attitudes to logical order is bound either to fail, or to reveal that Arnold was more inconsistent than he perhaps really was. Basically, his approach to ideas, for all his sophistication, was homespun, empirical, and intuitive in the everyday rather than philosophical meaning of that term. For example, he argues that a man is better off to take the forms of religious expression 'which have commended themselves most to the religious life of his nation' rather than battle for 'his own private forms', for he may thus ensure to himself the 'leisure and composure to satisfy other sides of his nature as well'.[17] Again, in surveying Amiel's work, he acknowledges that his 'sense for philosophy' is far from satisfying such a rationalistic critic as Frederic Harrison. 'But', he continues, 'I am too old to change and too hardened to hide what I think; and when I am presented with philosophical speculations . . ., I persist in looking closely at them and in honestly asking myself what I find to be their positive value.'[18]

At the risk, therefore, of somewhat misrepresenting Arnold's studied vagueness, we may yet observe that when he speaks of 'truth' or implies standards for its measurement, he is likely to mean one of three things. He may have in mind the sort of certitude that nineteenth-century materialism held up as 'scientific truth', based on certain assumptions about the absolute truth of 'laws of nature'. By this standard, he rejects, for example, faith in miracles, although even here it should be noted that he is less concerned to prove that miracles do not happen, than that the temper of the times, the Zeitgeist, has rendered the whole question of miracles as obsolete as the problem of angels on a pinhead.[19] Secondly, under the influence of prevailing utilitarianism, he may make 'truth' essentially synonymous with utility. This pragmatic approach is especially evident in his religious writings, where the 'human truth' of Christianity is proved by its rich adequacy, when put to the test of practice, to man's needs. Finally, Arnold may employ still another notion of truth, namely, aesthetic or 'poetic' truth. The appeal to this kind of truth is equally prominent in his defence of Christianity; it is a debatable question whether it or the pragmatic argument is the more important in his apologetics, but I am inclined to favour the aesthetic.

Inevitably, Arnold's pragmatic defence of Christianity encounters certain difficulties. After all, though such a test may prove religion useful, it cannot prove it true unless the terms are defined as synonymous. Measured by any absolute standard, the utility of religion may be just what makes one suspicious of the existential truth of its assertions. To be sure, in appealing to the modern notion of practical 'verifiability', Arnold thought that he was providing his arguments on behalf of faith with a firmly scientific basis. But such a notion of 'verifiability' is close to being a travesty of scientific operationalism. The scientist who develops a theory adequate to the data in his possession never loses awareness of the hypothetical and, by any absolutist standards, tentative nature of his 'truth'. Furthermore, when a scientific hypothesis is made subservient to any set of psychological needs or to any value system, it is at once in the gravest danger of losing its scientific validity; when it is treated as an absolute it has already lost its validity.

At the same time, scientific method and discipline teach wariness of those hypotheses which seem subjectively most 'adequate', for they are most likely to be rationalizations. Hence a rigorous critical method was developed which, as it became part of the psychological set of the thinking portion of mankind, worked against acceptance of the pragmatic argument for religious truth.

The louder it is asserted, 'Religious truth is proved by its adequacy to man's needs; try it and see', the more surely the critical response is likely to become, 'All that such adequacy really proves is that the religious view of life is manufactured out of those very needs.' For in the sphere of religion, however latitudinarian, certain absolutes are demanded, and in effect created, by the very nature of faith. Job's cry, 'Though He slay me, yet will I trust in Him', may be employed here as a touchstone. Such faith, beyond reason, in the existence of the Absolute is incommensurable with the provisional assent lent to any scientific theory whatsoever. And here was Arnold's difficulty, for he appears to have been incapable of appreciating the state of mind of those whose hunger for faith was such that the objective, material truth of a doctrine was a fundamental concern.[20]

While Arnold was rejecting all those parts of religion, such as miracles and the historical accuracy of the Scriptures, which were contradicted by modern science, he was also apparently aware of the defects of the pragmatic approach. Consequently, he makes his primary appeal to aesthetic standards of truth to establish the validity of religion. That is, religion may be 'true' as a novel, play, poem, or any work of art is true—by embodying a satisfactory organization of responses to both externally given and inward data, facts and feelings (Wordsworth's 'impassioned expression on the countenance of all science'). Viewed in this way, religion is not explanatory, but expressive, hence exempt from corrosion by science. At a mythopoeic stage of civilization, with the universe taken as homocentric, there would be little difference between scientific and aesthetic truth, as data and responses are not sharply differentiated. T. S. Eliot has argued that the metaphysical poets of the early seventeenth century were the last to possess this 'unified sensibility'; it may seem strange to think so, but perhaps from this point of view the Romantics were the heirs of the metaphysicals, representing a last desperate effort to reassert this fusion of thought and feeling in the face of what came to seem by Arnold's time the inevitable triumph of scientific standards of truth. The development of Keats's thought in his letters may be taken as an example of this effort; the whole letter to Reynolds of May 3, 1818, which contains the famous remark 'axioms in philosophy are not axioms until they are proved upon our pulses', is a central document, as the remark itself is a summary expression of

Keats's version of the fusion of thought and feeling which he sought.

But as the data came to be organized in ways which increasingly made of man a phenomenon or at most a mere observer, man found himself squeezed from the centre of action, while science developed methods of analysis and criteria of certitude quite different from those of art. The word *satisfactory*, used above in the characterization of aesthetic truth, becomes crucial, for conceptual organizations which satisfy the demands of critical method are not the same as expressive organizations which satisfy our aesthetic sense of how things ought to be. The most obvious difference is in what is appealed to: scientific demonstration must meet standards which are somehow independent of me or of any man; these standards may 'satisfy' me in so far as I accept them emotionally, but my acceptance is, on the other hand, quite irrelevant to their validity. But no such objective or self-subsistent standards are available for measuring artistic truth; in art assent is gained by methods analogous to persuasion, not demonstration. The futile efforts of Zola and the Naturalists to turn art into science and the work of art into a laboratory demonstration was a characteristic nineteenth-century expedient.

For the great Romantics, typically, poetry was an article of faith. They believed that its truth was on an equal footing with, if it was not indeed superior to, scientific truth. 'What the imagination seizes as Beauty must be truth—whether it existed before or not', proclaimed Keats in an important letter of November 22, 1817. Both the psychology and the philosophy they accepted provided a rationale: since the mind itself was a plastic, shaping force, there did not exist a radical split between data and responses. Another way of putting this, in Wordsworthian terms, is that Nature is a living spirit infusing and infused by the human mind. Consequently, to have attributed artistic truth to religion would in no way have detracted for them from its truth in other senses. But for succeeding generations the matter was more difficult. Science was rapidly organizing itself into patterns which left no room for or were totally indifferent to human response (although this process had been going on since Bacon had banished final causes from scientific discourse). One understood these organizations or did not, but one's emotions regarding them were irrelevant except to another system of such organizations called psychology. Under

these circumstances, what becomes of 'aesthetic truth'? Not by
canard or conspiracy, but merely because of the inevitable progress
of science, the valuation placed on it diminished. And what
becomes of religion? On the one hand there was the last-ditch
effort to keep alive the belief in its scientific truth—fundamenta-
lism. This seemed to Arnold not only hopeless, but undesirable,
for then the highest expression of man's spirit (for it was in such
humanistic terms that he conceived of religion) would become
ossified in a set of dubious material facts. Pragmatism, on the other
hand, is a struggle in quicksand which draws the struggler deeper.
Arnold could flirt with this approach in his prose, but in his poetry
where his intuitions were more certain he recognized its inadequacy, and sternly denied that the world was in any sense created
to satisfy us; it has its laws, we have ours.

Thus, while Shelley, for example, could see poetry as the true
organizer of the moral order and could somehow believe in its
divine function (and Yeats wanted to study *Prometheus Unbound*
as a sacred book), Arnold could not. He tried hard, to be sure. But
where Shelley believed that he was describing what was, Arnold
was pleading for what he hoped *might be*. Thus Shelley argued
from a position of strength, Arnold from a position of weakness;
Shelley fully believed in the truth of poetry as a fact of the universe,
Arnold could not; Shelley defined, Arnold defended. Unlike the
rebellious, passionate Yeats, Arnold was too much a willing child
of his time for it to be otherwise. Beneath his aesthetic cloak, he
was a believer in certitude. Science possessed certitude, but did not
satisfy; poetry satisfied, but alas possessed no certitude.[21]

If aesthetic truth, which was necessary to support religion, was
itself falling victim to scientific standards of certitude, if truth and
poetry were coming to be virtual antonyms, as they are to this day
in the popular cliché, what was Arnold to do? In his debate with
Huxley over education ('Literature and Science'), Arnold again
appealed to the standard of utility, this time to defend poetry; my
respected ancestor the ring-tailed baboon, it seems, was born
with a need for it. Now let us review the steps of the argument:
First, science tells us that the statements of religion lack material
truth; very well, religion still possesses aesthetic truth. But then
aesthetic truth turns out to be usefulness. However, the actual or
potential user who is needed to validate the standard of usefulness
may fail to perceive that quality in what is offered unless it measures

up to his standards of certitude, no matter how much he desires to believe. It may then be argued that he is missing a great deal, and he may even agree, but no logical argument is left to convince him of the *truth* of art or religion. The attempt to prove pragmatically the truth of either has not only failed, but it has opened the door to the possibility of all sorts of bad art (e.g., 'socialist realism') or sentimental religion (e.g., 'the power of positive thinking)'. As far as art is concerned, there was only one more step to take in this direction, or rather in desperate opposition to it, and aestheticism took that step: art is supremely valuable because it is useless.

Actually, Arnold's aesthetic defence of religion and religious defence of poetry can be plausible if one does really conceive highly enough of poetry. But it has been only a rare spirit since the time of Shelley and the Romantics who has been capable of it, while prior to that time it was unnecessary.[22] Arnold tried to hold and to propagate such a conception, but couldn't succeed; in his own language, the Zeitgeist was against him. And it can scarcely be doubted that the breach in our society's attitude between 'truth' and 'poetry' is wider than ever, although faith in certitude is no longer a part of the critical method of advanced scientific thought. But because man still hungers, he feeds himself insatiably on what is neither aesthetically nor scientifically 'true'. In his flight from the twin demons of boredom and despair he voraciously consumes in alarming quantities the meretricious and the ersatz in the arts, and the soothing religiosity of popular 'psychologists', weekly magazine preachers, and billboard slogans.

IV. ARNOLD AND THE ROMANTICS

Finally, we must review Arnold's evaluation of the Romantic poets and movement. His ranking of the five poets is still controversial. For one thing, Blake has now, and quite properly, assumed his rank as one of the major poets of the period; probably my own opinion that he and Wordsworth share the supreme rank is fairly common. In taking up the five poets whom Arnold did deal with, we must recognize that the qualities he most highly valued were power and breadth of achievement. He badly underestimated Shelley, but, considering his critical premises, his view of Coleridge as a poet is quite understandable. Coleridge's significance as an intellectual force can hardly be overestimated, but as a poet his accomplishment, after all, was the production of a very few masterpieces on the basis of which he has his own special but minor place. Again, Arnold's relative ranking of Byron and Keats is in accord with his general principles, although of course other premises are defensible. This placement is certainly in opposition to much current opinion, but it is possible that our contemporary tendency to elevate Keats, the artist of profound genius but narrow accomplishment, over Byron, a lesser genius of ampler scope, is symptomatic of our own Romantic provinciality. At any rate, one formidable controversialist, F. R. Leavis, finds himself in complete agreement with Arnold's relative evaluation from first to last.[23]

Whatever personal attraction Arnold may have felt toward Romanticism, and whatever virtues he may have found in some of the poets, his lack of critical sympathy is evident from the way he used the term itself. Sometimes he was condescendingly affectionate, as in the delicately ironic panegyric on Oxford which he apostrophizes as an 'adorable dreamer, whose heart has been so romantic!' and as a 'queen of romance' steeped in sentimental moonlight, 'so unravaged by the fierce intellectual life of our century'. This tone is closely related to the momentary attraction of the cloister in *Stanzas from the Grande Chartreuse* or of the passion and charm of the impractical Celtic temperament, an attraction that Knowledge and Duty may permit or even momentarily encourage for the sake of 'refreshment', but then must proscribe. In his notebook Arnold copied a sentence out of Pater's *Renaissance* characterizing the Romantic and Hellenic spirits: 'The Romantic spirit—its adventure, its variety, its deep subjectivity; Hellenism—its transparency, its rationality, its desire for beauty.'[24] This may be more of what Douglas Bush has referred to as 'Romantic Hellenism', but there is no doubt which of these two spirits claimed Arnold's critical allegiance. His most definitely damning comment on the Romantic, calling it by name, is backed by the authority of Sainte-Beuve in a passage of *On Translating Homer*. There a remark of Ruskin's on a phrase from the *Iliad* elicits the following response:

> It reminds one, as, alas! so much of Mr. Ruskin's writing reminds one, of those words of the most delicate of living critics: 'Comme tout genre de composition a son écueil particulier, *celui du genre romanesque, c'est le faux.*' [Arnold's italics.] . . . It is not true, as a matter of general criticism, that this kind of sentimentality,

eminently modern, inspires Homer at all. 'From Homer and
Polygnotus I every day learn more clearly', says Goethe, 'that in
our life here above ground we have, properly speaking, to enact
Hell:'—if the student must absolutely have a keynote to the *Iliad*,
let him take this of Goethe, and see what he can do with it; it will
not, at any rate, like the tender pantheism of Mr. Ruskin, falsify
for him the whole strain of Homer.[25]

I have omitted the details of the argument for they are not relevant
here; the important thing to notice is Arnold's linking of 'romantic',
le romanesque, with words like *sentimentality* and *tender pantheism*.
A quarter of a century later, Arnold still recalled Sainte-Beuve's
words when he again referred to *le faux* as the special danger 'of
the romantic artist'.[26]

Arnold's belief that falsity was the particular stumbling-block of
the romantic artist was entirely consonant with his conviction that
'the burst of creative activity in our literature, through the first
quarter of this century' was premature, that the poetry it produced 'did not know enough'. For expressing a similar opinion,
Maurice de Guérin is praised for judging 'the romantic school and
its prospects like a master'. Since this poetry had its 'source in a
great movement of feeling, not in a great movement of mind', its
inadequacy must eventually be recognized as the world pursues
its relentless course of attempting to understand the real nature of
things. In *Memorial Verses* and elsewhere, Arnold associated the
period of the Romantics with other intellectually primitive ages—
the Elizabethan, the medieval, and the pre-philosophic antique.
Himself and his own times, on the other hand, he associated with
the clear-eyed disillusion of a Lucretius and his epoch: 'The infancy
of the world was renewed with all its sweet illusions but infancy
and its illusions must for ever be transitory, and we are again in
the place of the Roman world, our illusions past. . . .'[27]

To *know*—that was the great impulse of the mid-Victorians.
Literary England had travelled far from Wordsworth's 'It is the
hour of feeling'. This intellectual bias is reflected in many other
poets of the period and in a considerable body of critical opinion
on the Romantics which was similar to Arnold's.[28] Consequently,
Arnold's own critique of the Romantic movement was not startlingly independent, although it did not represent majority opinion.[29]
The Romantics have not lacked defenders ready to point out
Arnold's deficiencies of sympathy, understanding, or judgement,

Jacques Barzun, for example, in *Romanticism and the Modern Ego*, deplores the fact that the Romantic poets' output should have come to us filtered through Arnold's 'sentimental critical taste'. He frankly blames Arnold for 'our incomplete view of Byron and Wordsworth', for helping to create the legend of Shelley as an ineffectual angel, and for numerous other crimes against the reputations not only of the Romantics, but of Burns, Dryden, Pope, and Swift.[30] In a sense it is flattering to Arnold's own reputation to have so much power imputed to him, but surely we may wonder whether any one critic could have caused so much unmerited damage. Still, after allowance is made for exaggeration, some residue of justice remains in Barzun's indictment of Arnold. If we cannot ignore him in approaching the Romantics, we have certainly found it necessary to supplement and transcend him.

However, Arnold's services as a critic of the Romantics should not be forgotten. It was Arnold who helped not only to popularize Wordsworth, but who reminded an earnest generation that Wordsworth was, above all, a great poet. It was Arnold who, in his poetry and lectures *On the Study of Celtic Literature*, spoke out on behalf of Byron at a time when English taste had turned against him. It was Arnold, too, who saw and insisted on pointing out that there was something deeper and something stronger in Keats than the aesthetes or the perpetuators of the Johnny Keats legend could see. At the same time, Arnold made important discriminations. If he did not believe that the English Romantics possessed the towering stature that parochial English taste found in them, it is yet to his credit that he paid them the compliment of measuring them against the broad and ample standards of a European literature that included Homer, Sophocles, Virgil, Dante, Shakespeare, and Goethe. Finally, in Arnold's appraisal of the movement as a whole, he demonstrated his power to prophesy with considerable accuracy what taste would be a century later. Arnold's frankest and simplest expression of this evaluation is to be found in a letter he wrote to his brother Thomas on December 28, 1857

> A great transformation in the intellectual nature of the English, and, consequently, in their estimate of their own writers, is, I have long felt, inevitable. When this transformation comes the popularity of Wordsworth, Shelley, Coleridge, and others, remarkable men as they were, will not be the better for it.[31]

On the whole he was right. It has not been.

APPENDIX

EXPOSTULATION AND REPLY:
ARNOLD'S *RESIGNATION* AND WORDSWORTH'S
TINTERN ABBEY

MATTHEW ARNOLD'S *Resignation* has received consistent appreciation
from his critics, and sources of its thought have been more or less
fruitfully sought in Lucretius, Goethe, Senancour, Spinoza, Carlyle,
and the *Bhagavad Gita*. Professors Tinker and Lowry in *The Poetry
of Matthew Arnold: A Commentary* summarize most of these researches
(pp. 63–9). In the course of their discussion they mention that this is
one of Arnold's 'very few poems dealing directly with the environment
of the poet's youth in the Lake District', and in a note they refer the
reader to another poem of Arnold's, *The Youth of Nature*, which takes
its inspiration not only from the Lake District, but specifically from
Wordsworth. Nevertheless, they do not mention Wordsworth's name
in connection with *Resignation*. Lionel Trilling, in his masterly interpretation of the poem, has quite justly called *Resignation* 'the assertion
of the way to human freedom in the abandonment of the romantic
temperament', and he does mention Wordsworth's name in discussing
it, as did Swinburne in his 1867 review of Arnold's *New Poems*.[1]
However, neither Trilling nor Swinburne followed up this hint, and in
spite of all the source-hunting of recent years, neither has anyone else,
although Mr. Paull F. Baum, in a book published since the present
study was written, briefly lists in a footnote some parallels between
Arnold's poem and Wordsworth's *Tintern Abbey*.[2] But certainly Wordsworth, Arnold's 'pure and sage master', could not have been far from
the later poet's consciousness when he was composing one of his few
poems dealing with the Lake District. If the theme of *Resignation* is
as Trilling says, and since it does offer some striking parallels with
Tintern Abbey, which was in turn a favourite poem of Arnold's, the later
poem seems openly to invite consideration as a response to the attitudes
of the earlier writer.

The most obvious parallels involve the setting and dramatic situation.
In both poems the speakers are revisiting a well-remembered rural
scene in July after a lapse of years, five for Wordsworth, ten for Arnold.
Both poets are accompanied by intimate woman friends who are
addressed and exhorted in the poems. Wordsworth plainly identifies

his as his sister Dorothy, and Arnold's 'Fausta' is his favourite sister 'K' (Mrs. Forster).[3] In both poems the woman is represented as the more impassioned and 'natural' personality, sensitive and responsive to experience, while the male narrator is relatively subdued, chastened, and philosophical. Of course, these similarities are fairly external; nevertheless, their importance should not be underestimated, for if they are obvious to us, it is impossible that Arnold should have been unaware of them. He grew up in the shadow of Wordsworth, was finding the Romantic tradition in general inadequate to his needs, and much of his poetry (e.g., *Empedocles on Etna, The Youth of Nature*) occupies itself with a dialogue, even a debate, with the attitudes of the elder poet. It therefore seems unlikely in the extreme that Arnold could have been aware of the parallels between the situation in *Tintern Abbey* and that in his own poem without exploiting so rich a possibility.

And, in fact, comparison of *Resignation* and *Tintern Abbey* suggests most forcefully that Arnold's poem is almost a direct answer to Wordsworth's. In a central passage of *Tintern Abbey*, Wordsworth says that he was

> well pleased to recognise
> In nature and the language of the sense
> The anchor of my purest thoughts, the nurse,
> The guide, the guardian of my heart, and soul
> Of all my moral being.

R. D. Havens, commenting on these lines, defines Wordsworth's faith in nature as 'positive and creative as opposed to the inhibitive and corrective'.[4] The lessons Arnold derives from nature are, on the contrary, consistently 'inhibitive and corrective'. As Arnold's Empedocles says,

> We mortals are no kings
> For each of whom to sway
> A new-made world up-springs,
> Meant merely for his play;
> No, we are strangers here; the world is from of old.

> In vain our pent wills fret,
> And would the world subdue.
> Limits we did not set
> Condition all we do;
> Born into life we are, and life must be our mould.[5]

Similarly, in *Resignation*, Arnold argues that the poet finds no real home in the world of sense, for

> The world in which we live and move
> Outlasts aversion, outlasts love,
> Outlasts each effort, interest, hope,
> Remorse, grief, joy. . . .

Consequently he prefers to withdraw in advance from experience:

> Blame not thou, therefore, him who dares
> Judge vain beforehand human cares.

This stoic resignation of one

> Whom schooling of the stubborn mind
> Hath made, or birth hath found, resign'd

is at the opposite pole from Wordsworth's dynamic vision of a human soul, passionately involved in the greater life around it and developing from stage to stage [*Tintern Abbey*, ll. 65–111 *et passim*]. So strikingly negative is the attitude of the speaker in Arnold's poem that one might almost be tempted to take the whole as a piece of dramatic irony, with the speaker playing Mephistopheles, 'der Geist der stets verneint', to Fausta, the female Faust, if the speaker were not so manifestly sincere, and if his attitudes did not accord so well with those of the Arnold we know. Unlike Wordsworth, Arnold's speaker desires not to partake of life, but only of 'the general life', a quietist impulse.[6] To be sure, he characterizes this 'general life' partly in Wordsworthian language: 'The life of plants, and stones, and rain'; however, we recall that Wordsworth's Lucy was passively

> Rolled round in earth's diurnal course,
> With rocks, and stones, and trees

because she was dead. Wordsworth himself, intensely alive in his 'wise passiveness', has an ear attuned not only to the beauties and terrors of nature, but to 'The still, sad music of humanity', which Arnold terms merely, while urging a rather fastidious withdrawal from it, 'men's business' and 'clouds of individual strife'. Looking at an encampment of gipsies, the speaker in Arnold's poem points out that they might struggle and quarrel with their fate, but are much more contented if they go through the normal cycles of life with animal resignation:

> . . . they rubb'd through yesterday
> In their hereditary way,
> And they will rub through, if they can,
> Tomorrow on the self-same plan.

Could Arnold have been thinking of Wordsworth's poem *Gipsies*, with its diametrically opposed attitude? Wordsworth's gipsies, not having stirred during the course of a long day, provoke the following outburst:

> —oh, better wrong and strife
> Better vain deeds and evil than such life![7]

But Wordsworth possesses more than a feeling for the intensities of common human experience. In *Tintern Abbey* he gives thanks also for

> a sense sublime
> Of something far more deeply interfused

that disturbs him with 'the joy / Of elevated thoughts'. By means of this 'deep power of joy, / We see into the life of things'. In Arnold, on the other hand, there is no such 'power of joy'; Wordsworth's 'sense sublime' has been replaced by Arnold's 'sad lucidity of soul'. Arnold's speaker resigns all hope of joy and would be willing to settle for peace:

> That general life, which does not cease,
> Whose secret is not joy, but peace.

The world of things, according to Arnold, is far from sharing the Wordsworthian vitality. Where Wordsworth in *Tintern Abbey* could achieve his *O altitudo !* with a vision of the 'life of things', and elsewhere could express his faith 'that every flower / Enjoys the air it breathes' (*Lines Written in Early Spring*), Arnold can only feel about the things of nature that they 'Seem to bear rather than rejoice'. And the dimming of the 'celestial light' of romanticism has perhaps never been more poignantly revealed than in the decay of Wordsworth's 'something far more deeply interfused' into Arnold's 'something that infects the world'. Inevitably, Arnold's poet, as described in *Resignation*, does not possess Wordsworth's penetrating vision 'into the life of things'. Instead, says Arnold, 'Not deep the poet sees but wide'. The Arnoldian poet asks only to lean on a gate while

> Before him he sees life unroll,
> A placid and continuous whole.

Wordsworth, on the other hand, had sought and believed he had found communion with a vital principle, an active force far from placid:

> A motion and a spirit, that impels
> All thinking things, all objects of all thought,
> And rolls through all things.

In view, then, of both the structural similarities between the two poems and the striking number of points at which contradictory attitudes are expressed or implied, it is difficult for me not to see in *Resignation* a conscious reply to Wordsworth's *Tintern Abbey*, a reply which is a part of Arnold's lifelong debate in prose and verse with the romanticism of his own temperament and of an earlier generation of poets. As collateral evidence, it might be pointed out that many of the ideas expressed in *Resignation* were developed further in *The Youth of Nature*, a poem which is partly an elegy for Wordsworth and partly a philosophical debate with Wordsworth's spirit.[8] And finally, *Resignation* is drenched with Wordsworthian diction and imagery, as Swinburne pointed out; one example may suffice:

> He sees the drowsy new-wak'd clown
> In his white quaint-embroider'd frock
> Make, whistling, tow'rd his mist-wreathed flock—
> Slowly, behind his heavy tread,
> The wet, flower'd grass heaves up its head.

NOTES

List of Abbreviations

FOR convenience, the following abbreviations are used throughout the notes.

I. BOOKS BY MATTHEW ARNOLD

CA — *Culture and Anarchy*, ed. J. Dover Wilson, 1948.

Celtic — *On the Study of Celtic Literature* (bound with *Homer*), 1907.

EC I — *Essays in Criticism* (first series), 1889.

EC II — *Essays in Criticism: Second Series*, 1924.

EC III — *Essays in Criticism: Third Series*, ed. Edward J. O'Brien, 1910.

GB — *God and the Bible*, 1901.

Homer — *On Translating Homer* (including *Last Words on Translating Homer*; bound with *Celtic*), 1907.

Irish — *Irish Essays, and Others* (bound with *Mixed*), 1908.

LC — *The Letters of Matthew Arnold to Arthur Hugh Clough*, ed. H. F. Lowry, 1932.

LD — *Literature and Dogma*, 1883.

Letters — *Letters of Matthew Arnold*, 1848–1888, ed. G. W. E. Russell, 2 vols., 1896.

Mixed — *Mixed Essays* (bound with *Irish*), 1908.

NB — *The Note-Books of Matthew Arnold*, ed. H. F. Lowry, K. Young, and W. H. Dunn, 1952.

PW — *The Poetical Works of Matthew Arnold*, ed. C. B. Tinker and H. J. Lowry, 1950.

UL — *Unpublished Letters of Matthew Arnold*, ed. A. Whitridge, 1922.

Works — *The Works of Matthew Arnold*, ed. de luxe, 15 vols., 1903–4.

II. OTHER TITLES

CBEL — *The Cambridge Bibliography of English Literature*, ed. F. W. Bateson, 4 vols., Cambridge, 1941. Vol. V (Supplement), ed. George Watson, Cambridge, 1957.

Com — C. B. Tinker and H. F. Lowry, *The Poetry of Matthew Arnold: A Commentary*, 1950.

JEGP — *Journal of English and Germanic Philology*.

MLN — *Modern Language Notes*.

MP — *Modern Philology*.

OW — *The Poetical Works of William Wordsworth*, Oxford Standard Edition, ed. T. Hutchinson, 1933.

PMLA — *Publications of the Modern Language Association of America*.

RES — *Review of English Studies.*
Shedd — *The Complete Works of Samuel Taylor Coleridge*, ed. W. G. T.
Shedd, 7 vols., 1884.
TLS — *Times Literary Supplement.*

II. SUCH NEED OF JOY: WORDSWORTH

[1] *UL*, pp. 65–6. This letter was written May 28, 1872: Arnold did not meet Newman until May 12, 1880 (see *Letters*, II, 195–6).

[2] 'Wansfell! this Household has a favoured lot', XLII of *Miscellaneous Sonnets*. See Thomas Arnold, *Passages in a Wandering Life*, pp. 11, 39–44, and A. P. Stanley, *Life and Correspondence of Thomas Arnold*, I, 30, 280.

[3] Thomas Arnold, *Passages*, p. 45.

[4] *LC*, p. 29.

[5] *Letters*, I, 255, 386, and II, 58, 126, 186, 378–9.

[6] Although Wordsworth was appreciated and even claimed by representatives of various religious opinions, including the Catholics, his most notable influence seems to have been on such free-thinkers as Leslie Stephen, George Eliot, John Stuart Mill, and Matthew Arnold.

[7] *NB*, p. 123. See *Ecclesiastical Sonnets*, Part I, Sonnet VII. In *EC I*, p. 3, Arnold suggests that Wordsworth was much better employed in making his Preface than in writing the *Ecclesiastical Sonnets*, and in 'Wordsworth' he placed them among the work which can generally be enjoyed only by the Wordsworthians (*EC II*, p. 161).

[8] *The Prelude*, V, 359–63, 573–7; *NB*, p. 406.

[9] *Discourses in America*, p. 205. Wordsworth has 'that' instead of 'which'; *Poems Dedicated to National Independence and Liberty*, Part II, poem XXXIII.

[10] See, among other places, *LD*, p. 37, and *GB*, pp. x, 139. 'Stream of tendency' is from *The Excursion*, IX, 87.

[11] 'I am a Liberal tempered by experience, reflection, and renouncement.' *CA*, p. 41. (As J. Dover Wilson points out in a note in his edition, Arnold is glancing at the Liberal slogan 'Peace, retrenchment, reform'.) Elsewhere he called himself 'a Liberal of the future rather than a Liberal of the present'. *Irish*, p. 381.

[12] Katherine M. Peek, *Wordsworth in England: Studies in the History of His Fame*, pp. 247–60, offers a summary of Wordsworth's political views, quoting from a number of commentators such as Orville Dewey, William Hale White, Edith Batho, etc.

[13] Later in life, Arnold did make more of an effort to reach the Populace; see, for example, his speech 'Ecce, Convertimur ad Gentes', 1879 (*Irish*), in which he expressed discouragement over the progress of the middle class.

[14] See last paragraph of Wordsworth's *Guide to the Lakes*, Section Second (pp. 57–9 of fifth edition, 1835), for one of his most striking descriptions of this idyllic but vanishing culture.

[15] 'Emerson', *Discourse in America*, p. 196.

[16] 'A Study of Matthew Arnold', *Sewanee Review*. X (1902), 153.

[17] *Matthew Arnold*, p. 176.

[18] *NB*, pp. 294, 329; *EC II*, pp. 2, 3. See also *EC I*, p. 5.

[19] *EC II*, p. 96. See also *ibid.*, p. 36: 'Are Dryden and Pope poetical classics? . . . Wordsworth and Coleridge, as is well known, denied it; but the authority of Wordsworth and Coleridge does not weigh much with the young generation.'

[20] *NB*, p. 329, from *The Prelude*, I, 150.

[21] *The Prelude*, IV, 297–8, 304–6; *NB*, pp. 406, 519.

[22] *Palladium*, 11. 9–11; cf. *The Prelude*, XIV, 38 ff.

[23] *NB*, pp. 350, 514; from a letter of Wordsworth to Lady Beaumont, 1807.

[24] *NB*, p. 63, and used as close of 'Wordsworth', *EC II*, p. 162; from a letter of Wordsworth to Lady Beaumont, 1807.

[25] *Ibid.*, p. 329.

[26] *Memorial Verses*, l. 57.

[27] *EC II*, p. 154, from *The Recluse*. Incidentally, the stanza form of *Westminster Abbey* is reminiscent of that in the third stanza of Wordsworth's *Immortality Ode*.

[28] 'Charles Dickens', *Quarterly Review*, CXCVI (1902), 37. Swinburne's disaffection from Arnold goes back at least to the Wordsworth and Byron prefaces, in which Arnold had ranked Byron above Swinburne's beloved Shelley and Coleridge, but Swinburne was also exacerbated, no doubt, by reading in Arnold's *Letters*, published in 1895, a characterization of himself as 'a sort of pseudo-Shelley'. See *Letters*, I, 227.

[29] John Duke Coleridge's observation was published in *The Christian Remembrancer*, XXVII, 312, cited in *Com*, p. 37. Lines 102–3 of *Mycerinus* seem to reflect ll. 147–8 of the *Immortality Ode*:

> Might shrink half startled, like a guilty man
> Who wrestles with his dream . . .
> ARNOLD

> High instincts before which our mortal Nature
> Did tremble like a guilty Thing surprised:
> WORDSWORTH

On Melville, see Walter E. Bezanson, 'Melville's Reading of, Arnold's Poetry', *PMLA*, LXIX (1954), 378–9. Melville had noticed that the opening lines of Arnold's *The Youth of Nature*, an elegiac poem on Wordsworth, echoed Wordsworth's *Remembrance of Collins*, which in turn alludes to Collins' own *Ode on the Death of Mr. Thomson*. The same passage did not elude Swinburne's sharp observation; see his essay on 'Collins', *Miscellanies*, p. 60.

Robert E. Lovelace in 'A Note on Arnold's "Growing Old",' *MLN*, LXVIII (1953), 21–3, argues that Arnold's poem is related in theme and imagery to the passage on old age in *The Excursion* (IX, 50–92) and to the doctrine of recollection in the *Immortality Ode*, rather than to Browning's *Rabbi Ben Ezra*, as had been maintained by W. C. DeVane in *A Browning Handbook*, p. 260.

Lionel Trilling, in *Matthew Arnold*, pp. 104–5, hears echoes of Wordsworth (and Burke) in *Fragment of an 'Antigone'* which stresses the importance of deep ties of blood and clan, and also in *The Sick King in Bokhara* where the theme of a criminal who has committed a breach of the blood-bond seeking his own punishment has been anticipated by Wordsworth in III and XII of the *Sonnets on the Punishment of Death*.

Geoffrey Tillotson, in *Criticism and the Nineteenth Century*, p. 223n, notes that in spite of Arnold's strictures on the inadequacies of the English ballad metre, Arnold uses the metre Wordsworth had employed in many of the *Lyrical Ballads* when he sets out to write 'poems of thinking' in the two Obermann poems.

Louis Bonnerot, *Matthew Arnold, Poète*, p. 224, finds examples of Wordsworthian *primitivisme* in the close of *Parting* and in ll. 53–5 of *The Youth of Nature*. Also, Bonnerot asserts that in *The Future* Arnold 'a . . . repris le thème' of Wordsworth's *Immortality Ode*: 'Il n'y a pas imitation à proprement parler, mais adaption si discrète qu'elle n'a pas été perçue, jusqu'ici, par les critiques.' It seems to me that the close of *Parting* is more Shelleyan than Wordsworthian—e.g.:

> Blow, ye winds! lift me with you!
> I come to the wild.
> Fold closely, O Nature!
> Thine arms round thy child.

For other examples of what seem to be Wordsworthian echoes, see *Rugby Chapel*, ll. 145–6 (the poet is addressing his father):

> And through thee I believe
> In the noble and great who are gone.

which may be compared with *The Prelude*, XI, 393–5:

> There is
> One great society alone on earth:
> The noble Living and the noble Dead.

Also, ll. 60–6 of *Rugby Chapel* are thematically similar to Wordsworth's sonnet 'The world is too much with us'; Arnold's 'Gather and Squander' of l. 63 is an obvious echo of Wordsworth's 'Getting and spending'. In Arnold's *To a Gipsy Child by the Sea-Shore* there is an interesting blend of Keatsian and Wordsworthian elements in ll. 53–6:

> Ah! not the nectarous poppy lovers use,
> Not daily labour's dull Lethæan spring,
> Oblivion in lost angels can infuse
> Of the soil'd glory, and the trailing wing.

(Shelley's 'Lost angel of a ruined Paradise', *Adonais*, l. 88, may also have contributed something to this passage.) Sometimes merely a cadence from a much-read poet may unconsciously be transmitted:

> shapes
> Of joyless daylight; when the fretful stir
> Unprofitable, and the fever of the world . . .
> [*Tintern Abbey*, ll. 51–3]

> breath
> Of the night-wind, down the vast edges drear
> And naked shingles of the world.
> [*Dover Beach*, ll. 26–8]

On other occasions slight phrasal echoes may be heard, such as Arnold's 'See, in the blue profound' (*Obermann Once More*, l. 32) and Wordsworth's 'And rolls the planets through the blue profound' (*Miscellaneous Sonnets*, XI). Query: did Shelley pick up his device of making two adjectives serve as adjective-noun (e.g., 'intense inane') from Wordsworth?

30 Swinburne, *Essays and Studies*, p. 145; Bonnerot, *Matthew Arnold, Poète*, p. 222; Bush, *Mythology and the Romantic Tradition*, p. 254; Brown, *Matthew Arnold: A Study in Conflict*, p. 194. Swinburne is quite emphatic in the essay cited (a review of Arnold's *New Poems*, 1867) on the subject of Wordsworth's influence on Arnold: 'The good and evil influence of that great poet, perverse theorist, and incomplete man, upon Mr. Arnold's work is so palpable and so strong as to be almost obtrusive in its effects.'

31 *Letters*, I, 378.

32 *EC II*, p. 155.

33 See Appendix, pp. 219–23.

34 Arnold's poetic 'ideas' have been widely discussed by his critics; it seems not only more modest but more useful to deal here with some of the ways in which these 'ideas' find expression. For an analysis of Arnold's poetic views of Nature, see Joseph Warren Beach, *The Concept of Nature in Nineteenth Century English Poetry*, pp. 397–405.

35 Saintsbury sees in the leading ideas of the Preface a blending of Wordsworth with Aristotle; *A History of Criticism and Literary Taste in Europe*, III, 518–19.

36 Cf. the following passage from a letter from Arnold to his sister, Mrs. Forster ('K'), probably of 1849; 'More and more I feel bent against the modern English habit (too much encouraged by Wordsworth) of using poetry for thinking aloud, instead of making anything.' Had he in mind Keats on the 'égotistical sublime'? See Keats's letters of October 27, 1818, to Woodhouse, February 3, 1818, to Reynolds, November 22, 1817, to Bailey, and December 28, 1817, to George and Thomas Keats.

37 *Letters*, I, 66; see Bush, *Mythology and the Romantic Tradition*, pp. 261–2.

38 There may be some question about how well Arnold manages the third quality, plainness of thought; he is probably most successful

with the fourth, nobility. *Homer*, p. 149. On *Sohrab and Rustum* see Bush, *Mythology and the Romantic Tradition*, pp. 262–3, and J. B. Broadbent, 'Milton and Arnold', *Essays in Criticism*, VI (1956), 404–17.

[39] *LC*, p. 126.

[40] That is, in serious poetry. A rare, if not unique, example of verbal wit in Arnold's poetry occurs in the turn on the word *came* in *The Scholar-Gipsy*, ll. 39–40:

> And came, as most men deem'd, to little good,
> But came to Oxford and his friends no more.

The same poem contains what seems to be an echo of Pope, probably the only one in all Arnold's work, in l. 203: 'this strange disease of modern life'; cf. *Epistle to Arbuthnot*, l. 132, 'This long disease, my life'. In a letter of December 28, 1857, to his brother Thomas, Arnold conceded that in the age of Pope 'certainly poetry was a power in England ... which it is is not now—now it is almost exclusively "virginibus puerisque" and not for the sanest and most promising of these—then it was for *men* at large'. His remark later in the letter that poetry now interests 'only a small handful of sectaries' is an interesting foreshadowing of his later effort to rescue Wordsworth from the Wordsworthians. See Lowe, 'Two Arnold Letters', *MP*, LII (1955), 263.

[41] F. R. Leavis, *New Bearings in English Poetry*, p. 9.

[42] *Victorian Prose Masters*, p. 194.

[43] T. S. Eliot, *Ash Wednesday*, Part I.

[44] *Dover Beach*, ll. 30–4. The 'wintry clime' is from *Memorial Verses*, l. 42. Cf. Wordsworth's 'chilled age' in *Musings Near Aquapendente April, 1837*, l. 325.

[45] *Souvenirs d'enfance et de jeunesse*, quoted by Irving Babbitt, *Rousseau and Romanticism*, pp. 323–4.

[46] *Stanzas from the Grande Chartreuse*, ll. 85–7.

[47] *LC*, p. 146. Arnold himself thus seems to refute a recent critic who argues that the two great pastorals are not escapist; see Lawrence Perrine, 'Arnold's *The Scholar-Gipsy* and *Thyrsis*', *Explicator*, XV (February, 1957).

[48] *News Bearings*, p. 15.

[49] *Ibid.*, pp. 18–19.

[50] *UL*, p. 17.

[51] *LC*, p. 115. Wordsworth died April 23, 1850; Arnold's poem was published in June. Edward Quillinan, Wordsworth's son-in-law, was himself to be 'dirged' by Arnold the following year in *Stanzas in Memory of Edward Quillinan*.

[52] 'Mr. Arnold's New Poems', *Fortnightly Review*, VIII (1867), 426. Reprinted in *Essays and Studies*.

[53] *The Use of Poetry and the Use of Criticism*, p. 111.

[54] See Bonnerot, *Matthew Arnold*, p. 223n.

[55] John Keble, *Lectures on Poetry 1832–1841*, trans. E. K. Francis,

2 vols., Oxford, 1912. Keble had been a close friend of Dr. Arnold until ecclesiastical and political disagreements broke the friendship. He was also Matthew Arnold's godfather, and in spite of the coolness which had developed between him and Dr. Arnold, Matthew and his brother Thomas visited him at his home while they were at Winchester. See Thomas Arnold, *Passages*, p. 15. It was through Keble that Matthew Arnold became interested in Bishop Wilson's *Maxims*; Keble published a biography of Wilson in 1866. It is interesting that Keble wrote a pamphlet against the Deceased Wife's Sister Bill (one of Arnold's favourite bugbears in *Culture and Anarchy*) as early as 1849.

[56] *EC II*, p. 18. Arnold's note identifying these lines as *Inferno*, XXXIII, 39–40, is in error; they are really lines 49–50. Grandgent's edition of Dante instead of *impietrai*. at the end of the first line has *impetrai*:.

[57] Suggested by Brown, *Matthew Arnold*, p. 40.

[58] ' "Viewed from the heights of reason", Goethe wrote, "all life looks like some malignant disease and the world like a madhouse".' Thomas Mann, *Freud, Goethe, Wagner*, p. 59.

[59] *Virgil's Works*, trans. J. W. Mackail, Modern Library, p. 321.

[60] 'On the Modern Element in Literature', *EC III*, pp. 75, 79–80. The tribute to Wordsworth appears in 'Wordsworth', *EC II*, p. 162: 'It is not for nothing that one has been brought up in the veneration of a man so truly worthy of homage. . . . No Wordsworthian has a tenderer affection for this pure and sage master than I. . . .'

[61] The quotations are from *Below the Surface-stream* and *The Buried Life*.

[62] 'The French Play in London', *Irish*, p. 440.

[63] 'Goethe knew very well that this matter of being a genius is to a great extent a question of luck: that it is important to be at the right place in the right moment. "When I was eighteen", he says, "Germany was just eighteen too—a man could do something. I am glad I began then and not today, when the demands on one are so much greater."' Mann, *Freud, Goethe, Wagner*, p. 92.

[64] *EC III*, pp. 113–14.

[65] Arnold is probably remembering Faust's speech to Wagner on the two souls; *Faust*, Part One, 'Vor dem Tor', l. 1110 ff.

[66] 'but I leave / Half my life with you'. ll. 131–2. This seems to be one of those Tennysonian bits which would creep in: 'One has him so in one's head', Arnold wrote to John Duke Coleridge, 'one cannot help imitating him sometimes; but except in the last lines I thought I had kept him out of "Sohrab and Rustum". Mark any other places you notice, for I should wish to alter such.' *Life and Correspondence of Lord Coleridge* (1904), I, 210, letter of 1853. Cf. *In Memoriam*, LVII, 6: 'But half my life I leave behind'. Arnold's poem is dated November, 1849, but it was not published until 1852, two years later than *In Memoriam*. Kathleen Tillotson argues in 'Arnold, Clough, Walrond, and *In Memoriam*', *RES*, n.s. IV (1953), 136, that Arnold had once felt strongly the attraction of Tennyson, and that his strictures against

him are partly to be understood as reaction. With respect to the passage in question here, however, Mrs. Tillotson informs me that she is inclined to think that both poets were recalling Horace's 'et serves animae dimidium meae' (*Odes*, I, 3).

67 *Com.*, p. 188.

68 *The Concept of Nature*, p. 402.

69 *Revaluation*, p. 163.

70 'The Study of Poetry', *EC II*, p. 5.

71 *Homer*, p. 293. Arnold misquotes Wordsworth.

72 'Wordsworth', *EC II*, pp. 140–1. Here Arnold quotes accurately (except for capitalization).

73 See, for example, George H. Ford, *Keats and the Victorians*, p. 61n.

74 They are paired again for their 'natural magic' in 'A Guide to English Literature', *Mixed*, p. 147 (a book review first published in *Nineteenth Century*, December, 1877).

75 *Celtic*, p. 129.

76 *EC I*, p. 7.

77 'Emerson', *Discourses in America*, p. 160. See also *Letters*, II, 182–3.

78 *EC II*, pp. 135, 155, 158–9.

79 'Wordsworth', *Appreciations*, p. 43; first published in *Fortnightly Review*, April, 1874.

80 *Letters*, I, 191.

81 *Homer*, pp. 288–90. See also pp. 291–3 for Arnold's discerning illustrations of the relation between tone and verse form in specific passages of Wordsworth.

82 *Ibid.*, pp. 262–4. It is worth mentioning that the favourite lines 'The marble index of a mind for ever / Voyaging through strange seas of thought, alone', are a late addition and a clear exception to Arnold's generally low opinion of Wordsworth's late 'tinkerings'.

83 *Mixed*, p. 200.

84 *LC*, p. 133. Arnold is referring to an article by Lockhart in *Quarterly Review*, XCII (1852), 182–236, which he calls 'very just though cold'.

85 The quotations in this paragraph come from *EC II*, pp. 135–7, 154–6.

86 Douglas Bush, 'A Minority Report,' *Wordsworth: Centenary Studies*, ed. Gilbert T. Dunklin, pp. 10–11. F. R. Leavis, *The Common Pursuit*, pp. 219–20; cf. *Revaluation*, pp. 163–4.

87 It is by no oversight that I refer to Arnold's quarrel with an attitude, rather than with Leslie Stephen, because except for a few unfortunate phrases in Stephen's 'Wordsworth's Ethics', there was no real controversy between the two men. In 'Wordsworth's Ethics' itself, Stephen is at some pains to distinguish between poetic and prosaic methods of getting at truths. In 'Wordsworth's Youth', a later essay stimulated by Legouis's *La Jeunesse de Wordsworth*, he says even more emphatically that Wordsworth was a poet, not a philosopher. Finally, in 'Matthew Arnold', Stephen once again distinguished between the poetic and the prosaic methods, and rounded off the non-existent controversy by praising Arnold for having said 'precisely the right word about Byron and Wordsworth'. 'Wordsworth's Ethics' may be

found in *Hours in a Library*, Vol. III, and the two later essays in *Studies of a Biographer*, Vols. I and II. For more on the relation between poet and philosopher, see also Stephen's 'Coleridge', *Hours in a Library*, IV, 356–9.

[88] *EC I*, p. 7. But books alone would not have sufficed (Coleridge and Shelley had great reading) in the absence of a cultural climate which could support and give substance and application to ideas; *ibid.*, pp. 8–9.

[89] Even didactic poetry 'counts too, sometimes, by its biographical interest partly, not by its poetic interest pure and simple; but then this can only be when the poet producing it has the power and importance of Wordsworth, a power and importance which he assuredly did not establish by such didactic poetry alone'. *EC II*, p. 139.

[90] J. Dover Wilson in *Leslie Stephen and Matthew Arnold as Critics of Wordsworth* accuses Arnold of trying to eat his cake and have it too; G. H. Ford in *Keats and the Victorians* agrees. Professor Wilson's book, originally a lecture, is a defence of Leslie Stephen's 'Wordsworth's Ethics' against Arnold. Today it is possibly Arnold who needs defending more than Stephen; see C. F. Harrold in *Bibliographies of Studies in Victorian Literature 1932–1944*, p. 290: 'Professor Wilson seems curiously unaware of recent scholarship on Wordsworth and of the absence of any need to champion Stephen against Arnold's rejection of Wordsworth the "thinker".' A reviewer in the *Times Literary Supplement*, July 22, 1939, p. 437, considers too that Wilson has somewhat distorted Arnold's opinions of Wordsworth, and that these are 'more faithful to the master than Professor Wilson will allow'.

[91] *EC II*, pp. 148–9, 150. Peek in *Wordsworth in England*, p. 217, seems to miss the main point when she writes that 'the distinction between applying moral ideas to life, and applying moral ideas *systematically* to life may seem to be a slight and on the whole a meaningless one'. On the contrary, Arnold would insist, it is no more slight and meaningless than the distinction between the *Oresteia* and the *Nicomachean Ethics*.

[92] Edith C. Batho, *The Later Wordsworth*, pp. 341–2; Bush, 'A Minority Report', *Wordsworth: Centenary Studies*, ed. Dunklin.

[93] *In Harmony with Nature*, ll. 12–13.

[94] 'The instinct of delight in Nature and her beauty had no doubt extraordinary strength in Wordsworth himself as a child. But to say that universally this instinct is mighty in childhood, and tends to die away afterwards, is to say what is extremely doubtful. In many people, perhaps with the majority of educated persons, the love of nature is nearly imperceptible at ten years old, but strong and operative at thirty.' *EC II*, p. 151.

[95] *Irish*, p. 440.

[96] 'Wordsworth' and 'The Long Poem in the Age of Wordsworth' in *Oxford Lectures on Poetry*, 1909. Another interesting study of Wordsworth's relation to the 'cloud of destiny' is Lionel Trilling's essay

'Wordsworth and the Iron Time' in *Wordsworth: Centenary Studies*, reprinted in *The Opposing Self*, 1955. Others who insist, against what Arnold is supposed to have said, on the role of darkness, suffering, alienation, etc. in Wordsworth's poetry are G. Wilson Knight, *The Starlit Dome*, p. 5, and Karl Kroeber, 'The Reaper and the Sparrow: A Study in Romantic Style', *Comparative Literature*, X (1958), 204–5.

[97] *Letters*, I, 11.

[98] *Macmillan's Magazine*, XLVIII (1883), 155. The address may also be found in *Transactions of the Wordsworth Society*.

[99] *Letters*, II, 192.

[100] 'The Function of Criticism at the Present Time', *EC I*, pp. 13–14.

[101] 'Introduction', *ibid.*, p. v.

[102] 'Heinrich Heine', *ibid.*, p. 177.

[103] *Ibid.*

[104] *EC II*, p. 148.

[105] *Biographia Literaria*, ed. J. Shawcross, II, 7.

[106] *EC II*, pp. 152–3. Cf. Arnold's letter to his wife, after the meeting on May 2, 1883: 'The speech is over, and I got through it pretty well. The grave would have been cheerful compared to the view presented by the Westminster Chamber and the assembled Wordsworth Society when I came upon the platform. The hall was not full, the worthy —— having rather muddled things, and the Society is not composed of people of a festive type. . . . The papers were awfully boring, except Stopford Brooke's, which was saved by his Irish oratorical manner.' *Letters*, II, 245–6. 'The worthy ——' is probably William Knight, Honorary Secretary of the Society. See 'Report of Meeting' in *Transactions of the Wordsworth Society*, No. 5, p. 3.

[107] Presumably Brooke's *Theology in the English Poets*, 1874, and de Vere's essay 'The Genius and Passion of Wordsworth', first published in two parts in *Month*, 1880, and reprinted with two later papers on Wordsworth in *Essays Chiefly on Poetry*, 2 vols., 1887. De Vere was unable to attend the meeting at which Arnold spoke, but sent a paper to be read. Stopford Brooke gave a paper 'On Wordsworth's *Guide to the Lakes*'. See *Transactions of the Wordsworth Society*, No. 5, pp. 13, 25.

[108] 'Address to the Wordsworth Society, May 2, 1883', *Macmillan's Magazine*, XLVIII (1883), 154–5.

[109] In *Matthew Arnold: A Study in Conflict*. Trilling comments in the preface to the second edition of his *Matthew Arnold*: 'A very able scholar recently wrote a book chiefly to show that Arnold did not in actual practice always exemplify the virtues of mind he praised in his writing—despite all his talk of disinterestedness, he himself was often passionate and unfair, and so on. But does this matter and is it not a symptom of our confusion to remark it—an evidence of our losing the sense of human limits, therefore of human processes, of our turning to the desperate absolute, thus to make it a reproach to a man that he did not achieve the perfection of his ideal ?' For a study of the rhetorical element in Arnold's criticism—'the rhetoric which Arnold attacked, the rhetoric he taught, and the rhetoric he used in his appeals to the

public'—see Everett Lee Hunt, 'Matthew Arnold: The Critic as Rhetorician', *Quarterly Journal of Speech*, XX (1934), 483–507.

[110] Although I have tried to chart my own course, the following discussion is inevitably indebted in a general way to Chapter XI, 'Joy Whose Grounds Are True', in Trilling's *Matthew Arnold*.

[111] *Empedocles on Etna*, Act II, ll. 258–5.

[112] *Letters*, I, 60.

[113] *GB*, p. x. The quotation is from 'The pibroch's note, discountenanced or mute'.

[114] T. S. Eliot, 'Arnold and Pater', *Selected Essays*, pp. 385–90. Eliot apparently was following Paul Elmer More, who respected Arnold but saw in his criticism tendencies which resulted in the descent of Arnold to Pater to Wilde; *Shelburne Essays, Seventh Series*, 1910, pp. 230–3. Eliot's view is challenged by Leonard Brown, 'Matthew Arnold's Succession: 1850–1914', *Sewanee Review*, XLII (1934), 158–79. On Eliot and Arnold see also M. L. S. Loring, 'T. S. Eliot on Matthew Arnold', *Sewanee Review*, XLIII (1935), 479–88, and Douglas Bush, *Mythology and the Romantic Tradition*, Chapter XV.

[115] *EC I*, p. 160. Cf. letter to Lady de Rothschild, August 9, 1868, *Letters*, I, 458–9.

[116] *Obermann Once More*, ll. 237–40.

[117] *LD*, p. 188. Arnold had previously discussed this difference between ethics and religion in 'Marcus Aurelius', *EC I*.

[118] *GB*, p. 137.

[119] *Mixed*, p. 251.

[120] H. M. Margoliouth, *Wordsworth and Coleridge 1795–1834*, pp. 176–7.

[121] William E. Buckler, *Matthew Arnold's Books*, pp. 132–42. The quotation is from p. 141.

[122] The poems added to the section 'Lyrical Poems' are *To the Same* ('Bright flowers, whose home is everywhere!') following *To the Daisy*; *The Green Linnet*, which was added at the request of the poet's grandson (see note 142 below), following *I Wandered Lonely as a Cloud*; *The Cuckoo Again* ('Yes, it was the mountain Echo') following *To the Cuckoo*; and *The Primrose of the Rock* at the end of the section. To the section 'Reflective and Elegiac Poems', Arnold added *A Poet's Epitaph* following *The Fountain*. A few minor changes and corrections were made in titles or in table of contents entries. The remaining alterations of contents were in the 'Sonnets' section. The following sonnets were dropped from the original list:

1. 'Pelion and Ossa flourish side by side'
2. 'Adieu, Rydalian Laurels! that have grown'
3. 'Degenerate Douglas! oh, the unworthy Lord'
4. 'Sacred Religion! "mother of form and fear"'
5. 'They called Thee MERRY ENGLAND, in old time'
6. 'There's not a nook within this solemn Pass'

The following six sonnets were added to the original list:

1. 'Surprised by joy—impatient as the Wind'

2. 'They dreamt not of a perishable home'
3. 'From low to high doth dissolution climb'
4. 'Such age how beautiful! O Lady bright'
5. 'Methought I saw the footsteps of a throne'
6. 'In my mind's eye a Temple, like a cloud'

Five other sonnets were moved to locations different from those they had occupied originally.

[123] Cf. Thomas M. Raysor, 'The Establishment of Wordsworth's Reputation', *JEGP*, LIV (1955), 65: 'the later fame of Wordsworth, even in his own day, has certainly not been founded on *The Excursion*, or indeed on any poetry of Wordsworth after 1807'.

[124] As a matter of fact, it was Arnold's private opinion that Wordsworth's 'body of work is more interesting than Milton's though not so great'. *Letters*, II, 182.

[125] 'Wordsworth', *Fortnightly Review*, n.s. XV (1874), 455 ff. Reprinted in *Appreciations*. It seems unlikely that Arnold could have missed this essay when it first appeared, but there is no certain evidence that he read it until 1880, during which year he copied out some passages from it into his notebook. *NB*, p. 341.

[126] *Oxford Lectures on Poetry*, p. 127.

[127] 'Matthew Arnold's Essay on Wordsworth', *Evolution and Repentance*, 1935. This paper was first read at a meeting of the Modern Language Association of America, December, 1926. In revised form it was first published in *The Bookman*, LXIX (1929), 479–84, where it caught the attention of G. G. Sedgewick, who made a telling reply in 'Wordsworth, Arnold, and Professor Lane Cooper', *Dalhousie Review*, X (1930), 57–66.

[128] 'Emerson', *Discourses in America*, p. 178.

[129] *Matthew Arnold*: pp. 94–5.

[130] *CA*, p. 37; *EC III*, p. 37.

[131] The book is dated 1873, but the Introduction and the first four chapters appeared in *Cornhill Magazine* in 1871.

[132] See esp. pp. vi–vii, ix, x, xiii–xiv of *LD*.

[133] *Letters*, II, 313.

[134] For example, Arnold wrote to T. H. Huxley on February 13, 1873: 'I think . . . we shall see in our time a change in religion as great as that which happened at the Reformation, and, like that, a decided advance on the whole: though like that, by the mere fact of it being a popular movement and embracing numbers of men, it will carry with it a large part of blunder and misconception.' W. H. G. Armytage 'Matthew Arnold and T. H. Huxley: Some New Letters 1870–1880', *RES*, n.s. IV (1953), 349.

[135] T. Sturge Moore, 'Matthew Arnold', *Essays and Studies by Members of the English Association* (1938), offers a refreshingly sympathetic but brief appraisal of the meaning and present value of Arnold's religious efforts; see pp. 7–17. William Robbins in *The Ethical Idealism of Matthew Arnold* cites evidence that Arnold's religious writings exerted

a considerable influence; see pp. 176–81. In a note on p. 236 Robbins quotes Frederic Harrison who wrote that the Arnoldian transformation of Anglicanism 'sank deep into the minds of many thinking men and women, who could neither abandon the spiritual poetry of the Bible nor resist the demonstrations of science'.

[136] *St. Paul and Protestantism and Last Essays on Church and Religion*, pp. 157–8.

[137] *Letters*, II, 175; see also pp. 176–7.

[138] *Irish*, p. 376.

[139] *Letters*, II, 41. Similar concerns are expressed in the preface to *Mixed Essays*.

[140] *EC II*, pp. 2–3, 149.

[141] See *Letters*, II, 158, March 11, 1877: 'I have promised Macmillan to make a volume out of the best of Hales and Whichcote, and Cudworth's two sermons. I shall write twenty pages of introduction, and call the volume *Broad Church in the Seventeenth Century*. I think it will do good.' Arnold and Macmillan corresponded about this project in the first three months of 1877; see Buckler, *Matthew Arnold's Books*, pp. 158–9. On January 22 Arnold, replying to Macmillan's suggestion that he do the Wordsworth selections, wrote to express interest (Buckler, pp. 132–3). Across the top of the letter, however, he added the postscript (not reproduced by Professor Buckler): 'Don't forget, however, the Hales and Co.—and the Johnson. I am against having many notes. Let us not aim at a school-book, but rather at a literary book which schools can and will use.'

[142] *LC*, p. 97. The letter to Miss Quillinan from which I quote is unpublished; it is in the library of Dove Cottage Museum, Ambleside. Thanks to the kind permission of the Chairman of the Trustees, and to the help of the Honorary Librarian, Mr. Johnson, I can offer it here in full:

> Cobham, Surrey.
> Jan. 20th 1880.

My dear Mima

I found your letter here on my return from Woodhouse. Very many thanks to you for copying out for me Willie Wordsworth's remarks on my little volume of selections from his dear grandfather's poems. What I had to think of, both in the preface and in the selection, was the great public; it is the great public which I want to make buy Wordsworth's poems as they buy Milton's. Many poems which Wordsworth's friends and admirers like, I have therefore excluded; the first poem mentioned by Willie Wordsworth is a case in point; he may like it, but to the great public it would appear inane. Kilchurn Castle I should like to have put in, but there was so much blank verse already, & blank verse is not popular. Rob Roy is interesting, but not good enough in proportion to its length, I thought, for my volume. The Green Linnet I perhaps ought to have inserted; so many people like it, and such good judges; perhaps I was in this case misled by the poem's not being a special favourite with myself. I put in everything biographical, & therefore some sonnets not of high value as poetry were inserted; two of them, however, I have struck out from the second edition. The little book is doing very well; I think nearly 4000 are sold. The large paper edition is indeed beautiful; if you have not got it, you must let me give it to you.

We have just had a letter from Dick; Fan will have told you the good report of him which reached us a day or two ago. If anything could console us for the dear, dear boy's absence, it would be the knowledge that it is doing him good to be where he is.

ever affectionately your,
Matthew Arnold

P.S. Lord Cranbrook has today taken charge of a copy of the little Wordsworth for Lord Lytton, the Viceroy, tell Willie W.

143 *Works* ed. Cook and Wedderburn, III, 82n; cited in Peek, *Wordsworth in England*, p. 183.

144 'Byron', *EC II*, p. 203.

145 *EC II*, p. 161.

146 See the article cited above in note 127.

147 See Arnold's letter to Miss Quillinan on April 21, 1879, *Letters*, II, 182–3. There are several remarks on textual matters in Arnold's letters to Macmillan published in Buckler, *Matthew Arnold's Books*; see e.g., p. 137. In a letter to Craik of the house of Macmillan on August 27, 1879, Arnold requests that copies be sent to various people, including Miss Quillinan because she 'has been of help to me in restoring the text of the poems in several places'. Buckler, p. 142.

148 *EC II*, p. 206.

149 Sir Henry Taylor, *Autobiography*, II, 61; cited in Peek, *Wordsworth in England*, p. 183.

150 See letter to Miss Jemima Quillinan given in note 142 above.

151 Arnold commented in his opening remarks on the honour of his being chosen president although he was not a member, and explained why he had declined membership. However, in the List of Members published in *Transactions of the Wordsworth* Society, No. 1, p. 17, his name appears.

152 Patrick Cruttwell, 'Wordsworth, the Public, and the People', *Sewanee Review*, LXIV (1956), 75, 76n, 78–9, *et passim*.

III. THE ANGUISH OF GREATNESS: BYRON

1 *EC II*, p. 172.

2 'Byron', *From Anne to Victoria*, ed. Bonamy Dobrée, p. 602; reprinted in *On Poetry and Poets*, 1957. These juvenile verses may still be seen in the bound volumes of the Smith Academy *Record*, St. Louis, 1904–5, in the library of Washington University.

3 See *Com*, p. 321.

4 Cf. T. S. Omond, 'Arnold and Homer', *Essays and Studies by Members of the English Association*, III (1912), 71–91.

5 Thomas Arnold, *Passages*, p. 15. The speech is from Act V, sc. iii,

of *Marino Faliero*: 'I speak to Time and to Eternity'.

[6] *LC*, p. 25, from a letter of Clough to J. C. Shairp.

[7] See Trilling, *Matthew Arnold*, Chapter I, and Thomas Arnold, *Passages*, p. 57.

[8] See Trilling's interesting analysis, *Matthew Arnold*, pp. 96–7. However, we do not know, as Trilling has it, that Mycerinus was calmed; Arnold says 'It may be'.

[9] Cf. *Childe Harold*, Canto III, stanza xiv.

[10] Act II, l. 23. Cf. *Obermann*, ll. 93–6:

> Ah! two desires toss about
> The poet's feverish blood.
> One drives him to the world without,
> And one to solitude.

[11] *Obermann*, ll. 79–80.

[12] Tinker and Lowry call attention to ll. 33–4 of *Parting*, and also to the figured arras of *Tristram and Iseult*, II, 147–53, which echoes *The Siege of Corinth*, ll. 620–1; *Com*, pp. 154, 114–15. In addition, the famous lines from *Stanzas from the Grande Chartreuse*,

> Wandering between two worlds, one dead,
> The other powerless to be born

may echo *Don Juan*, XV, stanza 99: 'Between two worlds life hovers like a star.' In his Byron anthology Arnold givest his stanza as the concluding selection of 'Personal, Lyric, and Elegiac' poetry, and entitles it 'Life'. The phrase 'between two worlds' was a commonplace of the times, however, and may also be found in Maurice de Guérin and Alfred de Musset.

[13] *EC I*, p. 161.

[14] Cf. H. J. C. Grierson, 'Lord Byron: Arnold and Swinburne', *The Background of English Literature*, pp. 73–4.

[15] See Samuel C. Chew, *Byron in England: His Fame and After-fame*, p. 194 ff., on the reactions of other famous and not so famous mourners.

[16] *Letters*, II, 151.

[17] *LC*, p. 92.

[18] *Letters*, I, 11. The unpleasant note of snobbery will be heard again in the essay on Keats, and may have played a part in Arnold's fairly easy treatment of Byron's sexual transgressions.

[19] This comment and the two which follow are quoted from the collection made by Edith Batho in an appendix to *The Later Wordsworth*. Those I have quoted may be found there on pp. 363 and 364.

[20] Dowden and White are quoted in Chew, *Byron in England*, pp. 297, 309–10.

[21] 'Byron, Goethe, and Mr. Matthew Arnold', *Contemporary Review*, XL (1881), 184–5. Mark Van Doren, in 'Poets and Trimmers', *Sewanee Review*, LIII (1950), 53, quotes what Kierkegaard wrote in 1843: 'Let others complain that the age is wicked, my complaint is

that it is wretched; for it lacks passion. Men's thoughts are thin and flimsy like lace, they are themselves pitiable like the lacemakers. The thoughts of their hearts are too paltry to be sinful.' Cf. an epigram also by Kierkegaard: 'What our age lacks is not reflection but passion', discussed by Walter Kaufmann, *Existentialism from Dostoevsky to Sartre* (New York, 1957), p. 18.

22 Quoted by J. A. Symonds in his introduction to Byron for Ward's *English Poets.*

23 In this purpose, as in so many others, Arnold considered himself a continuator of his father's mission. He praised his father in many places for being, relative to his time, so European in his historic sense. See, e.g., *Letters*, II, 5. On Byron's impact in France, Alfred de Musset gives arresting testimony in the second chapter of *Confessions of a Child of the Century.*

24 *EC II*, pp. 196–7.

25 E. D. H. Johnson, *The Alien Vision of Victorian Poetry*, p. 199.

26 *EC I*, pp. 176–8. Senancour is distinguished from Byron, however, not only by his greater intellectuality, but by his 'severe sincerity' in dealing with the great question of St. Bernard: 'Bernarde, ad quid venisti?' Byron, Rousseau, and Chateaubriand, on the other hand, are too often 'attitudinising and thinking of the effect of what they say on the public'. *EC III*, p. 114. Arnold's high esteem for force of character is both Carlylean and Goethean. Thomas Mann has observed that Goethe 'knew, and said, that it was only through the character and personality of the author that a work actually had influence and became a monument of culture. "One must *be* something in order to *do* anything".' *Freud, Goethe, Wagner*, p. 55.

27 *EC II*, p. 193.

28 *Letters*, I, 278, to J. Dykes Campbell, September 22, 1864. Arnold is declining an invitation to review Tennyson on the grounds that depreciatory criticism of a contemporary poet 'would inevitably be attributed to odious motives'.

29 Slightly altered from the famous passage on the dying gladiator in *Childe Harold*, IV, cxli. This canto, the major influence on Arnold's Rugby prize poem, apparently remained his favourite poem of Byron. In the anthology of 1881 he gave seventy-five stanzas from this canto alone, compared with one hundred and four from the whole of *Don Juan.*

30 *Letters*, II, 224. Other correspondence, between Arnold and his publisher, relating to this volume may be found in Buckler, *Matthew Arnold's Books*, pp. 146–50.

31 *EC I*, p. 177. Cf. *LC*, p. 65: 'The poet's matter being the *hitherto experience of the world, and his own*, increases with every century. . . . For me you may often hear my sinews cracking under the effort to unite matter. . . .' See also *EC III*, 'On the Modern Element in Literature', pp. 38–9.

32 *EC I*, pp. 192, 193.

33 *EC III*, pp. 62, 77.

34 *EC I*, pp. 6–7. First published in *National Review*, November, 1864.

[35] *EC I*, p. 10.

[36] As a safeguard against the oversimplified 'Lost Leader' view, *The Prelude*, X, 470–80 should be remembered:

> When a taunt
> Was taken up by scoffers in their pride,
> Saying, 'Behold the harvest that we reap
> From popular government and equality,'
> I clearly saw that neither these nor aught
> Of wild belief engrafted on their names
> By false philosophy had caused the woe,
> But a terrific reservoir of guilt
> And ignorance filled up from age to age,
> That could no longer hold its loathsome charge,
> But burst and spread in deluge through the land.

[37] *EC I*, p. 11.

[38] Arnold's racialist notions have been studied by Frederic E. Faverty, *Matthew Arnold the Ethnologist*, 1951.

[39] *Letters*, I, 279.

[40] *Ibid.*, I, 234.

[41] Two modern critics have discussed the Scottish element in Byron: J. D. Symon, *Byron in Perspective*, 1924, and T. S. Eliot in 'Byron', cited above note 2. Eliot stresses the environmental rather than the racial force of Byron's Calvinist upbringing and the part it played in his un-English sense of guilt, and he relates Byron's best work in *Don Juan* to the Scottish colloquial tradition in poetry. F. R. Leavis too believes that Byron's satire 'has less affinity with Pope than with Burns'. *Revaluation*, p. 150.

[42] *Celtic*, p. 115. Arnold was evidently unfamiliar with Anglo-Saxon poetry.

[43] *Ibid.*, pp. 117–19. Perhaps Arnold exaggerates the explicability of Faust's motivation. However, almost as though to bear out his opinion of German reasonableness, there is Goethe's clear, reasonable, and unfounded explanation of Manfred's secret, quoted in Nichol's *Byron*, pp. 117–18. Incidentally, Arnold never explained why the Anglo-Saxon (Germanic) Philistine was so deficient in reasonableness. But we must not press him too hard; he wore his theories very loosely, and could have taken this one only half-seriously.

[44] *Ibid.*, pp. 130–2.

[45] Cf. J. B. Orrick, *Matthew Arnold and Goethe*, p. 20.

[46] Brown, *Matthew Arnold*, p. 217n. The Shelley volume was written by J. A. Symonds, who also contributed the 'Byron' introduction to Ward's *English Poets*.

[47] This brief publishing history is based in part on correspondence between Arnold and his publishers in Buckler, *Matthew Arnold's Books*, pp. 146, 148, letters of May 21 and December 2, 1880.

[48] For the material in this pargraph and the next I am indebted to Chew, *Byron in England*, Chapter XIII.

[49] *CBEL* lists only two selections of Wordsworth's poems between his

death (1850) and Arnold's volume (1879). One is the Tauchnitz edition of 1864 in two volumes, the other was edited by Palgrave for the Moxon Series, 1865.

[50] *EC II*, p. 49.

[51] Buckler, *Matthew Arnold's Books*, p. 148.

[52] A few of the pieces had been incorporated into *The Prelude* or *The Excursion*, but had first been published separately, e.g., 'There was a boy' and 'Margaret'.

[53] Swinburne, 'Wordsworth and Byron', *Nineteenth Century*, XV (April and May, 1884), 583–609, 764–90, reprinted in *Miscellanies*, 1895. Grierson, 'Lord Byron: Arnold and Swinburne', *The Background of English Literature*, pp. 70–1.

[54] 'Fiction, Fair and Foul', first published in five parts in *Nineteenth Century*, June, 1880, to October, 1881. Reprinted in *Works*, ed. Cook and Wedderburn, XXXIV. The end of Part II (August, 1880), all of Part III (September), and the opening of Part IV (November) are the relevant portions.

[55] See Chew, *Byron in England*, pp. 307–13, and Peek, *Wordsworth in England*, pp. 186–7, 220–33 for discussions of this controversy.

[56] From Swinburne's preface to the volume of Byron selections he edited for the Moxon Series in 1865. Reprinted in *Essays and Studies*; the quotation is from p. 239. Arnold's essay of 1881 with its ranking of Byron above Keats, Coleridge, and Shelley, contributed to Swinburne's later violent anti-Byron position.

[57] *Essays and Studies*, pp. 242, 254.

[58] See White, 'Byron, Goethe, and Mr. Matthew Arnold', *Contemporary Review*, XL (1881), 183; Edward Dowden, *The French Revolution and English Literature*, pp. 261–2; and W. E. Henley's review in the *Athenaeum*, June 25, 1881, reprinted in *Views and Reviews: Literature*, p. 56 ff.

[59] Arnold is referring to the great vogue of the earlier part of the century; except for references to Swinburne and Nichol, he seems to ignore the Byron revival of the seventies. One of the sources of Swinburne's anger, incidentally, was probably this bland assumption on Arnold's part that no other adequate volume of Byron selections existed, although a second edition of Swinburne's had appeared in 1875.

[60] At this point in the essay (*EC II*, p. 173) appears some material on Taine's and Scherer's criticism of Byron, which had first been used in slightly different form in the periodical version of 'Wordsworth', but had been deleted when that article was reprinted as the preface to *Poems of Wordsworth*. E. K. Brown, in *Studies in the Text of Matthew Arnold's Prose Works*, quite overlooked this later use of the suppressed passage when he called it, in discussing 'Wordsworth', 'in irreconcilable contradiction with the paper on Byron published two years later. It is of capital importance for the historian of Matthew Arnold's literary opinions to note that the puzzling fervour of his admiration for Byron was a development of the last decade.' (p. 121.) Since the passage in question, which is not favourable to Byron, was reproduced

almost verbatim in the later paper, Brown's comment can only lead to confusion. The removal of the passage from 'Wordsworth' indicates neither an increasing nor a puzzling fervour of admiration for Byron, but merely that, first, Arnold may, during the several months between the periodical and book publication of 'Wordsworth', have already begun to think of a companion volume on Byron, and second, that a controversial discussion of Byron's reputation was out of keeping with both the tone and contents of 'Wordsworth'.

[61] Act I, sc. i, 138–40; Act II, sc. ii, 403–4.

[62] Henley, in the review cited above (note 58), did argue that not only was the touchstone method inadequate in itself, but that Arnold was unfair in his use of it by comparing the feeblest of Byron's verse with gems from Leopardi and Wordsworth.

[63] *EC II*, pp. 175–6. Cf. T. S. Eliot, 'Byron', *From Anne to Victoria*, p. 611: 'Of Byron one can say, as of no other English poet of his eminence, that he added nothing to the language, that he discovered nothing in the sounds, and developed nothing in the meaning, of individual words.' Eliot concludes that Byron's best work is that which is in the colloquial tradition, not that in which he was trying to be 'poetic'. Many modern critics concur; see, e.g., Ronald Bottrall, 'Byron and the Colloquial Tradition in English Poetry', *Criterion*, XVIII (1939), 204–24. Both Eliot's and Bottrall's essays have conveniently been reprinted in a recent publication, *English Romantic Poets: Modern Essays in Criticism*, ed. M. H. Abrams, New York, 1960.

[64] One of the quoted passages,

> All shall be void
> Destroy'd

from *Heaven and Earth*, I, iii, 94–5, is even given twice. Swinburne parodied this sort of verse in his 1884 attack on Byron (*Miscellanies*, p. 83):

> ... let such vile verse—why should it not?—
> Rot.

[65] *Homer*, pp. 263–4; *Mixed* ('A French Critic of Milton'), p. 200; *EC II* ('Milton'), p. 62.

[66] Arnold jotted excerpts from these articles in his 1880 notebook, *NB*, pp. 343, 347. Ruskin's attack on Wordsworth, and his elevation of Byron, were in turn prompted by Arnold's 'Wordsworth' of 1879.

[67] 'Inscriptions: xiii', *OW*, p. 550; 'The Longest Day', *OW*, p. 90. See Ruskin, *Works*, XXXIV, 322, 332.

[68] It derives mostly from Swinburne's 1865 essay-preface; some passages are almost verbatim.

[69] Arnold's use or abuse of Goethe quotation was first discussed in a review by William Hale White cited above (note 21); this review was reprinted in *Pages from a Journal*, 1901. Orrick, *Matthew Arnold and Goethe*, covers the subject of Arnold and Goethe more generally. He argues that Arnold restricted Goethe, choosing what he wanted for his own purposes, and also that Arnold's view of Goethe was derived

largely from Carlyle. The pages relevant to Arnold's 'Byron' are pp. 17–27.

[70] Nichol had translated the German *Talent* as 'genius'; Arnold was willing to admit that Byron had talent, but denied him genius: '... talent gives the notion of power in a man's performance, genius gives rather the notion of felicity and perfection in it'. *EC II*, p. 182.

[71] *EC II*, p. 185. This statement, which Arnold uses to explain Byron's 'real source of weakness both as a man and as a poet', is the Goethe quotation which is most misleadingly wrenched out of context, as William Hale White pointed out.

[72] White, *Contemporary Review*, XL (1881), 184.

[73] See Buckley, *Poetry and Morality*, p. 65, for a further discussion of the pragmatic 'sleight-of-hand' by which Arnold interchanges 'healthful' and 'true'.

[74] Cf. Arnold's opinion that Goethe 'is the greatest poet of modern times, not because he is one of the half-dozen human beings who in the history of our race have shown the most signal gift for poetry, but because, having a very considerable gift for poetry, he was at the same time, in the width, depth, and richness of his criticism of life, by far our greatest modern man'. *Mixed* ('A French Critic on Goethe'), p. 234.

[75] *Matthew Arnold*, p. 189.

[76] *LC*, p. 128.

[77] *Matthew Arnold*, p. 130. Cf. Buckley, *Poetry and Morality*, pp. 44–5.

[78] See I. A. Richards's noble but, I think, finally unsatisfactory attempt to attach some clear meaning to this term; *Practical Criticism*, Part III, Chapter 7.

[79] Byron himself was well aware of the difference between the *personae* of the narrators of the first two cantos of *Childe Harold*, and of the last two, and of *Don Juan*, and between all of these and the Lord Byron who wrote the poems, although to be sure he was not always consistent in keeping the distinctions clear in practice.

[80] *From Anne to Victoria*, p. 611.

[81] Arnold's description of Heine, but equally appropriate here. *EC I*, p. 192.

[82] Orrick, *Matthew Arnold and Goethe*, pp. 22–3.

[83] *Matthew Arnold*, p. 372. Trilling calls him 'perfectly' indifferent, but this surely does not square with the outburst in 'Shelley' or even with the few moral comments Arnold permitted himself in 'Byron'.

[84] *Ibid.*

[85] This and the following quotation from 'Count Leo Tolstoi' are in *EC II*, pp. 275–76.

[86] *EC I*, p. 216.

[87] W. E. Henley in the *Athenaeum*, June 25, 1881, p. 840.

[88] R. W. Chambers, 'Ruskin (and Others) on Byron', *Man's Unconquerable Mind*, p. 313.

[89] *Irish*, p. 440.

[90] See Trilling, *Matthew Arnold*, p. 376.

[91] Dowden, *The French Revolution and English Literature*, pp. 261–2.

IV. THE STRAYED REVELLER: KEATS

[1] See Ford, *Keats and the Victorians*, pp. 74–5; H. W. Garrod, 'Matthew Arnold's 1853 Preface', *RES*, XVII (1941), 310–21; Kathleen Tillotson, 'Rugby 1850', *RES*, n.s. IV (1953), 122–40. Ford devotes three chapters to Arnold and Keats; although I have tried to cover the ground independently, this chapter is necessarily much indebted to his excellent study.

[2] See *EC II* ('John Keats'), p. 120.

[3] *Com*, p. 115. Arnold's later apostrophe to the hunter (ll. 186–93) ends with an effect of chill and distancing in time especially reminiscent of the end of *The Eve of St. Agnes*.

[4] *Ibid.*, p. 227.

[5] *Letters*, I, 147.

[6] H. W. Garrod, *Keats*, pp. 95–7. See also M. R. Ridley, *Keats' Craftsmanship*, pp. 208–9; Bonnerot, *Matthew Arnold*, pp. 476–7, 483; *Com*, p. 212; and J. D. Jump, *Matthew Arnold*, pp. 98–9.

[7] *Letters*, I, 378. Tinker and Lowry observe that 'the indebtedness to Theocritus, save for the name "Thyrsis" and the references in the ninth, tenth, and nineteenth stanzas, is of a very general sort'. *Com*, p. 218.

[8] Cf. Ford, *Keats and the Victorians*, p. 65.

[9] Jump, *Matthew Arnold*, p. 101, following Leavis, *Revaluation*, pp. 190–1.

[10] *LC*, p. 146. The late Professor Tinker, in a private letter to me, placed *The Scholar-Gipsy* among Arnold's romantic poems, but not *Thyrsis*. I have not found it necessary for the present discussion to distinguish in detail between the two poems.

[11] *LC*, p. 96. Keats's *Life and Letters* by Monckton Milnes appeared in early September, 1848; *The Strayed Reveller, and Other Poems* by 'A.' in late February, 1849. The letter to Clough in which Arnold expressed his agitation is undated, but Lowry assigns it to the 1848–9 period on the basis of handwriting. It seems unlikely to the point of impossibility that Arnold would not have read the letters as soon after publication as possible, especially when they came recommended by Clough, who in turn had been in communication with Milnes before they were published.

[12] *Matthew Arnold*, p. 97.

[13] *LC*, p. 97.

[14] *Ibid.*, p. 63.

[15] *Ibid.*, p. 97. The allusion to Horace (characteristically misquoted) makes clear just how contemptuous he was:

> Ambubaiarum collegia pharmacopolae,
> Mendici, mimae, balatrones, hoc genus omne.

In the English of D. B. Wyndham Lewis: 'The community of doxies, quacks, beggars, mummers, rascals, and all their kind'. Horace, *Satires*, I, 2.

16 *Matthew Arnold*, pp. 97–101.

17 Arnold underlined the word *new* in writing to Clough about *The New Sirens*, *LC*, pp. 105–7. In this poem the Siren's voice almost quotes Keats: 'Judgment shifts, convictions go; . . . Only, what we feel we know.'

18 *LC*, pp. 65, 97.

19 *Ibid.*, p. 97.

20 *Ibid.*, p. 99.

21 However, at least two passages seem to be conscious allusions to Keats's *Ode on a Grecian Urn*. In the first, Ulysses questions Circe about the identity of the mysterious youth:

> What youth, Goddess,—what guest
> Of Gods or mortals?
> [ll. 94–5]

This may be compared with Keats's

> What men or gods are these? What maidens loth?
> What mad pursuit?

In the second, Ulysses is again the speaker. He is dilating on the social usefulness of the 'divine bard, / By age taught many things', who would delight 'The chiefs and people' with his songs

> Of Gods and Heroes,
> Of war and arts,
> And peopled cities,
> Inland, or built
> By the grey sea.—
> [ll. 118–28]

This is surely reminiscent of Keats's famous

> What little town by river or sea shore,
> Or mountain-built with peaceful citadel. . . .

22 Emery E. Neff, *A Revolution in European Poetry 1660–1900*, p. 151, and Trilling, *Matthew Arnold*, p. 144. See also Ford, p. 80.

23 See *Com*, pp. 287–9. Within the last few years *Empedocles on Etna* has received the sort of careful analysis which has been long overdue; see Walter E. Houghton, 'Arnold's "Empedocles on Etna",' *Victorian Studies*, I (1958), 311–36, and Frank Kermode, *Romantic Image*, 1957. Although my own study of the poem was written before I had read Kermode's book, I take pleasure in acknowledging the points of similarity between his interpretation and my own.

24 *The Modern Temper*, p. 16.

25 *EC I*, p. 112.

26 *Homer*, p. 203.

27 *Keats and the Victorians*, pp. 74–5.

28 *LC*, pp. 65, 124.

29 *Keats and the Victorians*, p. 75.

30 Cf. Bush, *Mythology and the Romantic Tradition*, p. 247. Frederic E. Faverty, ed., *The Victorian Poets: A Guide to Research*, pp. 133–4, gives an excellent brief summary of the views of Bush, Ford, and

Garrod. All three critics agree on the importance of Keats's influence, and all point out the disparity between Arnold's opinions and his most successful poetry.

[31] Allen Tate discusses Arnold's 'eighteenth century view of poetic language as the rhetorical vehicle of ideas' in 'Literature as Knowledge: Comment and Comparison', *Southern Review*, VI (1941), 631–3.

[32] The first quotation about style is from *LC*, p. 65; the second, on the grand style, is from *Homer*, p. 265.

[33] *LC*, p. 124.

[34] *Ibid.*, p. 101. This Goethean idea is also expressed in *EC I* ('The Literary Influence of Academies'), p. 45: '. . . the *ethical* influence of style in language,—its close relations, so often pointed out, with character,—are most important'.

[35] *Ibid.*, p. 65.

[36] *Letters*, I, 147.

[37] *Gentleman's Magazine*, November, 1848, quoted in J. R. MacGillivray, *Keats: A Bibliography and Reference Guide*, p. lvii.

[38] MacGillivray, *Keats*, pp. lxi–lxii.

[39] *LC*, pp. 99, 126, 130–1; cf. *Letters*, I, 72–3.

[40] *EC II*, p. 120. Arnold wrote to Colvin on June 26, 1887, after reading the latter's *Keats* in the English Men of Letters Series: 'What is good in *Endymion* is not, to my mind, so good as you say, and the poem as a whole I could wish to have been suppressed and lost. I really resent the space it occupies in the volume of Keats's poetry. The *Hyperion* is not a poetic success, a *work*, as Keats saw, and it was well he did not make ten books of it; but that, of course, deserves nevertheless the strongest admiration, and its loss would have been a signal loss to poetry; not so as regards the *Endymion*.' E. V. Lucas, *The Colvins and Their Friends*, p. 193.

[41] *LC*, pp. 124, 98–9.

[42] *EC II*, p. 120. Arnold does not state explicitly at this point, but is obviously still (1880) assuming a distinction between minor and major forms, a distinction which is substantially that of the Renaissance and of neo-classicism. As a footnote to the history of criticism, it is worth observing that by 1875 Swinburne could state as self-evident that the two highest kinds of poetry are the lyric and dramatic. Thus he can neatly set Milton aside, even while praising him, and put Shakespeare and Shelley on the pinnacle of Parnassus. See the passage quoted in Sylva Norman, *Flight of the Skylark*, p. 232n.

[43] *EC III* ('On the Modern Element in Literature'), pp. 39–40.

[44] *LC*, p. 124.

[45] *Ibid.*, p. 97. From Goethe Arnold derived a similar comparison (which he used in the last paragraph of his 1853 Preface) between two kinds of dilettanti. The one who seeks to be a poet by acquiring the craft, without the 'soul and matter', harms only himself; the other, who ignores craft and thinks 'spirituality and feeling' are enough, harms his art.

[46] *University of Toronto Quarterly*, I (1932), 333–51.

[47] Arnold's italics. The quotation is from a letter from Matthew Arnold to his brother Thomas, December 22, 1857, expatiating on the concept of 'adequacy' which he had discussed in his inaugural lecture ('On the Modern Element in Literature'). Robert Lidell Lowe, 'Two Arnold Letters', *MP*, LII (1955), 263.

[48] *Homer*, p. 162.

[49] The discussion of Shakespeare is in the 1853 Preface (*PW*, pp. xxiv–xxv). See also *EC I* ('The Literary Influence of Academies'), pp. 53–4; nowhere is Arnold's view of poetic language expressed in more neo-classical terms. Cf. Tate, 'Literature as Knowledge', *Southern Review*, VI (1941), 631–3, and Saintsbury, *Matthew Arnold*, p. 35.

[50] *LC*, p. 97. Arnold uses Keats's ignorance as an indirect weapon against Chapman: 'Chapman's translation has often been praised as eminently Homeric. Keats's fine sonnet in its honour every one knows; but Keats could not read the original, and therefore could not really judge the translation.' *Homer*, p. 161.

[51] *LC*, p. 65.

[52] *Ibid.*, pp. 100–1. In this context, 'form' evidently refers to 'form of expression' or perhaps 'metrical form' rather than architectonics.

[53] De Quincey: 'And yet upon his mother tongue, upon this English language, has Keats trampled as with the hoofs of a buffalo.' Clough: 'Keats, who was indeed no well of English undefiled, though doubtless the fountain-head of a true poetic stream.' Both quoted in MacGillivray, *Keats*, pp. lvii, lviii.

[54] *Homer*, p. 203.

[55] *EC II*, p. 29.

[56] *LC*, pp. 96–7.

[57] *Ibid.*, p. 124. Arnold's selection of Shelley's line about the clouds (*Prometheus Unbound*, II, i, 147) may be due to Ruskin's having singled it out for special praise in *Modern Painters*, Vol. I, Pt. II, Sec. III, Chap. 2 (*Works*, ed. Cook and Wedderburn, III, 364).

[58] This quotation and those from 'Maurice de Guérin' in the next paragraph are from *EC I*, pp. 81–2. For a perceptive discussion of this passage from another point of view, see Buckley, *Poetry and Morality*, pp. 31–5.

[59] *Celtic*, pp. 120–1.

[60] *Mixed*, pp. 146–7.

[61] *Celtic*, pp. 124–6.

[62] *Ibid.*, p. 129.

[63] *EC I*, p. 177; *Celtic*, p. 129. See also Ford, *Keats and the Victorians*, pp. 56–7, 76.

[64] Lucas, *The Colvins*, p. 193.

[65] *EC I*, p. 112. The long quotation immediately following is from *EC I*, p. 107.

[66] *Ibid.*, p. 109. 'If Keats could have lived he might have done any thing; but he *could not have lived*, his not living, we must consider, was more

than an accident.' Arnold to Colvin, June 26, 1887, Lucas, *The Colvins*, p. 194.

[67] Ford, *Keats and the Victorians*, p. 70; MacGillivray, *Keats*, pp. lxv–lxvi.

[68] *EC I*, p. 177.

[69] Saintsbury, *Matthew Arnold*, p. 85; Swinburne, 'Mr. Arnold's New Poems', *Fortnightly Review*, VIII (1867), 438–40.

[70] *LC*, p. 139.

[71] The quality I am trying to define need not be unmixed with shrewd psychological insight, however. Arnold's remark after quoting one of the more fulsome letters to Fanny undoubtedly hits the mark: 'A man who writes love-letters in this strain is probably predestined, one may observe, to misfortune in his love-affairs.' *EC II*, p. 103. As far as I know, Amy Lowell was the first to articulate the charge of snobbery against Arnold; see her *John Keats*, II, 125.

[72] Paul de Musset, *Biographie de Alfred de Musset: sa vie et ses œuvres*, mentions a few of his brother's *affaires*, and adds that there would be no point in listing them all, but where none are mentioned, they should be taken for granted. Quoted by Henry James, *French Poets and Novelists* (London, 1878), pp. 4–5. Arnold's opinion of de Musset's love-letters is given in *Letters*, I, 123.

[73] *LC*, p. 93. Lowry believes that the verse fragment is undoubtedly Arnold's own. Similar sentiments are expressed with much greater felicity and delicacy in *Horatian Echo* and with greater forcefulness and philosophical generality in *Resignation*. This fragment may be taken as a psychological footnote to the philosophical influence of Spinoza and the *Bhagavad Gita* which Trilling finds in the latter poem.

[74] *NB*, p. 510, quoted from Monckton Milnes' *Life, Letters, and Literary Remains of John Keats*, I, 163, letter of July 1818. There are several other quotations from Keats's letters in Arnold's notebooks, most of them of the sort to illustrate the poet's 'manly' side. In one place Arnold copied out the passage on 'negative capability', but unfortunately made no comment on it. *NB*, pp. 339, 349, 509 (five quotations), 510.

[75] The Latin quotation from Cicero's *Fragmenta* is found in *NB*, pp. 36, 84, 99, 548. The passage from Paul (Romans 8:6) is in *NB*, pp. 103, 164.

[76] *Matthew Arnold*, pp. 344–5. Arnold always interpreted the Beatitude about the 'pure in heart' sexually. In a very late religious essay he makes sex count for more than half of morality, and raises the virtue of chastity above that of humility in importance. 'A Comment on Christmas', *Contemporary Review*, XLVII (1885), 462.

[77] Arnold was not alone in regretting the publication of the letters to Fanny Brawne. Colvin, Swinburne, Charles Eliot Norton, William Watson, Frederick Tennyson, and many others objected. Edward Fitzgerald was an almost isolated dissenter, finding Keats to be a modern Catullus, until his friends made him retract. See Ford, *Keats and the Victorians*, p. 70.

[78] *EC II*, pp. 142–3: 'Yes, but so too, when Keats consoles the forward-bending lover on the Grecian Urn, the lover arrested and presented in immortal relief by the sculptor's hand before he can kiss, with the line, "For ever wilt thou love, and she be fair"—he utters a moral idea.' This sort of 'consolation' struck a resonant chord in Arnold's mentality. His tense bipolarity with regard to experience (see, e.g., *Obermann*, ll. 93–104) should have charged the whole *Ode on a Grecian Urn* with meaning for him. Yet this critic who demanded wholes dealt with this great poem only in atoms—one line quoted in 'Pagan and Medieval Religious Sentiment', the line just quoted in 'Wordsworth', and the concluding couplet quoted in 'John Keats', *EC II*, p. 116.

[79] See Ford, *Keats and the Victorians*, p. 71.

[80] 1853 Preface, *PW*, p. xviii.

[81] These are the works Arnold selected for Ward's anthology:

> From *Endymion*: 'Beauty', I, 1–24; 'Hymn to Pan', I, 279–92; 'Bacchus', IV, 193–203. 46 lines.
> From *I Stood Tip-Toe*: 'Endymion', 193–204; 'Cynthia's Bridal Evening', 215–38. 36 lines.
> From *Hyperion*: 'Saturn', I, 1–51; 'Coelus to Hyperion', I, 309–57; 'Oceanus', II, 167–243; 'Hyperion's Arrival', II, 346–78. 210 lines.
> From *The Eve of St. Agnes*: 'The Flight', last eighteen stanzas. 126 lines.
> Whole poems: *Ode to a Nightingale, Ode on a Grecian Urn, Ode* ('Bards of Passion and of Mirth'), *To Autumn, Lines on the Mermaid Tavern*.
> Sonnets: 'On First Looking into Chapman's Homer', 'Written in January, 1817' ('After dark vapours'), 'Written in January, 1818' ('When I have fears'), 'Addressed to Haydon' ('Great spirits'), 'On the Grasshopper and the Cricket', 'The Human Seasons', 'On a Picture of Leander' ('On an Engraved Gem of Leander'), 'Keats's Last Sonnet' ('Bright Star').
> From *Epistle to My Brother George*: 'The Bard Speaks', 71–111. 40½ lines.

All titles are given as Arnold gave them; in parentheses I have given part of the first line or the generally accepted title in use today when necessary to facilitate identification. The line numbers refer in all cases to the whole poem, and indicate the portions selected by Arnold.

[82] Ford, *Keats and the Victorians*, p. 31, seems to express an ironic sympathy with Arnold, Tennyson, and the other Victorians who 'saw Keats without the benefit of Mr. Murry'. But the general tenor of his argument indicates that they are more to be censured than pitied for the deficiency.

V. THE INTENSE INANE: SHELLEY AND COLERIDGE

[1] Fairchild, *Religious Trends*, III, 328.

[2] See the review of Gérard's book in *TLS*, September 21, 1956, p. 552. The review is interesting as a record of current taste, illustrating, for example, how radically different are present views on Keats as a poet of high seriousness from the common Victorian acceptance—or rejection—of him as a purely aesthetic poet.

[3] A. C. Bradley, *A Miscellany*, pp. 171–6. A. C. Swinburne, 'Shelley', *Chambers's Cyclopaedia of English Literature*, Vol. III; 'Coleridge', *Essays and Studies*; 'Wordsworth and Byron', *Miscellanies*.

[4] *EC I*, pp. 6–8.

[5] *EC II*, pp. 203–4.

[6] Shelley's name is absent from Arnold's lists of books to read until 1862, then appears with increasing frequency until 1880, after which it appears every year until the end except for 1886. It is among the last few entries in 1888, the year of Arnold's death, probably because of his planned essay on Shelley's poetry. Arnold did not always read the books he put on his lists, but even the increasing recurrence of intention is significant. *NB*, pp. 551–627.

[7] *Miscellanies*, p. 112. The poem is *A Question*.

[8] *Studies in Literature: Second Series*, pp. 62–3.

[9] *Shelley and the Unromantics*, pp. 3–4. Mrs. Campbell's book dates from 1924, and so comes soon after Quiller-Couch's lectures, but Q is, by his own proud admission, a belated Victorian, while Mrs. Campbell is clearly of a later era.

[10] Cf. Trilling, *Matthew Arnold*, pp. 83–5, and *Com*, pp. 289–90. However, a major source for Arnold is Carlyle, as Tinker and Lowry mentioned (*Com*, p. 300), and as Kathleen Tillotson elaborated in 'Matthew Arnold and Carlyle', *Proceedings of the British Academy*, 1956, pp. 144–6.

[11] J. D. Coleridge cited in *Com*, p. 156. Kathleen Tillotson, '"Yes: In the Sea of Life",' *RES*, n.s. III (1952), 346–64 Trilling hears 'accents reminiscent of Coleridge's vision of himself transformed by the music of the Abyssinian maid' in ll. 21–4 of *Urania* (*Matthew Arnold*, p. 126). I have wondered whether *Kubla Khan* might not have been in Arnold's head when he wrote these lines in *The Voice*:

> Like bright waves that fall
> With a lifelike motion.

[12] Bonnerot, *Matthew Arnold*, p. 268.

[13] Brown, *Matthew Arnold*, p. 217n.

[14] I do not mean that Shelley was the perfect metrist he is often credited with being, but that he did not write unpronounceable verse. His fault lay in the other direction, as Arnold said. He could get a melody or rhythm so firmly in his head or hand that he would not notice the discrepancy between it and what the words were saying. Compare, for example, the meaning with the movement in the opening stanza of *Death*:

> Death is here and death is there,
> Death is busy everywhere,
> All around, within, beneath,
> Above is death—and we are death.

Shelley may have seen death as a dear, busy, little housekeeping fairy, but most other people do not.

[15] *Studies in Literature*, p. 241.

[16] Hugh Kingsmill (pseud.), *Matthew Arnold*, p. 69.

[17] *Matthew Arnold*, p. 67.

[18] Tinker and Lowry (*Com*, p. 154) call the passage ending with these lines Byronic, and there is certainly a touch of Byronism in young Arnold's Alp-worship, but the rush of the lines seems to me more Shelleyan. In this poem of ninety lines, incidentally, there are nine 'Ah's', all but two with exclamation points, of which there are altogether twenty-eight in the poem.

[19] Fairchild, *Religious Trends*, III, 339–40, provides a convenient summary of Shelley's ideas on Christianity, quoting many characteristic passages.

[20] *Life of Percy Bysshe Shelley*, 1913, p. 270, quoted by Fairchild, *loc. cit.* Medwin sounds like some of the later critics of Arnold's religious thought, when he asks how Shelley, in reducing Christianity to a code of morals, differs 'from the Unitarians'.

[21] Fairchild, *Religious Trends*, III, 355; W. G. H. Armytage, 'Matthew Arnold and T. H. Huxley; Some New Letters, 1870–1880', *RES*, n.s. IV (1953), 350.

[22] William J. Robbins, *The Ethical Idealism of Matthew Arnold*, 1959, analyses in considerable depth the philosophical and religious similarities between Arnold and Coleridge.

[23] Trilling, *Matthew Arnold*, pp. 323–4; Jump, *Matthew Arnold*, p. 42.

[24] Dr. Arnold writing to W. W. Hull, Esq., November 16, 1836:

> We have got Coleridge's Literary Remains, in which I do rejoice greatly. I think with all his faults old Sam was more of a great man than any one who has lived within the four seas in my memory. It is refreshing to see such a union of the highest philosophy and poetry, with so full a knowledge, on so many points at least, of particular facts. But yet there are marks enough that his mind was a little diseased by the want of a profession, and the consequent unsteadiness of his mind and purposes; it always seems to me that the very power of contemplation becomes impaired or perverted, when it is made the main employment of life.

A. P. Stanley, *The Life and Correspondence of Thomas Arnold, D.D.*, II, 61.

[25] Reprinted in Shairp's *Studies in Poetry and Philosophy*, 1868.

[26] First quotation in *NB*, 1866, p. 40, repeated condensed 1867, p. 50. Second quotation 1866, p. 40, repeated 1867, p. 50, and 1868, p. 72. See *CA*, p. 96.

[27] *NB*, p. 518.

[28] 'A Comment on Christmas', first published in *Contemporary Review*, XLVII (1885), 457–72, was reprinted only in the 1887 popular edition of *St. Paul and Protestantism*. See H. D. Traill, *Coleridge*, pp. 184–6.

[29] *Letters*, I, 442. In another letter, of November 13, 1869, Arnold did couple the names of Coleridge and Dr. Arnold, but only in connection with the criticism of a third person who disagreed with both; II, 23.

[30] I am characterizing Arnold's view, not mine. For Arnold on Maurice, see *LD*, p. 312, and 'A Comment on Christmas', p. 463, where he also comments on Green. Arnold may have been unfair to Maurice; certainly their positions were close in many ways. Thomas Hughes,

the novelist of Dr. Arnold's Rugby, defended Maurice in his Preface to the latter's *Friendship of Books*. John Stuart Mill, who knew and liked Maurice personally, is more sympathetic in tone than Arnold, but regretfully arrived at similar conclusions (*Autobiography*, Oxford World Classics, pp. 129–30).

31 Dr. Arnold placed *Aids to Reflection* and *Literary Remains* among the few works in English capable of greatly improving the mind.

32 The passage from 'Johnson's Lives' may be found in *EC III*, p. 210, and see *Biographia Literaria*, ed. Shawcross, I, 4. I have arranged all the references to Coleridge in Arnold's works below in chronological order. Such an arrangement brings out most vividly the gap during the years between 1866 and 1878, the years when Arnold was writing the books for which he should have found Coleridge most useful. Brackets signify that Arnold drew upon a secondary source instead of Coleridge's own work.

1848   *LC*, p. 80. Arnold reminds Clough of a letter contributed by Wordsworth to *The Friend*, which they had presumably read together and discussed at Oxford. Shedd, II, 362.

1858   Preface to *Merope*. Most editors of Arnold's poems have not seen fit to reprint this preface, but it may be found in *The Poems of Matthew Arnold*, ed. Quiller-Couch, 1913. On p. 306 in that volume there is a reference to Coleridge on comic relief in Shakespeare. The reference appears to be so twisted to help Arnold make his point that I am not sure which of several passages in *Literary Remains* he may have had in mind. Cf. R.H. Super, ed., *Matthew Arnold on the Classical Tradition* (Ann Arbor, 1960), p. 233 n.

1861   *Homer*, pp. 150, 161. The first of these is a quotation of a line and a half of blank verse. These lines were first published in *On the Constitution of Church and State* (Shedd, VI, 143), and were not collected until the publication of Coleridge's *Poetical and Dramatic Works*, 1877–80, according to a note by E. H. Coleridge in his edition of *The Poems of Samuel Taylor Coleridge*, 1951, p. 487. This quotation and the one listed below under '1865' are the only certain evidence of Arnold's reading of *Church and State*. The second reference in *Homer* quotes Coleridge on Chapman's version. *Notes and Lectures upon Shakespeare*, Shedd, IV, 373.

1864   *EC I*, p. 31. Arnold alludes to Coleridge's phrase about the ability of the Bible to 'find' us. *Confessions of an Inquiring Spirit*, Shedd V, 580.

1864   *EC I*, p. 278. This is the only reference in 'Joubert' to a specific idea in Coleridge, namely his denial of genius to French literature. *The Friend*, Shedd, II, 384 ff.

1865   In a letter to the *Pall Mall Gazette*, December 22, 1865, Arnold gives 'these lines of Wither, quoted by Coleridge':

> Let not your King and Parliament in one,
> Much less apart, mistake themselves for that
> Which is most worthy to be thought upon,
> Nor think they are essentially the State.
> But let them know there is *a deeper life*
> *Which they but represent;*
> *That there's on earth a yet auguster thing,*
> *Veil'd though it be, than Parliament and King.*

The letter is reprinted in *Essays, Letters, and Reviews by Matthew Arnold*, ed. Fraser Neiman, 1960, p. 106. The italics are Arnold's. Arnold omits four lines between the fourth and fifth line as given above; this omission necessitates a verbal change in the fifth line above. Arnold also alters the punctuation somewhat in minor ways suggesting that he was quoting from memory. The lines as given by Coleridge may be found in *Church and State*, Shedd, VI, 90.

[1866   *Celtic*, periodical version only, *Cornhill Magazine*, XIV (1866), 127–8. Arnold quotes from *Aids to Reflection* (Shedd, I, 363): 'Evidences of Christianity! I am weary of the word! make a man feel the want of Christianity.' The passage, suppressed in the book version of 1867, is quoted by E. K. Brown, *Studies in the Text of Matthew Arnold's Prose Works*, pp. 15–16. Almost certainly Arnold took the quotation from Shairp's article in the *North British Review* for December, 1865, from which he copied other passages into his notebook early in 1866.]

1878   Preface to Johnson's *Lives*, EC III, p. 210. A garbled reference to *Biographia Literaria*, discussed in text above, p. 168; and in the beginning of this note.

1879   'Wordsworth', *EC II*, pp. 123–214. A general comment on Coleridge's influence upon young men of ability, especially at Cambridge, during the 1830's.

1880   'The Study of Poetry', *EC II*, p. 36. An appeal to the authority of Wordsworth and Coleridge to support Arnold's adverse opinion of Dryden and Pope. Coleridge, however, was capable, as Arnold apparently was not, of appreciating Pope's genius. He did not find gold in Pope's poetry, but he did call it 'a highly wrought vase of pure silver from the hand of a master'. *Church and State*, Shedd, VI, 89n.

[1885   'A Comment on Christmas', *Contemporary Review*, XLVII (1885), 463–4. References to Green's *Spiritual Philosophy* and to Traill's *Coleridge*, discussed above, pp. 166–7, and see note 28 above.]

1886   *Letters*, II, 398. A quotation attributed by Arnold to Colridgee, unique in Arnold's correspondence: 'Where every man may take liberties, no man can enjoy any'. I have been unable to locate the source.

³³ The Decade was a discussion club whose membership included, along with Arnold and Clough, such thoughtful young men as J. D. Coleridge, Jowett, Shairp, and Stanley.

³⁴ A recent article makes available some of Arnold's earlier reading lists. On the September page of the 1845 diary appears the entry 'Coleridge passim. read.' Mr. Kenneth Allott, the author of the article, is uncertain of the meaning of the reference, but suggests that it might refer to the *Encyclopaedia Metropolitana* (28 vols., 1845), an encyclopaedia 'on a methodical plan projected by Samuel Taylor Coleridge' and introduced by Coleridge's *Treatise on Method*. Coleridge appears again, twice, on the 1846 reading list: 'Biographia Litteraria (*sic*) vol. i.' and 'S. T. Coleridge Appendix', a rather mysterious entry for which Mr. Allott finds no satisfactory explanation. Kenneth Allott, 'Matthew Arnold's Reading-Lists in Three Early Diaries', *Victorian Studies*, II (1959), 259, 260.

[35] Arnold's late reading lists show an increasing or returning interest in Milton, Jonson, Shakespeare, Spenser, Chaucer, and also Pope, Swift, Sterne, Boswell, and the letters of Walpole.

[36] *Biographia Literaria*, ed. Shawcross, 'Introduction', I, xii.

[37] *Letters*, II, 37, June 7, 1870. The 'new book' is Sir Joseph Dalton Hooker's (1817–1911) *The Student's Flora of the British Islands*, 1870. Babington is the botanist Charles Cardale Babington (1808–1895). For an expression of Arnold's high faith in science in general and botany in particular, when well taught, to help form the mind see his letter of January, 1866, to his sister. *Letters*, I, 364–6.

[38] *Ibid.*, I, 287; see also *LC*, p. 97.

[39] Coleridge, however, distinguished between the Church militant whose head is Christ and the national Church. See Robbins, *Ethical Idealism*, p. 145.

[40] Quoted from *Church and State* by C. R. Sanders, *Coleridge and the Broad Church Movement*, p. 87.

[41] Sanders, *Broad Church*, p. 64. The quotations are, respectively, from *Church and State*, Shedd, VI, 67, and *Biographia Literaria*, ed. Shawcross, I, 182.

[42] Elton, *A Survey of English Literature, 1780-1830*, II, 129; Fairchild, *Religious Trends*, III, 315.

[43] For a sympathetic discussion of Coleridge's 'pragmatism', see Sanders, *Broad Church*, pp. 49, 65–7; for an unsympathetic view see Fairchild, *Religious Trends*, III, 315–19.

[44] *EC I*, p. 258.

[45] *LD, Works*, VII, 325.

[46] Arnold repeatedly insisted that he was not preaching his new gospel to believers in the old. He accepted the necessity of both esoteric and exoteric doctrine until the time when all mankind would be sufficiently civilized to accept purely essential religion without the existential. See Trilling, *Matthew Arnold*, p. 365, and Fairchild, *Religious Trends*, IV, 504.

[47] *Aids to Reflection*, Shedd, I, 234.

[48] Dr. Arnold quoted by Sanders, *Broad Church*, p. 98.

[49] *Aids to Reflection*, Shedd, I, 158, 224, 363, 233. Arnold seems almost to be quoting Coleridge in the passage from *Literature and Dogma* cited in the preceding paragraph. Cf. Spinoza, *Tractatus Theologico-Politicus*: '. . . a religion to be tested not by reason, but by the excellence of the life to which it lends support'.

[50] Robbins, *Ethical Idealism*, p. 85.

[51] *Aids to Reflection*, Shedd, I, 166. Cf. Arnold's 'Marcus Aurelius', *EC I*, pp. 346–7.

[52] *Ibid.*, p. 138.

[53] 'Spinoza and the Bible', *EC I*, p. 336.

[54] Trilling, *Matthew Arnold*, pp. 339–40, who cites Bradley's *Ethical Studies*.

[55] However, had Coleridge lived to read Arnold's books he would certainly have considered their author 'Minimi-fidian'. The following

description is prophetically apt: 'Again, there is a scheme constructed on the principle of retaining the social sympathies, that attend on the name of believer, at the least possible expenditure of belief; a scheme of picking and choosing Scripture texts for the support of doctrines, that have been learned beforehand from the higher oracle of common sense; which, as applied to the truths of religion, means the popular part of the philosophy in fashion. Of course, the scheme differs at different times and in different individuals in the number of articles excluded; but, it may always be recognized by this permanent character, that its object is to draw religion down to the believer's intellect, instead of raising his intellect up to religion. And this extreme I call Minimi-fidianism.' *Aids to Reflection*, Shedd, I, 238–9.

⁵⁶ I John 2:4, quoted by Coleridge in *Aids to Reflection*, Shedd, I, 149, and elsewhere.

⁵⁷ *EC II*, pp. 163–4. Cf. a sentence in 'Wordsworth', *EC II*, p. 139: 'If it were a comparison of single pieces, or of three or four pieces by each poet, I do not say that Wordsworth would stand decisively above Gray, or Burns, or Coleridge, or Keats, or Manzoni, or Heine.' The name of Coleridge in this comparison was an afterthought; it was added when a new edition of the Wordsworth anthology was being prepared in 1884. See Buckler, *Matthew Arnold's Books*, p. 145.

⁵⁸ Cf. Quiller-Couch, *Studies in Literature: Second Series*, p. 47.

⁵⁹ Quoted by Willis W. Pratt, *Shelley Criticism in England 1810-1890*, unpublished dissertation, Cornell University, 1935; see pp. 203–15.

⁶⁰ A reviewer in the *Saturday Review*, LXII (December 18, 1886), 820, had called Shelley 'a master of word-craft apart from meaning', apparently intending his comment as a compliment. Arnold pounced upon it and recorded it in his notebook, *NB*, p. 424.

⁶¹ *EC I*, pp. 111–12. This opinion should sufficiently gloss a remark Arnold made in a letter of August 6, 1858, that Shelley was superior in 'natural power' to Tennyson. *Letters*, I, 72.

⁶² Cf. Carlyle: 'Hear a Shelley filling the earth with inarticulate wail; like the infinite, inarticulate grief and weeping of forsaken infants.' 'Characteristics', quoted by Newman I. White, *Shelley*, II, 413.

⁶³ Preface to *GB*, pp. xii–xiii.

⁶⁴ From a transcript of an unpublished letter to George Macmillan, March 6, 1878, in the collection of Professor William E. Buckler of New York University, quoted with his permission.

⁶⁵ 'Dr. Stanley's Lectures on the Jewish Church', *Essays by Matthew Arnold*, Oxford edition, p. 431 (reprinted from *Macmillan's Magazine*, February, 1863).

⁶⁶ *EC II*, pp. 312–13. The sentence dealing with the image from *Adonais* contains Arnold's only definite praise of a specific poem of Shelley's, but the context indicates to what extent the praise is not for the 'truth' but for the 'poetry', thought of as a separable element.

⁶⁷ *EC I*, p. 294, and *EC II*, pp. 203–4. This likeness has been pointed out by W. S. Knickerbocker in a note, 'Arnold, Shelley, and Joubert', *MLN*, LV (1940), 201. Arnold also says that Wesley, 'this amiable and

gracious spirit, but intellectually slight and shallow compared to St Paul, beat his wings in vain', *St. Paul and Protestantism*, p. 62. The figure probably derives from St. Paul; see I Corinthians 9:26. Like Joubert, Coleridge had reservations about Plato. Wallace Stevens quotes his phrase about 'Plato's dear, gorgeous nonsense' in *The Necessary Angel*, 1951, p. 3.

[68] *EC II*, p. 164.

[69] 'A Friend of God', *EC III*, p. 239.

[70] *EC II*, p. 184. Even Shakespeare was not always proof against this romantic temptation, according to Arnold. See his interesting, brief critique of *Hamlet*, which anticipates some of the views of J. M. Robertson and T. S. Eliot on that play. *Letters of an Old Playgoer*, ed. Brander Matthews, 1919, pp. 51–3; also in *Works*, IV, 273–4.

[71] *Letters*, I, 289–90.

[72] Bonnerot, *Matthew Arnold*, pp. 521–2. The article was in *Revue des deux-mondes*, September 15, 1854. Writing to his sister, Mrs. Forster, on October 10, 1854, Arnold warned: 'The article in the Revue des deux Mondes is a confused affair—a piece of theorising—the author having a mania for finding everything in Shelley, whether it is there or no.' *UL*, p. 25.

[73] *EC I*, pp. 111–12. Palgrave, incidentally, did not include *Adonais*.

[74] *EC I*, p. 112n. This footnote lingered and rankled in Swinburne's elephantine memory for forty years. Writing on Shelley for *Chambers's Cyclopaedia of English Literature* in 1903, he said of the *Lines Written among the Euganean Hills* that 'the rush of rolling song, the glory of impassioned colour, the music of sublime emotion, combine to raise it far above the probable sympathy of a minor poet or the possible estimate of a self-complacent critic'. Vol. III, p. 109. This personal gibe at the long-dead Arnold by the irascible old man must have been incomprehensible to most of his readers by that late date. For Arnold on the comparative difficulty of music and poetry, see his poem *Epilogue to Lessing's Laocoön*.

[75] Arnold's comment was quoted by Alfred Austin from an unpublished letter in his obituary notice of Arnold, 'Matthew Arnold', *National Review*, XI (1888), 416, and again in his *The Bridling of Pegasus*, p. 7. The recent comment is from an article called 'Poetry and Reality', *TLS*, October 5, 1956, p. 585.

[76] *Mixed*, pp. 152–3.

[77] *EC II*, p. 53.

[78] *Ibid.*, pp. 164–6, 196, 203–4.

[79] *Miscellanies*, pp. 63–156.

[80] *Ibid.*, p. 102; see also pp. 119–20. Arnold apparently had in mind Stopford Brooke, who had extolled Shelley in this manner in 'Some Thoughts on Shelley', *Macmillan's Magazine*, XLII (1880), 129. By taking certain sentiments out of context, however, Arnold rather distorts Brooke.

[81] *Matthew Arnold and France*, p. 237n. Mrs. Sells informs me that she read the letter when she was a young girl, but took no transcript and

cannot recall it in any detail. She very kindly made inquiry of surviving members of the Arnold family in Hobart, only to discover that in various removals the letter has apparently been lost.

[82] See *EC II*, p. 238.

[83] Sanders, *Broad Church*, p. 129.

[84] Pater, for example, expressed such an opinion in his 'Coleridge', *Appreciations*, p. 88.

[85] Fairchild, *Religious Trends*, III, 287, 304. Cf. stanza VI of Coleridge's *Dejection: An Ode*. H. D. Traill, although sympathetic, also suggested such a view, as did Leslie Stephen.

[86] Dr. Arnold writing to Mr. Justice Coleridge, March 2, 1836: 'What a great man your uncle was, that is, intellectually! for something I suppose must have been wanting to hinder us from calling him a great man ἁπλῶς. But where has he left his equal?' Stanley, *Life of Arnold*, II, 34. The austere, moralistic Dr. Arnold, it seems, could be more forgiving than his free-thinking, poetic son of Coleridge's weaknesses.

[87] *EC I*, p. 275.

[88] *Coleridge*, p. 177.

[89] *EC II*, p. 108.

[90] Sanders, *Broad Church*, p. 102, who cites Dr. Arnold's preface to his *History of Rome* and Stanley's *Life of Arnold*.

[91] *EC I*, pp. 292–3.

[92] Among the pertinent replies are:

> Edward Dowden, 'Last Words on Shelley', *Fortnightly Review*, XLVIII, n.s. XLII (1887), 461–81. Although a defence of Shelley, it is by no means uncritical of him. Reprinted in *Transcripts and Studies* (London, 1896).
>
> Alfred Austin, 'Mr. Matthew Arnold on the Loves of the Poets', *National Review*, X (1888), 768–78. Takes issue with the British habit of confusing moral and literary criticism; very witty about Arnold's comparison of the Byron-Shelley circle with that of Keble-Copleston-Hawkins.
>
> Sir Arthur Quiller-Couch, 'Byron' and 'Shelley', *Studies in Literature: Second Series* (New York, 1922). Arnold is dead wrong in almost every way: 'The only void in which Shelley ever beat his luminous wings in vain was a void in Mr. Arnold's understanding.' Interesting as a document of early twentieth-century taste; supposes that Francis Thompson's essay is the finest criticism ever written on Shelley.
>
> Olwen Ward Campbell, *Shelley and the Unromantics* (New York, 1924). See especially pp. 69, 140. Ardent but sensible. 'It had apparently never entered [Arnold's] head that Shelley might have whole-heartedly agreed with him' in his disgust with Godwin, the Duke of Norfolk, etc.
>
> A. C. Bradley, 'Shelley and Arnold's Critique of his Poetry', *A Miscellany* (London, 1929), pp. 139–62. As usual, Bradley is good-tempered and judicious, and hence succeeds far better than some of Shelley's more fervent defenders. His essay is not a reply to 'Shelley', but to the Shelley criticism in Arnold's 'Maurice de Guérin' and 'Byron'.
>
> Finally, Swinburne's 'Wordsworth and Byron', already referred to on numerous occasions, ought to be mentioned, although it was written in 1884, four years before Arnold's 'Shelley'.

[93] He ignored a principle he elsewhere swore allegiance to, Bishop Butler's maxim: 'Things and actions are what they are, and the consequences will be what they will be; why then should we desire to be deceived?' Quoted by Arnold in 'Bishop Butler and the Zeit-Geist', *Last Essays on Church and Religion, Works*, IX, 261. See also Arnold's approving quotation from Amiel in the essay devoted to that writer, collected in the same volume with the 'Shelley': 'Pious fiction is still fiction. Truth has superior rights. The world must adapt itself to truth, not truth to the world.' *EC II*, p. 330.

[94] Trilling, *Matthew Arnold*, p. 372; *LC*, p. 115.

[95] These innuendoes are what aroused Mark Twain's chivalrous ardour and stimulated him to write his almost book-length essay *In Defense of Harriet Shelley*. Twain knew and referred to Arnold's 'Shelley'.

[96] *Letters*, II, 433.

[97] *Studies in Literature: Second Series*, p. 80.

[98] *EC I*, pp. 314, 341.

VI. BETWEEN TWO WORLDS: MATTHEW ARNOLD AND ROMANTICISM

[1] E. K. Brown, 'Matthew Arnold and the Eighteenth Century', *University of Toronto Quarterly*, IX (1940), 213; Ludwig Lewisohn, 'A Study of Matthew Arnold', *Sewanee Review*, X (1902), 150; George H. Ford, *Keats and the Victorians*, p. 53. To F. L. Lucas, Arnold is 'our last great neo-classic'. *Eight Victorian Poets*, p. 52.

[2] For supporters of Arnold, see Norman Foerster, 'Matthew Arnold and American Letters Today', *Sewanee Review*, XXX (1922), 298 ('When it was written, this diagnosis of the Romantic movement [that it did not "know enough"] was plausible: to-day it is conclusive.'); F. R. Leavis, 'Matthew Arnold', *The Importance of Scrutiny*, ed. Eric Bentley, pp. 90, 97; T. S. Eliot, *The Use of Poetry and the Use of Criticism*, p. 104. A leading opponent of Arnold's view of the Romantics is Jacques Barzun, *Romanticism and the Modern Ego*, pp. 148–9.

[3] *Matthew Arnold*, p. 379.

[4] *EC III*, pp. 208–9.

[5] *Ibid.*, p. 215.

[6] *Ibid.*, p. 68.

[7] *Ibid.*, pp. 43, 89. After saying of Dante that he effaces the world in presence of the spirit, Arnold seems to be inconsistent in reproving other critics for placing too much emphasis on the allegory in the *Divine Comedy*.

[8] Cf. Bush, *Mythology and the Romantic Tradition*, p. 247. On this point cf. D. G. James, *Matthew Arnold and the Decline of English Romanticism*. I am pleased to acknowledge the similarity of many of my conclusions in this chapter to those of Professor James in this

recent (1961) publication of his Gregynog lectures, published since the present study was written.

[9] John H. Muirhead, *Coleridge as Philosopher*, p. 28.

[10] I do not mean the total ego in the psychological sense, but the more limited poetic ego or sense of self-as-poet and poet-as-seer.

[11] Cf. Bonnerot, *Matthew Arnold*, pp. 233–4, 264.

[12] *CA*, p. 139.

[13] *Matthew Arnold*, p. 67. Jump is alluding to F. R. Leavis, who had traced the ancestry of the feebler sort of Georgian nature poetry to Matthew Arnold.

[14] Bonnerot, *Matthew Arnold*, p. 184. Cf. Beach, *The Concept of Nature in Nineteenth Century English Poetry*, p. 403, and H. F. Lowry's introduction to *LC*, pp. 33–4.

[15] Fairchild, *Religious Trends*, III, 299.

[16] *Letters*, II, 10. Cf. Jump, *Matthew Arnold*, p. 64, and Trilling, *Matthew Arnold*, p. 79.

[17] *CA*, p. 15.

[18] *EC II*, p. 308. Cf. a very striking passage from the preface to the first edition of *EC I* (1865), later suppressed:

> ... the truth is, I have never been able to hit it off happily with the logicians, and it would be mere affectation in me to give myself the airs of doing so. They imagine truth something to be proved, I something to be seen; they, something to be manufactured, I, as something to be found. I have a profound respect for intuitions, and a very lukewarm respect for the elaborate machine-work of my friends the logicians. I have always thought that all which was worth much in this elaborate machine-work of theirs came from an intuition to which they gave a grand name of their own. How did they come by this intuition? Ah! if they could tell us that. But no; they set their machine in motion and build up a fine showy edifice; glittering and unsubstantial like a pyramid of eggs; and then they say 'Come and look at our pyramid!' And what does one find it? Of all that heap of eggs, the one poor little fresh egg, the original intuition, has got hidden away far out of sight and forgotten. And all the other eggs are addled!

Quoted by Brown, *Studies in the Text of Matthew Arnold's Prose Works*, p. 2.

[19] See *LD*, Chapter V.

[20] Cf. Alan Harris, 'Matthew Arnold: The "Unknown Years"', *Nineteenth Century and After*, CXIII (1933), 500.

[21] Cf. Arnold's discussion in *Literature and Dogma* of '*Aberglaube*'. He quotes from Goethe the maxim 'der Aberglaube ist die Poesie des Lebens', then proceeds to comment: '*Extra-belief*, that which we hope, augur, imagine, is the poetry of life, and has the rights of poetry. But it is not science. . . .' *LD*, p. 70.

[22] Cf. Jacques Rivière, quoted and translated by Martin Turnell, *Jacques Rivière* (New Haven, 1953), p. 50: 'If in the seventeenth century, anyone had taken it into his head to ask Molière and Racine why they wrote, they would probably only have been able to answer: "To

amuse people". It was only with Romanticism that the art of writing began to be thought of as a raid on the absolute and its result a revelation. At this time literature garnered the heritage of religion and organised itself on the model of the thing it was replacing. The writer became a priest; the sole aim of his gestures was to produce in the host that literature had become "the real presence". The whole of nineteenth-century literature is a vast incantation towards the miraculous.' Cited by William A. Madden, 'The Divided Tradition of English Criticism', *PMLA*, LXXIII (1958), 78n.

23 'Matthew Arnold', *The Importance of Scrutiny*, p. 97.
24 *NB*, p. 513.
25 *Homer*, pp. 148–9.
26 *Letters of an Old Playgoer*, ed. Brander Matthews, p. 24 (December 6, 1882).
27 *Com*, p. 270.
28 R. G. Cox, 'Victorian Criticism of Poetry: The Minority Tradition', *Scrutiny*, XVIII (1951), 2–17. William A. Jamison, *Arnold and the Romantics* (Anglistica, vol. 10: Copenhagen, 1958), is primarily concerned with placing Arnold's criticism of the Romantics against its Victorian background.
29 T. S. Eliot called it 'startlingly independent' in *The Use of Poetry*, p. 104.
30 *Romanticism and the Modern Ego*, pp. 148–9.
31 Lowe, 'Two Arnold Letters', *MP*, LII (1955), 262–3.

APPENDIX

1 Trilling, *Matthew Arnold*, p. 100; Swinburne, *Essays and Studies*, pp. 149–51 (reprinted from *Fortnightly Review*, vol. VIII, 1867).
2 Paull F. Baum, *Ten Studies in the Poetry of Matthew Arnold*, pp. 25–6n.
3 *Com.*, p. 64.
4 R. D. Havens, *The Mind of a Poet*, p. 117.
5 *Empedocles on Etna*, Act I, sc. ii, ll. 177–86.
6 Cf. Trilling, *loc. cit.*, and Arnold's poem *The World and the Quietist*.
7 I quote the lines as given in the early editions, 1807–15. In 1820 Wordsworth softened 'Better vain deeds and evil than such life!' to '(By nature transient) than such torpid life'; and in 1827 he changed 'such' to 'this'.
8 Cf. Beach, *The Concept of Nature in Nineteenth-Century English Poetry*, pp. 401–2.

BIBLIOGRAPHY

I. MATTHEW ARNOLD

A. *Works by Matthew Arnold*

THE following list, alphabetically arranged, includes only those editions of Matthew Arnold's works which have been used for this study. No complete bibliography exists for Matthew Arnold, although presumably one will appear in conjunction with the new edition of Arnold's works being published under the auspices of the University of Michigan. For the present, the nearest to a complete Arnold bibliography is that of Thomas Burnet Smart in Volume XV of *The Works of Matthew Arnold*, Edition de Luxe, 15 vols., London, 1904. This may be supplemented by Theodore G. Ehrsam, Robert H. Deily, and Robert M. Smith, *Bibliographies of Twelve Victorian Authors*, New York, 1936, and Marion Mainwaring, 'Notes Toward a Matthew Arnold Bibliography', *MP* XL (1952), 189–94. Some important recent contributions to Arnold bibliography have been reported periodically by Fraser Neiman and Robert H. Super.

'Address to the Wordsworth Society', *Macmillan's Magazine*, XLVIII (1883), 154–5.
'The Bishop and the Philosopher', *Macmillan's Magazine*, VII (1863), 241–56.
'Charles Augustin Sainte-Beuve', *Encyclopaedia Britannica*, 11th ed., XXIII, 1023–4.
Civilization in the United States: First and Last Impressions of America, Boston, 1888.
'A Comment on Christmas', *Contemporary Review*, XLVII (1885), 457–72.
Culture and Anarchy, ed. with an introduction by J. Dover Wilson, Cambridge, 1948.
Discourses in America, London, 1896.
England and the Italian Question, London, 1859.
Essays by Matthew Arnold, Oxford edition, 1914.
Essays in Criticism, London and New York, 1889.
Essays in Criticism: Second Series, New York, 1924.
Essays in Criticism: Third Series, ed. Edward J. O'Brien, Boston, 1910.
A French Eton: or, Middle Class Education and the State, London and Cambridge, 1864.
General Grant: An Estimate, Boston, 1887.

261

God and the Bible: A Review of Objections to 'Literature and Dogma', New York, 1901.

'Introduction', Volume I (*Poets*), *The Hundred Greatest Men*, 8 vols. in 4, London, 1879.

Letters of an Old Playgoer, ed. with an introduction by Brander Matthews, New York, 1919.

Literature and Dogma: An Essay Towards a Better Apprehension of the Bible, New York, 1883.

Mixed Essays; Irish Essays, and Others, New York, 1908 (2 vols. bound as one).

On the Study of Celtic Literature and *On Translating Homer*, New York, 1907 (2 vols. bound as one).

The Poems of Matthew Arnold, ed. Sir Arthur Quiller-Couch, London, 1913.

The Poetical Works of Matthew Arnold, ed. C. B. Tinker and H. F. Lowry, London, New York, Toronto, 1950.

The Popular Education of France with Notices of that of Holland and Switzerland, London, 1861.

'Schools', *The Reign of Queen Victoria*, ed. T. H. Ward, 2 vols., London, 1887, II, 238–79 (with 'A Note on Scottish Education', *ibid.*, pp. 280–7).

St. Paul and Protestantism with an Essay on Puritanism & the Church of England and *Last Essays on Church & Religion*, New York, 1898 (2 vols. bound as one).

The Works of Matthew Arnold, Edition de Luxe, 15 vols., London, 1904.

B. *Works Edited by Matthew Arnold*

Isaiah of Jerusalem in the Authorized English Version with an Introduction, Corrections, and Notes by Matthew Arnold, London, 1883.

Letters, Speeches and Tracts on Irish Affairs by Edmund Burke, collected and arranged by Matthew Arnold with a preface, London, 1881.

Poems of Wordsworth, London, 1879 (1st ed.; later editions also consulted).

Poetry of Byron, London, 1881.

C. *Letters and Notebooks of Matthew Arnold*

The first five items are the principal editions of Arnold's letters and notebooks. Other letters are listed after these in alphabetical order according to the name of the author who published them.

Letters of Matthew Arnold 1848-1888, collected and arranged by George W. E. Russell, 2 vols., New York and London, 1896.

The Letters of Matthew Arnold to Arthur Hugh Clough, ed. with an introductory study by Howard Foster Lowry, London and New York, 1932.

Unpublished Letters of Matthew Arnold, ed. Arnold Whitridge, New Haven and New York, 1922.

Buckler, William E., *Matthew Arnold's Books: Toward a Publishing Diary*,

Geneva and Paris, 1958. (Selections from Arnold's letters to his publishers, although Professor Buckler's running commentary gives this book a value beyond that of a mere collection of letters.)

The Note-Books of Matthew Arnold, ed. Howard Foster Lowry, Karl Young, and Waldo Hilary Dunn, London, New York, and Toronto, 1952.

Armytage, W. H. G., 'Matthew Arnold and W. E. Gladstone: Some New Letters', *University of Toronto Quarterly*, XVIII (1949), 217–26.

—, 'Matthew Arnold and Richard Cobden in 1864: Some Recently Discovered Letters', *RES*, XXV (1949), 249–54.

—, 'Matthew Arnold and T. H. Huxley: Some New Letters, 1870–80', *RES*, n.s. IV (1953), 346–53.

Collins, John Churton, *Letters from Matthew Arnold to John Churton Collins*, London 1910. 'Edition Limited to Twenty Copies'.

Dove Cottage Museum, Ambleside, unpublished letter from Matthew Arnold to Miss Jemima Quillinan dated Jan. 20th, 1880. Transcript by the Honourable Librarian published here with the permission of the Chairman of the Trustees.

Drinkwater, John, 'Some Letters from Matthew Arnold to Robert Browning', *Cornhill Magazine*, n.s. LV (1923), 654–64.

Galton, Arthur, *Two Essays upon Matthew Arnold with some of His Letters to the Author*, London, 1897.

Gordon, Ian A., 'Three New Letters of Matthew Arnold', *MLN*, LVI (1941), 552–4.

Gosse, Edmund, 'Matthew Arnold and Swinburne', *TLS*, Aug. 12, 1920, p. 517 (six letters from Arnold to Swinburne).

Lowe, Robert Liddell, 'Matthew Arnold and Percy William Bunting: Some New Letters 1884-1887', *Studies in Bibliography*, ed. Fredson Bowers, VII (1955), 199–207.

—, 'Two Arnold Letters', *MP* LII (1955), 262–4.

Smart, Thomas Burnet, 'Matthew Arnold and Sainte-Beuve', *Athenaeum*, XXXIV (1898), 325. (Eight further letters to Sainte-Beuve have been published by Bonnerot; see Bonnerot entry in general section below.)

II. GENERAL

The following list makes no pretence to exhaustiveness, beyond including all the works consulted in preparing the present study. Numerous significant works on Wordsworth, Byron, Keats, Shelley, and Coleridge have been omitted. However, an attempt has been made to include studies of these authors which have immediate relevance to my subject, or which Arnold himself read.

Brackets round the name of an author indicate anonymous publication.

Allott, Kenneth, 'Matthew Arnold's Reading-Lists in Three Early Diaries', *Victorian Studies*, II (1959), 254–66.

Annan, Noel G., *Leslie Stephen*, Cambridge, Mass., 1952.

Arnold, Thomas, *Passages in a Wandering Life*, London, 1900.

Austin, Alfred, *The Bridling of Pegasus*, London, 1910.
—, 'Matthew Arnold', *National Review*, XI (1888), 415–19.
—, 'Mr. Matthew Arnold on the Loves of the Poets', *National Review*, X (1888), 768–78.
Babbitt, Irving, *The Masters of Modern French Criticism*, Boston and New York, 1912.
—, 'Matthew Arnold', *The Nation*, CV (1917), 117–21.
—, *The New Laokoon*, Boston and New York, 1910.
—, *Rousseau and Romanticism*, Boston and New York, 1919.
Bagehot, Walter, *Literary Studies*, 2 vols., Everyman's Library, London and New York, 1916.
Barnard, Cyril C., 'Byron: A Criticism of Matthew Arnold's Essay', *Englische Studien*, LXV (1930/31), 211–16.
Barzun, Jacques, *Romanticism and the Modern Ego*, Boston, 1944.
Bate, Walter Jackson, *From Classic to Romantic*, Cambridge, Mass., 1949.
Batho, Edith C., *The Later Wordsworth*, Cambridge, 1933.
Baum, Paull F., *Ten Studies in the Poetry of Matthew Arnold*, Durham, N.C., 1958.
Beach, Joseph Warren, *The Concept of Nature in Nineteenth-Century English Poetry*, New York, 1936.
Benn, Alfred William, *The History of English Rationalism in the Nineteenth Century*, 2 vols., London, New York, and Bombay, 1906.
Bernbaum, Ernest, *Guide Through the Romantic Movement*, New York, 1949.
Bezanson, Walter E., 'Melville's Reading of Arnold's Poetry', *PMLA*, LXIX (1954), 365–91.
Bonnerot, Louis, *Matthew Arnold, poète: Essai de biographie psychologique*, Paris, 1947. (Includes in an appendix an exchange of letters between Arnold and Sainte-Beuve.)
Bottrall, Ronald, 'Byron and the Colloquial Tradition in English Poetry', *The Criterion*, XVIII (1939), 204–24.
Bowra, Cecil Maurice, *The Romantic Imagination*, Cambridge, Mass., 1949.
Bradley, A. C., *A Miscellany*, London, 1929.
—, *Oxford Lectures on Poetry*, London, 1909.
Broadbent, J. B., 'Milton and Arnold', *Essays in Criticism*, VI (1956), 404–17.
Brooke, Stopford A., 'Some Thoughts on Shelley', *Macmillan's Magazine*, XLII (1880), 124–35.
—, *Theology in the English Poets*, London, 1904.
Brown, Edward Killoran, *Matthew Arnold: A Study in Conflict*, Chicago, 1948.
—, 'Matthew Arnold and the Eighteenth Century', *University of Toronto Quarterly*, IX (1940), 202–13.
— 'Matthew Arnold and the Elizabethans', *University of Toronto Quarterly*, I (1932), 333–51.
—, *Studies in the Text of Matthew Arnold's Prose Works*, Paris, 1935.

Brown, Leonard, 'Arnold's Succession: 1850–1914', *Sewanee Review*, XLII (1934), 158–79.

Brownell, W. C., *Victorian Prose Masters*, New York, 1902.

Buckley, Jerome H., *The Victorian Temper*, Cambridge, Mass., 1951.

Buckley, Vincent, *Poetry and Morality*, London, 1959.

Bulwer-Lytton, E.G.E.L., 'Charles Lamb and Some of His Contemporaries', *Quarterly Review*, CXXII (1867), 1–29.

Bush, Douglas, *Mythology and the Romantic Tradition*, Cambridge, Mass., 1937.

Byron, George Gordon, Lord, *The Poetical Works of Lord Byron*, Oxford Standard Authors Series, New York and London, 1945.

Campbell, Olwen Ward, *Shelley and the Unromantics*, New York, 1924.

Chambers, Raymond W., *Man's Unconquerable Mind*, London, 1939.

Chew, Samuel C., *Byron in England: His Fame and After-fame*, New York, 1924.

Churchill, R. C., 'Gray and Matthew Arnold', *The Criterion*, XVII (1939), 426–31.

Clough, Arthur Hugh, *The Poems and Prose Remains of Arthur Hugh Clough*, ed. Mrs. Clough, 2 vols., London, 1869.

Coleridge, Samuel Taylor, *Biographia Literaria*, ed. with his Aesthetical Essays by J. Shawcross, 2 vols., London, 1949.

—, *The Complete Works of Samuel Taylor Coleridge*, ed. W. G. T. Shedd, 7 vols., New York, 1884.

—, *The Poems of Samuel Taylor Coleridge*, ed. E. H. Coleridge, London and New York, 1951.

Collins, John Churton, *Posthumous Essays*, ed. L. C. Collins, London and New York, 1912.

Colvin, Sir Sidney, *John Keats: His Life and Poetry, His Friends, Critics, and Afterfame*, New York, 1917.

Cooper, Lane, *Evolution and Repentance*, Ithaca, New York, 1935.

Cox, R. G., 'Victorian Criticism of Poetry: The Minority Tradition', *Scrutiny*, XVIII (1951), 2–17.

Cruttwell, Patrick, 'Wordsworth, the Public, and the People', *Sewanee Review*, LXIV (1956), 71–80.

De Vere, Aubrey, *Essays Chiefly on Poetry*, 2 vols., London and New York, 1887.

Donovan, Robert Alan, *Matthew Arnold's Literary Criticism*, unpublished doctoral dissertation, Washington University, St. Louis, Mo., 1953.

Dowden, Edward, *The French Revolution and English Literature*, New York, 1887.

—, 'Last Words on Shelley', *Fortnightly Review*, XLVIII, n.s. XLII (1887), 461–81.

—, *The Life of Percy Bysshe Shelley*, 2 vols., London, 1886.

Dunklin, Gilbert T., ed., *Wordsworth: Centenary Studies Presented at Cornell and Princeton Universities*, Princeton, 1951.

Dyson, A. E., 'The Last Enchantments', *RES*, n.s. VIII (1957), 257–65.

Eliot, T. S., 'Byron', *From Anne to Victoria: Essays by Various Hands*, ed. Bonamy Dobrée, London, Toronto, Melbourne, and Sydney, 1937.

Eliot, T. S. *On Poetry and Poets*, New York, 1957.
—, 'The Second-Order Mind', *Dial*, LXIX (1920), 586–689.
—, *Selected Essays*, New York, 1950.
—, *The Use of Poetry and the Use of Criticism*, Cambridge, Mass., 1933.
Elliott, G. R., 'Byron and the Comic Spirit', *PMLA*, XXXIX (1924), 897–910.
Elton, Oliver, 'The Present Value of Byron', *RES*, I (1925), 24–39.
—, *A Survey of English Literature 1780–1830*, 2 vols., London, 1912.
'The English Romantics', *TLS*, Sept. 21, 1956, p. 552.
Fairchild, Hoxie Neale, *Religious Trends in English Poetry*, Vols. III and IV (of 4 vols.), New York, 1949, 1957.
—, *The Romantic Quest*, Philadelphia, 1931.
Faverty, Frederic E., *Matthew Arnold, the Ethnologist*, Evanston, Ill., 1951.
—, ed., *The Victorian Poets: A Guide to Research*, Cambridge, Mass., 1956.
Fitch, Sir Joshua, *Thomas and Matthew Arnold and Their Influence on English Education*, New York, 1898.
Foerster, Norman, 'Matthew Arnold and American Letters Today', *Sewanee Review*, XXX (1922), 298–306.
Forbes, Duncan, *The Liberal Anglican Idea of History*, Cambridge, 1952.
Ford, George H., *Keats and the Victorians*, New Haven, 1944.
Fogle, Richard Harter, *The Imagery of Keats and Shelley*, Chapel Hill, N.C., 1949.
Furrer, Paul, *Der Einfluss Sainte-Beuve's auf die Kritik Matthew Arnold's*, Inaugural-Dissertation, Zürich, 1920.
Garrod, H. W., *Keats*, Oxford, 1926.
—, 'Matthew Arnold's 1853 Preface', *RES*, XVII (1941), 310–21.
—, *Poetry and the Criticism of Life*, Oxford, 1931.
Glanvill, Joseph, *The Vanity of Dogmatizing*, reproduced from the edition of 1661, with a bibliographical note by Moody E. Prior, published for the Facsimile Text Society by the Columbia University Press, New York, 1931.
Graves, Alfred P., 'Celtic Nature Poetry', *Essays by Divers Hands* (transactions of the Royal Society of Literature), n.s. VIII (1928), 81–105.
Grierson, H. J. C., *The Background of English Literature*, New York, 1926.
Harper, G. M., 'Matthew Arnold and the Zeit-Geist', *Virginia Quarterly Review*, II (1926), 415–31.
Harris, Alan, 'Matthew Arnold: The "Unknown Years",' *Nineteenth Century and After*, CXIII (1933), 498–509.
Harrison, Frederic, 'Culture: A Dialogue', *Fortnightly Review*, VIII (1867), 603–14.
Havens, R. D., *The Mind of a Poet*, Baltimore, 1941.
Hearnshaw, F. J. C., 'Coleridge the Conservative', *Nineteenth Century and After*, CXVI (1934), 104–13.
Henley, W. E., *Views and Reviews: Essays in Appreciation. Literature*, New York, 1902.

Highet, Gilbert, *The Classical Tradition*, New York and London, 1949.

Houghton, Walter E., 'Arnold's "Empedocles on Etna",' *Victorian Studies*, I (1958), 311–36.

—, *The Victorian Frame of Mind, 1830-1870*, New Haven, 1957.

Hughes, Thomas, 'Preface' to F. D. Maurice, *The Friendship of Books*, London and New York, 1893.

The Letters of Sara Hutchinson from 1800 to 1835, ed. Kathleen Coburn, Toronto, 1954.

Hunt, Everett Lee, 'Matthew Arnold: The Critic as Rhetorician', *Quarterly Journal of Speech*, XX (1934), 484–507.

James, D. G., *Matthew Arnold and the Decline of English Romanticism*, Oxford, 1961.

Jamison, William A., *Arnold and the Romantics*, Anglistica, Vol. X, Copenhagen, 1958.

Johnson, E. D. H., *The Alien Vision of Victorian Poetry*, Princeton, 1952.

Jump, J. D., *Matthew Arnold*, London, New York, and Toronto, 1955.

Keats, John, *Complete Poems and Selected Letters*, ed. C. D. Thorpe, New York, 1935.

Keble, John, *Lectures on Poetry 1832-1841*, trans. E. K. Frances, 2 vols., Oxford, 1912.

Kermode, Frank, *Romantic Image*, New York, 1957.

Kingsmill, Hugh (pseud. of Hugh Kingsmill Lunn), *Matthew Arnold*, New York, 1928.

Knickerbocker, Frances Wentworth, *Free Minds: John Morley and His Friends*, Cambridge, Mass., 1943.

Knickerbocker, W. S., 'Arnold, Shelley, and Joubert', *MLN*, LV (1940), 201.

Knight, G. Wilson, *The Starlit Dome: Studies in the Poetry of Vision*, London, New York, and Toronto, 1941.

Knight, William, untitled review of Arnold's *Poems of Wordsworth*, *Modern Review*, I (1880), 235–8.

Kroeber, Karl, 'The Reaper and the Sparrow: A Study in Romantic Style', *Comparative Literature*, X (1958), 203–14.

Krutch, Joseph Wood, *The Modern Temper*, New York, 1929.

Leavis, F. R., *The Common Pursuit*, London, 1952.

—, 'Matthew Arnold', *The Importance of Scrutiny*, ed. Eric Bentley, New York, 1948.

—, *New Bearings in English Poetry*, London, 1932.

—, *Revaluation*, New York, 1947.

Lewisohn, Ludwig, 'A Study of Matthew Arnold', *Sewanee Review* IX (1901), 442–56, and X (1902), 143–59, 302–19.

Liptzin, Sol, 'Heine, the Continuator of Goethe: A Mid-Victorian Legend', *JEGP*, XLIII (1944), 317–25.

[Lockhart, John G.], 'Memoirs of Wordsworth', *Quarterly Review*, XCII (1852), 182–236.

Logan, James Venable, *Wordsworthian Criticism*, Columbus, Ohio, 1947.

Loring, M. L. S., 'T. S. Eliot on Matthew Arnold', *Sewanee Review*, XLIII (1935), 479–88.

Lovelace, Robert E., 'A Note on Arnold's "Growing Old",' *MLN*, LXVIII (1953), 21–3.

Lowell, Amy, *John Keats*, 2 vols., Boston and New York, 1925.

Lucas, E. V., *The Colvins and Their Friends*, New York, 1928.

Lucas, F. L., *Eight Victorian Poets*, Cambridge, 1930.

Lynd, Robert, *Old and New Masters*, New York, 1919.

MacGillivray, J. R., *Keats: A Bibliography and Reference Guide with an Essay on Keats' Reputation*, Toronto, 1949.

Madden, William A., 'The Divided Tradition of English Criticism', *PMLA*, LXXIII (1958), 69–80.

Mann, Thomas, *Freud, Goethe, Wagner*, trans. H. T. Lowe-Porter and Rita Matthias-Reil, New York, 1942.

Marchand, Leslie A., *Byron: A Biography*, 3 vols., New York, 1957.

Margoliouth, H. M., *Wordsworth and Coleridge 1795–1834*, London, New York, and Toronto, 1953.

Mayne, Ethel C., *Byron*, 2 vols., London, 1912.

Milnes, Richard Monckton (Lord Houghton), *The Life and Letters of John Keats*, Everyman's Library, London, Toronto, and New York, 1927.

Moore, T. Sturge, 'Matthew Arnold', *Essays and Studies by Members of the English Association*, XXIV (1938), 7–27.

More, Paul Elmer, *Shelburne Essays: Seventh Series*, New York and London, 1910.

Morgan, Charles, *The House of Macmillan (1843–1943)*, New York and London, 1944.

Morley, John, *Studies in Literature*, London and New York, 1891.

Muirhead, John H., *Coleridge as Philosopher*, London and New York, 1930.

De Musset, Alfred, *Confessions of a Child of the Century*, trans. anon., New York, 1910.

Neff, Emery E., *A Revolution in European Poetry 1660–1900*, New York, 1940.

Nichol, John, *Byron*, English Men of Letters Series, London, 1902.

Norman, Sylva, *Flight of the Skylark: The Development of Shelley's Reputation*, Norman, Okla., 1954.

Omond, T. S., 'Arnold and Homer', *Essays and Studies by Members of the English Association*, III (1912), 71–91.

Orrick, James Bentley, *Matthew Arnold and Goethe*, Publications of the English Goethe Society, n.s. IV (1928).

Pater, Walter Horatio, *Appreciations*, London, 1897.

Paul, Herbert, *Matthew Arnold*, London, 1907.

Peek, Katherine Mary, *Wordsworth in England: Studies in the History of His Fame*, Bryn Mawr, Pa., 1943.

Perkins, David, 'Arnold and the Function of Literature', *Journal of English Literary History (ELH)*, XVIII (1951), 287–309.

Perrine, Lawrence, 'Arnold's *The Scholar Gipsy* and *Thyrsis*', *Explicator*, XV (Feb., 1957).

Pottle, Frederick A., 'The Case of Shelley,' *PMLA*, LXVII (1952), 589–608.

Pratt, Willis Winslow, *Shelley Criticism in England 1810–1890*, unpublished
    doctoral dissertation, Cornell University, Ithaca, New York, 1935.
Quiller-Couch, Sir Arthur T., *Studies in Literature*, New York, 1918.
—, *Studies in Literature: Second Series*, New York, 1922.
Raysor, Thomas M., ed., *The English Romantic Poets: A Review of
    Research*, New York, 1950.
—, 'The Establishment of Wordsworth's Reputation', *JEGP*, LIV (1955),
    61–71.
Ridley, M. R., *Keats' Craftsmanship: A Study in Poetic Development*,
    Oxford, 1933.
Robbins, William, *The Ethical Idealism of Matthew Arnold*, Toronto, 1959.
Ruskin, John, *The Works of John Ruskin*, Library Edition, ed. E. T. Cook
    and Alexander Wedderburn, Vol. XXXIV (of 39 vols.), London, 1908.
Russell, G. W. E., *Matthew Arnold*, New York, 1904.
Saintsbury, George, *Corrected Impressions*, New York, 1895.
—, *A History of Criticism and Literary Taste in Europe*, 3 vols., New York,
    Edinburgh, and London, 1904.
—, *Matthew Arnold*, New York, 1899.
Sanders, Charles Richard, *Coleridge and the Broad Church Movement*,
    Durham, N.C., 1942.
Sedgewick, G. G., 'Wordsworth, Arnold, and Professor Lane Cooper',
    Dalhousie Review, X (1930), 57–66.
Sells, Iris Esther, *Matthew Arnold and France*, Cambridge, 1935.
Shairp, John Campbell, *Studies in Poetry and Philosophy*, Boston and New
    York, 1872.
[—], 'Wordsworth: The Man and the Poet', *North British Review*, XLI
    (1864), 1–28.
Shelley, P. B., *The Works of Percy Bysshe Shelley*, ed. Harry Buxton
    Forman, 8 vols., London, 1880.
'Shelley, the Poet of Liberty', *TLS*, Nov. 23, 1956, p. 696.
Sherman, Stuart P., *Matthew Arnold: How to Know Him*, Indianapolis,
    1917.
Solve, Melvin T., *Shelley: His Theory of Poetry*, Chicago, 1927.
Stanley, Arthur Penrhyn, *The Life and Correspondence of Thomas Arnold*,
    2 vols. in 1, New York, 1903.
Stanley, Carleton, *Matthew Arnold*, Toronto, 1938.
Stephen, Leslie, *Hours in a Library*, Vols. III and IV (of 4 vols.), New
    York and London, 1904.
—, *Studies of a Biographer*, Vols. I and II (of 4 vols.), London, 1907.
Stewart, Herbert L., 'The Place of Coleridge in English Theology',
    Harvard Theological Review, XI (1918), 1–31.
Swinburne, Algernon C., 'Charles Dickens', *Quarterly Review*, CXCVI
    (1902), 20–39.
—, *Essays and Studies*, London, 1901.
—, *Miscellanies*, London, 1895.
—, 'Mr. Arnold's New Poems', *Fortnightly Review*, VIII (1867), 414–45.
—, 'Shelley', *Chambers's Cyclopaedia of English Literature*, 3 vols., London,
    1903, III, 107–18.

Symon, James D., *Byron in Perspective*, New York, 1925.

Symonds, J. A., 'Byron', *The English Poets*, 4 vols., ed. T. H. Ward, London, 1880.

—, 'Matthew Arnold's Selections from Wordsworth', *Fortnightly Review*, n.s. XXVI (1879), 686–701.

Tate, Allen, 'Literature as Knowledge: Comment and Comparison', *Southern Review*, VI (1941), 629–57.

Taylor, Sir Henry, *The Autobiography of Henry Taylor*, 2 vols., New York, 1885.

Tillotson, Geoffrey, *Criticism and the Nineteenth Century*, London, 1951.

Tillotson, Kathleen, 'Matthew Arnold and Carlyle', *Proceedings of the British Academy*, London, XLII (1956), 133–53.

—, 'Rugby 1850: Arnold, Clough, Walrond, and In Memoriam', *RES*, n.s. IV (1953), 122–40.

—, '"Yes: In the Sea of Life",' *RES*, n.s. III (1952), 346–64.

Tinker, C. B. and H. F. Lowry, *The Poetry of Matthew Arnold: A Commentary*, London, New York, and Toronto, 1950.

Traill, H. D., *Coleridge*, English Men of Letters Series, New York, 1884.

Transactions of the Wordsworth Society, 8 nos. in 5 vols., Edinburgh, 1882–7.

Trilling, Lionel, *Matthew Arnold*, New York, 1949.

Ward, Mrs. Humphry, *A Writer's Recollections*, 2 vols., New York, 1918.

Warner, Rex, 'An Introduction to Welsh Poetry', *TLS*, Aug. 6, 1954, special insert p. xxxviii.

Warren, Alba H., *English Poetic Theory 1825–1865*, Princeton, 1950.

Warren, Thomas Herbert, *Oxford and Poetry in 1911*, Oxford, 1911 (bound in a volume with other lectures by other authors, entitled on the binding: *Oxford Lectures on Literature 1907–1920*; no title page).

White, Greenough, ed., *Matthew Arnold and the Spirit of the Age*, New York and London, 1898.

White, Newman Ivey, *Shelley*, 2 vols., New York, 1940.

White, William Hale ('Mark Rutherford'), 'Byron, Goethe, and Mr. Matthew Arnold', *Contemporary Review*, XL (1881), 179–85.

Willey, Basil, *Nineteenth Century Studies*, London, 1949.

Wilson, John Dover, *Leslie Stephen and Matthew Arnold as Critics of Wordsworth*, Cambridge, 1939.

Wordsworth, William, *The Poetical Works of William Wordsworth*, Oxford Standard Edition, ed. Thomas Hutchinson, New York, 1933.

'Wordsworth's Experience', *TLS*, July 22, 1939, p. 437.

Yeats, William Butler, *Ideas of Good and Evil*, London and Stratford-upon-Avon, 1914.

INDEX

INDEX

Byron, *Marino Faliero*, 76
Vision of Judgment, The, 84, 113
'Byron' (Arnold's essay and preface), 42, 52, 71, 85, 87, 91,
98 ff., 109, 147, 148, 177, 186,
188, 198

Campbell, Mrs. Olwen, 153 f., 158,
189
Campbell, Thomas, 177, 202
Carlyle, Thomas, 28, 80, 81, 169,
192, 219
Cato, 84
Cavendish, 140
Celts, 92 f.; *see also On the Study
of Celtic Literature*
Chapman, George, 137
Chateaubriand, 140
Chaucer, Geoffrey, 3, 114, 138,
177, 202
Chew, S. C., 96
Church of Brou, The, 158
classicism, Arnold and, 205
Clough, Arthur Hugh, 7, 24, 27,
57, 72, 76, 77, 81, 105, 121,
122, 126, 132, 134, 137, 145,
182, 197
Colenso, John William, Bishop, 18,
67, 195
Coleridge, Derwent, 165
Coleridge, Hartley, 165
Coleridge, John Duke, 18, 155, 165
Coleridge, John Taylor, Judge, 165
Coleridge, Samuel Taylor, 3, 8, 11,
53, 55, 56, 58, 64, 88, 99, 108,
109, 112, 118, 139, 151 ff.,
191 ff., 202, 203, 207, 209,
210, 215
Christabel, 155, 177
Dejection: an Ode, 155, 177
Kubla Khan, 177
*Lectures and Notes on Shakes-
peare*, 167
Lewti, 177
Rime of the Ancient Mariner,
155, 156, 177
'Comment on Christmas, A', 167
compromise, Victorian, 2

consolation, Wordworth's in-
fluence and, 9 f.
Cooper, Lane, 65, 72
Courage, 84
Cowper, William, 46, 177, 202
criticisms, general, of Arnold, 1
Cromwell, 17, 75
Cudworth, Ralph, 71
Culture and Anarchy, 12, 67, 166
Cuvier, Baron, 140

Dante, 28 f., 31, 50, 103, 204, 218
'Dante and Beatrice', 204 f.
Davy, Mrs., 8
'Democracy', 68
democracy, 12
De Quincey, Thomas, 137, 192
De Vere, Aubrey, 55
Donne, John, 3, 21, 107, 202
Dover Beach, 22, 23, 120, 209
Dowden, Edward, 82, 83, 97, 109,
110, 114 f., 156, 160, 188, 189,
191, 195, 196 f., 199
Dryden, John, 3, 16, 21, 84, 107,
177, 202, 218
'Dudley, Arthur', 184

'Ecce, Convertimur ad Gentes', 70
editor, Arnold as, 72 f.
Eliot, George, 2
Eliot, T. S., 16, 27, 31, 58, 75, 107,
154, 180, 212
Elton, Oliver, 172
Elze, Karl, 96
Emerson, R. W., 165, 169
'Emerson', 66
Empedocles on Etna, 18, 20, 24, 36,
57, 76, 78 f., 116, 127, 128,
141, 155, 158, 207, 209, 220
Epictetus, 64
'Equality', 68
Essays in Criticism, 15, 54, 58, 83,
87, 91, 92 f., 120, 138, 148,
165, 179, 194, 210
European consciousness, Arnold's, 3

Faded Leaves, 161
Fairchild, H. N., 164, 173

272